THE BOOK OF
ELMSETT
From Sickle to Satellite

ELMSETT LOCAL HISTORY GROUP

HALSGROVE

First published in Great Britain in 2006

British Library Cataloguing-in-Publication Data.
A CIP record for this title is available from the British Library.

ISBN 1 84114 506 8
ISBN 978 1 84114 506 8

HALSGROVE

Halsgrove House
Lower Moor Way
Tiverton, Devon EX16 6SS
Tel: 01884 243242
Fax: 01884 243325
email: sales@halsgrove.com
website: www.halsgrove.com

Frontispiece photograph: *Horseman Tom Hiskey (1849–1921), aged 22.*

Printed and bound in Great Britain by CPI Bath Press, Bath.

Foreword

The changes which have taken place in village life in the last 50 years have been more far-reaching than at any time in history. Communities which were once self-sufficient, and relied on farming for employment and prosperity, found their inhabitants were moving into a wider, richer world. Equally, those seeking the peace, quiet and comradeship that village life can offer, were fleeing metropolitan life with a sigh of relief, to take up country living. Village life was changing dramatically.

In Elmsett, the upheavals have been as great as in any village in Suffolk. But the one thing that survives all the turbulence is the village's rich and varied history. There have been moments of high drama, of course, remembered by the memorial which marks the tithe seizure at Elmsett Hall in 1932. But, as this book serves to remind us, the bulk of the village's story is best portrayed in the ebb and flow of ordinary life. And all shades of life are to be found within this book. We read the desperately sad accounts of the accidental losses, both in peace and war; the ups and downs in agriculture which inevitably have set the tone of life in this rural community.

It is a mistake to look at a village and see only the streets, cottages, distant fields and woodlands, and believe you have a true picture of it. Without knowing something of the people who shaped it over generations you will never have a full appreciation of the place. There is now no excuse for not understanding what makes Elmsett tick, for it is set out here in fine detail, and paints as vivid a picture as could be provided by any artist. The voices of villagers past and present ring clear from the page, the trials and tribulations of generations long gone are as compelling as any dramatist could create. This is real village life. This is Elmsett.

Paul Heiney
Suffolk, March 2006

Book Research Team:

Colin Boniface
Hilary Furlong
Grace Hammond
Rachel Hitchcock
Richard Hitchcock
Julie Hunn
Jackie Parkinson
Joy Sillitoe

CONTENTS

Acknowledgements

We are grateful to the following for their help: Elmsett Parish Council for financial support, BBC Radio Suffolk, the Charity Commission, the Commonwealth War Graves Commission, the Family Welfare Association, the Ordnance Survey, Savannah Publications – compilers of 'Soldiers died in the Great War', Suffolk Record Office.

And also: Katy Charge, Ashley Cooper, Janet Cooper, Nicci Gerrard, Jim and Ann Higgins, Duncan McLennan, Paul Marshall (headmaster) and staff, Elmsett School, London Metropolitan Archives, Martin and Jackie Mitchell, Val Norrington, William Smith, Carol Twinch, Edwin Westren.

This book would not have been possible without the help of many of the residents of Elmsett. Many hours of interviews have been recorded, and extracts of these appear throughout the book. Some of these people are no longer alive, but their memories have been recorded here for future generations. They were: Cecil Barber (1904–94), Freddie Barber (1933–2003), Gerald Barber (1920–99), Brian Hiskey (1938–2004), Alfie Holder (1917–2001), Fred Holder (1917–2001), George Holder (1915–98), Lily Holder (1914–2002), Christine Ladbrook (1911–2001), Tony Skippings (1933–2003).

In 1993 Eva Osborne, who was born in 1911 and grew up at Lucy Wood Cottages in Elmsett, published a booklet about her life. *Eva's Story* is dedicated to the memory of her parents, Walter and Anna Pryke, 'who worked so hard to give us a happy childhood'. Charles Barber sent a copy to his uncle, Reg Barber (1902–99), who had also lived at Lucy Wood Cottages. It prompted Reg to contact Eva in her nursing home, and the two became regular correspondents. At the age of 92, Reg, inspired by *Eva's Story*, wrote his own memories, which he called *Reg's Life*. Extracts from these two fascinating accounts have been included in this book.

Other contributors: Margaret Aggis, Aubrey and Ellen Barber, Charles Barber, Chris Barber, Flo Barber, Sheila Barber, Andrew Barnes, Jenny Barnes, Elizabeth Bellamy, Elizabeth Bennett, Lee Boniface, Janice Bradbrook, Pam Bradbrook, Barbara Briscoe, Marion Brown, Robert Brown, Briony Clarke, Trevor Clarke, Lorraine Coleyshaw, Harold Cooper, Janet Cooper, Oliver and Miranda Cooper, Rupert Cooper, Owen and Judith Corble, Phil and Janet Crick, Roger and Brenda Edwards, Robert and Barbara Everett, Robert Fison, Trevor Ford, Howard and Rosemary Fox, John Furlong, Sean and Nicci Gerrard French, Trevor Gibbons, John and Alison Gillies, Alison Grant, Tony Gray, Bob Green, Mick and Joy Grimwade, Miriam Hawes, Gerald and Mavis Harrison, Sheila Herd, Sylvia Hiskey, Jenny Hitchcock, Matthew and Sue Hitchcock, Miles Hitchcock Brown, Peter Hitchcock, Robert Hitchcock, Witgar Hitchcock, Cissie Holder, Roger and Gwen Horne, Andrew and Julie Hunn, Robin Jeans, Betty Kemp, Ron and Anne Kerridge, Michael and Hazel King, John and Doreen Ladbrook, Cuthbert Lambert, Jean Lawrence, John and Hazel Lee, Russell and Margaret Leek, Edie Leeks, Jean Leeks, Robert and Sue Mackie, Muriel Mitchell, Paul Moore, Peter Moore, Allan Mountfield, Alan and Andrea Newman, Martin Page, John Parkinson, Richard Pryke, Lorna Quick, Anna Reily, Jim and Jean Roberts, Steve Robinson, Derek and Ruby Rose, Marion Rowe, Blanche Seager, John Simmons, Bill and Jean Simpson, Joyce Skippings, Percy (Taffy) and June Skippings, Dave Steward, Jim Steward, Mike and Kathryn Stock, Steve and Wendy Tawell, Catherine Thoroughgood, Ian Tippett, Jonathan and Rosemary Tricker, Richard Turner, Jeremy and Cynthia Walsh, Margaret Watkins, Pauline Watkins, Concie West, Edwin Westren, Hilary Wilson, Lesley Woor, Jeannie Wright, Mollie Yates.

We are also grateful to the following pupils of Elmsett School for sharing their memories with us: David Bray, Adam Coleyshaw, Matthew D'Sousa, Sam French, Alastair Grant, Emily Greenfield, Zoe Griggs, Alice Kempson, Paul Midgley, Oliver Mires, Edward Seeley, Katrina Seeley.

CHAPTER 1

The Origins of a Suffolk Village

EXTRACTS FROM A PAPER BY A.R. MOUNTFIELD

At the edge of the village there is a house whose origins are medieval and where a discovery was made whilst repairing the footings. At a depth of about a metre, and extending down to about two metres, were dozens of what at first appeared to be polished flint spearheads, but a little research revealed that they are something extraordinary. In fact they are fossils, known as belemnites, which are the stony remains of a type of squid. They are reputed to be 140 million years old. Not far away, on Red House Farm, two vertebrae, one of an ichthyosaur and one of a plesiosaur, were found. The belemnites and the dinosaur fossils serve to remind us that, like almost every other part of our land, the area was inhabited by other living creatures long before man came to these parts. Early man has, however, left his faint mark on our parish.

For the last 2,000 years, families have roamed over the land, finally settling, building houses and bringing up their children; they felled the ancient woodland, created and worked their fields and left their mark. Our countryside, and with it Elmsett, has been shaped, plundered, organised, fought over and civilised. The rich, fertile land of Britain has always been an attraction and the turbulent, but surprisingly cultured, tribal life of the indigenous British was altered forever by a succession of invaders. This island, with its huge mineral wealth and pleasant climate, has always been a magnet to others from across the North Sea.

Archaeological Finds

When man left his earliest mark on the land hereabouts there were no administrative boundaries set down to confine or control him. The hunter-gatherers of prehistory left little behind them, but two Mesolithic (10,000–4,000BC) flint axe-heads were found a few feet apart in 1975 on Manor Farm, showing that, at the time of the retreat of the last ice age, man lived and hunted over the tundra of eastern Britain. To the south-east of Park Wood, close to an ancient 'dropping well', is a ring ditch approximately 30 metres (100 feet)

The fossilised bones found in the parish. Left: *Ichthyosaur vertebra;* right: *plesiosaur vertebra.*

Drawing of a badge in the shape of a boar found at Poplar Hall and possibly belonging to a retainer of Richard III.

The Roman denarius found by Roger Horne.

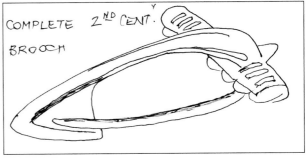

Drawing of a complete second-century bronze brooch – one of the recent finds at Poplar Hall.

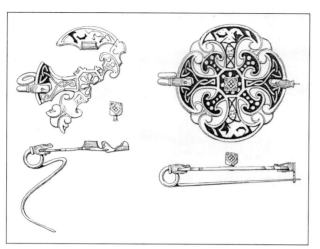

The drawing on the left shows fragments of a brooch discovered during the 1990s. On the right is the British Museum's reconstruction of what the whole brooch would have looked like.

The Elmsett Brooch. Dated to the ninth century, it is an extremely rare and fine example of Anglo-Saxon craftsmanship, and probably represents a special order from a wealthy local landowner to a skilled silversmith. The cross reflects the influence of the Church on the owner. It was found in several pieces and has been skilfully restored by Ipswich Museum, where it is on display.

(Photograph: David Baker, courtesy of Ipswich Museum)

in diameter, which is thought to be the ploughed-out remains of a Bronze Age enclosure, or barrow, revealed by aerial photography in 1996. This is the earliest evidence of habitation in our parish, but no more is known about the Bronze Age people who lived here, or how many there were. By the Bronze Age, family groups were settling into a less nomadic lifestyle, and it is at about 1000BC that one of our early inhabitants lost the tip of a bronze rapier-like knife, found at a site along Flowton Road, near to the turn-off for Flowton village. There is no way of knowing if this was a weapon point broken off while used in a fight, or whether it was part of a consignment of scrap lost while on its way for re-smelting. There have been other finds nearby. A silver coin, thought to be of

Amminus of the Cantii, was dated to between 100BC and AD42. Many Roman coins, brooches and pottery were found in the same field as the knife or spear point mentioned above. This site has yielded many other discoveries (mainly through metal detecting), including an early-Saxon sleeve or wrist clasp with a zoomorphic design, dated AD410–650. During the early 1980s, in a garden in Hadleigh Road, a Roman coin was found which Colchester Museum identified as a silver denarius, issued during the reign of Emperor Claudius between the years AD52 and AD54. Claudius ordered the invasion of Britain in AD43 and spent ten days in Colchester that year.

In 2002, finds have also been made at two sites on Poplar Hall's most southerly field, where it rolls down gently to a watercourse. This is a classic location favoured by the Romans. The first site, where there may have been a small group of Romano-British huts, has produced Roman bronze coins of the early first, second and fourth centuries, mostly badly corroded because of the acid soil. The second site, dated probably to AD100–310, produced shiny red Samian tableware, a complete second-century brooch which works in the same way as a modern safety pin, and more Roman coins, thimbles, buttons and brooches. In addition there is a denarius of Geta (AD209–12) a coin of Emperor Carausius (AD287–93) and some early sesterces. Confusingly, a King John coin (1199–1216), a Richard III (1483–85), retainer's badge in the form of a boar, a George I farthing from about 1720 and many late Victorian items have also been discovered. The site clearly awaits a full examination and explanation, but meanwhile the collection continues to grow. The finds are at present in the process of conservation.

Whilst there have been these Roman finds in the area of the village, there do not seem to be signs of important Roman occupation near to Elmsett, nor was there a significant Roman road close by, so whilst we know that members of the British tribe, the Trinovantes, lived hereabouts, we must move forward at least another 400 years before we can begin to make an educated guess at the beginnings of organised settlement in our village.

Immediately to the south of the Iron Age ring ditch, D. Baker and D. Cummings (junr) made a number of significant finds in 1991, which included a valuable Saxon brooch in the form of a cross, known as the Elmsett Brooch, which is now held in the Ipswich Museum, and two separate halves of a brooch, found at different times. In 1993 a buckle and a fragment of a silver coin of Edwald of East Anglia, dated AD798, were found at the same site. This could be evidence of our first Anglo-Saxon settlers. Other significant finds include a considerable amount of broken pottery discovered on the site of a medieval kiln right on the modern parish boundary, again on Manor Farm near Borley's Wood, and a late-Saxon cut halfpenny of Aethelred the Unready (978–1016).

This was found just off Whatfield Road, in the area of what was once the village green. Thus it is clear that organised human activity has been going on around Elmsett since before the Roman occupation, with others 'passing through' since the dawn of man.

The Roman Army had withdrawn from Britain by AD406 and local chieftains were left to take control. What we now know as Suffolk had a well-developed Iron Age field system, which would have been further developed by Romano-British farmers, but there was also a great area of largely uninhabited breckland, marsh, forest and fields. The area was ripe for the next phase in our history, which brought invasion, immigration and further settlement.

Dwellers among the Elm Trees

Settlement did not, of course, happen overnight, but within two centuries the native British (at least in the east of the country) had been absorbed into the culture of the settlers. Those who resisted the changes were driven into the west, mainly to Wales and Cornwall, and the east of England was firmly in the hands of the invaders.

Although we know of the Bronze Age ring ditch close to Park Wood, where the early British may have settled, and the possible Romano-British site on Poplar Hall, it is after the year AD450 that we can with more certainty pick up the story of the life of the family groups who settled here. We do not know their names, but we know where they came from and how they lived. We know their language, and their religion. We even know the type of ships they came in, and something of how they navigated. They were leaving traces on the ground for archaeologists to pick up, and giving us place names which have lasted to this day. We know of their skills and their art, their sympathy with, and closeness to, the land. Scholars have even made a very close copy of their early houses, for instance at West Stow Anglo-Saxon village, near Bury St Edmunds, as well as recreating something of the life of the communities formed from the family groups who first landed. The movement of people was not all peaceful, and the Danes were a tough bunch, but over the period AD400–600, and despite the turmoil, a new life blossomed in the land. Britain became England, the Welsh language of the Celts was replaced by that of the Angles, and the Kingdom of Anglia was hewn with plough and sword, the people making new dwellings in their own style.

Such, then, are the facts, scholarly reconstructions and archaeological evidence which create the picture of East Anglia in the two centuries following the decline and fall of the Roman Empire. By the seventh century, East Anglia had become the heartland of the famous dynasty of the Wuffings, with its residence in Rendlesham Forest. King Raedwald, who reigned from AD599 until his death in about AD625, is now

The reconstruction of an Anglo-Saxon village.
(PHOTOGRAPH COURTESY OF WEST STOW ANGLO-SAXON VILLAGE TRUST / ST EDMUNDSBURY BOROUGH COUNCIL)

thought to be the person interred in the great ship buried at Sutton Hoo. The fact that Raedwald had his palace at Rendlesham, 20 miles east of Elmsett, gives us guidance as to the likely Anglo-Saxon form of the early village of Elmsett.

Immigrants

Settlers travelled up the navigable rivers, the main river valleys and tributaries until they reached an acceptable spot. Later generations would have followed the same pattern, searching westward for good sites to claim and settle, not always without a fight. At some time in those dark ages of settlement by the Danes, a family group would have arrived here and named the place after a prominent feature – a stand of mature elm trees dominating the skyline. With some areas of wood and scrubland already cleared by the native Britons, the settlers would have set about laying claim to an area in which to plant their crops, close to a source of clean water, with a dry, sheltered place in which to build their house, or houses. The site would ideally have been within reach of neighbours, who would help them in such communal tasks as harvest, and with the supply of the goods they would need, or could trade items such as pottery, tools and cloth. Quickly they would have been absorbed into a growing rural culture which would survive in essence for the next 1,000 years.

There is little to be gained by searching for archaeological evidence of the early village settlement. Written references to Elmsett are not to be found until the tenth century, but it is difficult to dismiss the early years as being of no consequence, because the village developed into a wealthy estate. The recreated Anglo-Saxon village at West Stow gives an idea of what the early village of Elmsett would have looked like, and is well worth a visit.

Elmsett's First Mentions

The earliest written mentions of Elmsett found so far exist in two wills and in the Domesday Book. The wills were written about 100 years prior to Domesday. Elmsett was left in her will by Aelflaed to

King Aethelred (Ethelred the Unready) in about the year 1002. Through the wonderfully detailed work done by Miss Dorothy Whitelock, MA, in translating *Anglo-Saxon Wills* (published in 1930), we also know that Ylmesaetun (Elmsett) came to Aelflaed by inheritance from her family. Her father, Aelfgar, had left the estate to her brother, Aethelflaed, who in turn bequeathed it to his sister and her husband, Ealdorman Bryhtnoth, asking that it be left to the king in due turn. It is clear that the Elmsett estate was owned by her forebears for long enough for it to become a suitable gift to the king, and not just a little cluster of thatched houses!

Troubled Years

Harold became King of England in January 1066, having been Earl of East Anglia since 1045 and of Wessex since 1053. It was because of his command over East Anglia for the previous 21 years that recruits for his army were likely to have been drawn from here. Elmsett would have been called to send a great many of its young men into the service of the king.

On 25 September 1066, King Harold had marched his Army to the north, where they defeated the Norwegians at the battle of Stamford Bridge. Four or five days later, on hearing that Duke William had landed on the south coast, he force-marched his battle-hardened but weary men to London, then on to Hastings. The ensuing battle on 14 October was a bloody affair, with great loss on both sides. King Harold and his two brothers were killed. For William, the death of Harold and the loss of the English Army leaders constituted a triumph. Elmsett had lost its men, and ultimately the ownership of its land, to foreign rulers. East Anglia, which clearly belonged to and supported King Harold, would not have been looked on kindly by the Normans.

Domesday and After

The following years were terrible. The Norman Army subdued the country with great efficiency and ferocity. Our landed gentry, our thegns and earls, were displaced and our lands handed out to the foreign Norman invaders. Great estates were given as prizes to those Norman nobles and merchants who had lent money to support the invasion. Opposition was brutally crushed and the English were dispossessed. Over the next 20 years a sort of peace would come, along with an acceptance of the change. All this is poignantly recorded in the Domesday Book, named after the massive survey undertaken as a means of assessing the value of the whole land, and the taxes which would be collected. The first real civil servants had arrived!

The survey of England was done by an army of a different sort, armed only with writing materials.

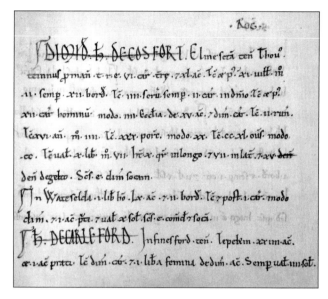

The entry for Elmsett in the Domesday Book.
(Reproduced with permission from the Suffolk Record Office)

They visited almost every town, estate and village, and asked the same questions wherever they went. They established what the position was before the Conquest and how it had changed by the time of the survey, and the whole project was finished within two years. It was ready by 1086. They used a sort of shorthand, which makes it very difficult to interpret, but the terms 'then' and 'now' are easy to understand: 'then' is before the conquest and 'now' is on the date of the survey. The entry for Elmsett translates as follows:

In the lands of Roger d'Auberville
Half-Hundred of Cosford
Tovi, a thane, held ELMSETT as a manor T.R.E; 6 carucates of land and 40 acres.
Then and later 11 villans [villeins], now 2; then as now 12 bordars. Then 4 slaves
Then as now 2 ploughs in demesne. Then and afterwards 12 ploughs belonging to the men, now 4
A church with 15 acres and half a plough.
Then 2 horses. Then 16 head of cattle, now 4. Then 30 pigs, now 20. Then 240 sheep, now 200.
Then it was worth £10; now £7.
It has 10 furlongs in length and 7 in width; 15d in geld.
St Edmund's has half the soke.

This document gives us brief and tantalising pictures of the village and estate of Elmsett in 1065, before Harold's brief reign, a second picture in the years after the Norman Conquest and a third picture 20 years later.

A plain translation leaves a lot to be guessed at. Under these circumstances, the final part of this early history of a Suffolk village is best presented as a summary using all available sources but with a little informed guesswork to make a more rounded picture.

Elmsett in the Reign of Edward the Confessor

In the Domesday entry, Elmsett had an almost modern spelling, being shown as 'Elmeseta'.

Earlier, in Aelflaed's will written about 975, it is written as 'Ylmesaetun'. Same name, same place, but this illustrates how much closer to modern English the written word had become.

In 1065 King Edward owned the greater part of Suffolk, although some parts were shared with the Church. The Elmsett estate was held by Tovi the Thegn, who paid his taxes half to the Church and half to the king. The manor lands extended to between 600 and 700 acres.

In addition to the cultivated land and grazing in the Elmsett estate, there was an area of woodland, and what we now know as Park Wood represents that today. Also, the village church had 'fifteen acres and half a plough' which could mean grazing and crops occupying about 65 acres. The estate was valued at ten pounds.

Tovi had the farm income from the manor; he also charged rent on the rest of the estate lands, where there were 11 substantial farms and a further 12 smallholdings, with more than 1,000 acres under cultivation, the whole estate amounting to something approaching 1,700 acres. The farms around the manor would have had sufficient draught animals to plough land for crops, and grazing for cattle, pigs and sheep in proportion. Compare this with the records for 1919, when the parish of Elmsett had taxable land of just over 1,933 acres. It comes as quite a surprise to learn that there was about as much land farmed in eleventh-century Elmsett as in the twentieth, but many scholars believe this to be so.

Elmsett after the Norman Conquest

At first the manor changed little, the number of farms in the hands of freemen remaining at 12, but over the next 20 years the number of freeman farmers fell to just two. The village changed hands, falling under the lordship of Roger d'Auberville. There is no record of the fate of Tovi the Thegn. The manor lands remain much the same in appearance, but the number of animals is much reduced. The horses have gone, there are only four head of cattle left on the manor, only 20 pigs, and the sheep flock is down from 240 to 200.

The value of the estate is now reduced to £7, the tax fixed at 15 pennyweight in gold. The farmers (villeins), who had numbered 11, are now two, while the number of smallholders remains at 12. The land under cultivation has fallen to about 400 acres.

These changes between 1065 and 1086 cannot be attributed directly to the loss of life at Hastings, because Domesday makes it clear that Elmsett remained in about the same condition immediately after the Conquest as before, but later the community came under the control of a foreign landlord and fell on very hard times. Yet there is a puzzle here, because other villages around Elmsett prospered. Aldham, for instance, lost three villeins, four slaves and three ploughs, meaning that about 300 acres reverted to grazing, but the number of cattle increased from ten to 18, the pigs are recorded as going from 80 to 60, and the sheep reduced from 140 to 60. The value of Aldham was increased from £8 to £15. This is a picture of a change in farming practice rather than decay. The value of part of Whatfield increased from 40s. to 50s. In Hintlesham the farms changed their practices, but the value increased from £10 to £22. In Wattisham all the animals increased in numbers; in Somersham there was no change. The wider picture tells the same story of a reviving, but changed, farming community. So why was Elmsett so badly out of line?

The answer is startling. Not one of Roger d'Auberville's holdings prospered, nor did those held by his brother, William. Roger's holdings in Elmsett, Finborough, Somersham (part), Blakenham, Offton, Bricett, Horswold and Henley at best remained static, but most fell in farming activity and value. William was as bad as his brother at managing his holdings. Ringshall fared badly, and the part of Bricett which he held tells a very interesting story. There, the 60 acres of land were rented to a freeman called Fulk:

Of the above 60 acres, Hugh of Houdain took 20 acres so William (d'Auberville) and the Hundred say; but Hugh himself is under the King's arrest and had therefore not been able to reply.

Dirty work afoot, perhaps? Those villages that prospered around us?
Hintlesham: 'the lands of Stigand, which William of Noyers keeps in the King's hand.'
Aldham: held by Aubrey de Vere, and part by St Edmund's.
Whatfield: fragmented but mainly held by Richard, son of Count Gilbert and partially by St Edmund's.
Flowton: fragmented, but owned by the king.
Somersham: fragmented, but owned by the king. Part held by Roger d'Auberville.

The only conclusion is that the Elmsett estate was callously neglected by its new lord. Roger d'Auberville was either back in Normandy, or perhaps too politically busy in London. Who knows?

The Rest of the Story

Slowly, as resistance faded, life in Elmsett fell under the control of a more relaxed regime and recovered, as it had in times before. In the late-medieval period, dairying developed and the wool trade flourished. The manorial system strengthened and brought

Elmsett Church by Thomas Gainsborough (1727–88).
(PHOTOGRAPH COURTESY OF THE BOWES MUSEUM, BARNARD CASTLE)

stability. The Church continued to be supported by tithes and offerings, as well as commandeering the common land, which the priest held as glebe; Elmsett's village green once stretched from the Old Rectory in a narrow triangle alongside Whatfield Road as far as the old mill. The rectory was relocated to overlook this green, and given a fashionable moat. Other wealthy residents built their houses around the edges of the green, while houses for smallholders and tradesmen were built in The Street. Fine timbered houses were built on brick foundations which avoided rot, so some are still with us today.

Two mills, not recorded in Domesday, were kept busy by the farms. By the eighteenth century corn was the main crop but in the nineteenth century arable farming became less profitable. The Napoleonic Wars temporarily encouraged high grain prices, but the repeal of the Corn Laws in the 1840s allowed the import of cheap corn. There was a respite during the Crimean War, when home production was again encouraged, but the bad harvests of the 1870s brought disaster to many farmers. By the end of the century Suffolk was one of the poorest and most depressed counties of England.

Glossary

Acre:	*A measure of land 220 yards (a furlong) long and 22 yards (a chain) wide that could be ploughed without having to turn the plough too often. Also the area which could be ploughed behind one ox in one day.*
Bordar:	*Smallholder or minor farmer who rented land from the lord of the manor.*
Carucate:	*Originally the area of land required to maintain a family at subsistence level. It became a basic unit of a nominal 120 acres for tax purposes.*
Demesne:	*Land held by the lord of the manor.*
Furlong:	*An eighth of a mile, 220 yards – originally the length of a furrow in a common field.*
Geld:	*Tax paid in gold*
Hundred:	*An administrative area.*
Plough:	*An area of land the size of which varied from region to region between 70 and 120 acres.*
Soke:	*Jurisdiction; Rental. (In Elmsett half paid to the king, half to St Edmund's Church)*
Thane:	*A land-owning Anglo-Saxon military companion of the king.*
TRE:	*In Temperae Regis Edwardis (In the time of King Edward). While compiling the Domesday book the inquisitors (scribes) were instructed to ask who held the land on the day Edward the Confessor died in 1066 (then) and who held it at the time of the survey (now).*
Villan/Villein:	*A feudal serf (peasant) renting land from the lord of the manor.*

CHAPTER 2

The War Years

Elmsett War Memorials

Elmsett has memorials commemorating the two great conflicts of the twentieth century. The memorial to those killed in the Second World War is a little unusual, as no residents of the village died on active service; they all died from a direct hit as a result of enemy action.

The First World War (1914–18)

As with every town and village in the United Kingdom, Elmsett sent men to fight in the First World War. The war memorial in the village church records that 11 men from the village were killed in action. Tracing these men and their records was not an easy task, as in many cases, when they volunteered, men seem to have given the names they used from day to day rather than their full names. However, we have listed the information we have found below.

Frederick William Barber: We have been unable to trace the service records or any other details of this man, but in the 1901 census a Frederick Barber, born in 1885, is listed as living in Whatfield Road, son of John and Louisa Barber.

Horace Lancelot Beaumont: The Beaumont family still had members living in Elmsett until the last quarter of the twentieth century. Horace is listed as being L/Cpl 46183 in the Machine Gun Corps (formerly 2055 Suffolk Yeomanry (TF). He served in France and in Flanders and was killed in action on 21 March 1918. He is also listed on the Pozières Memorial in France.

Sidney Thomas Clarke: Enrolled as Pte 2417 in the 5th Btn, Suffolk Regiment, he is shown as being the son of Mrs Polly Clarke of Eley's Cottages in Elmsett. He enlisted in Colchester with his friend Herbert John Keeble (note their consecutive numbers), and it emerges they both died on the same day in Gallipoli – 21 August 1915. He is listed on the Helles Memorial in Turkey. Two of his nieces still live in Elmsett.

William Cobbold: William is shown as having been born in 'Elmseth' and was baptised in Elmsett on 20 September 1896. He was the fifth of seven children born to Benjamin and Susanna Cobbold – the father's occupation is given as 'labourer'. He enlisted at Stowmarket, Sussex (sic). He was Pte 27328 in Prince Albert's (Somerset Light Infantry) formerly C/23465 East Surrey Regiment. He served in France and Flanders and was killed in action on 22 August 1917. He is also listed in the Hooge Crater Cemetery in Belgium.

Herbert John Keeble: Born in 1885, he was shown on the 1901 census as living in Elmsett with his parents, John and Mary Keeble. He is twice named in the baptismal register – in 1909 his son, Edward John, was baptised and the father's occupation given as 'labourer'. In 1915, when a daughter, Gladys, born on 26 August, was baptised on 17 October, his occupation is given as Pte, 5th Btn, Suffolk Regiment. Pte Keeble (2416) enlisted in Colchester and died of wounds on 21 August 1915 in Gallipoli five days before his daughter was born. He is also listed on the Helles Memorial in Turkey.

John Keeble: This man cannot be traced. However, there was a John T. Keeble, aged one, listed in the 1901 census as brother of the above Herbert John. Born to John and Mary Keeble on 3 May 1900, he is also entered in the school register in 1905. If this is the same person he was too young to enlist but could have given false information about his name and age.

John William Keeble: His parents were William and Mary Keeble of Ely, but he is shown living in Elmsett in 1901. He enlisted at Ipswich and was L/Cpl 10091, 1st Btn, Seaforth Highlanders. He was killed in action, aged 21, on 25 May 1916 in the Persian Gulf. He is also listed on the Basra Memorial in Iraq.

Wilfred John Kennington: The Kenningtons were builders who lived in the village at the beginning of the twentieth century and still live in the area. Wilfred John was born in Elmsett and was shown as living in Elmsett. He enlisted at Ipswich and was Pte 29658, 7th Btn, Royal Fusiliers (City of London Regiment). He served in France and Flanders and was killed in action on 23 April 1917. He is also listed on the Arras Memorial in France.

George Leeks: George was born in Elmsett and enlisted at Ipswich. He was Pte 16807, 7th Btn, Suffolk Regiment, served in France and Flanders and was killed in action on 13 January 1916. He is also listed in the Guards Cemetery, Windy Corner, Cuinchy, France.

Thomas William Mowles: Thomas is shown both as being born and as living in Elmsett. He enlisted in Ipswich as Pte 29651 and served with the 7th Btn, Royal Fusiliers (City of London Regiment). His number is only seven lower than Wilfred Kennington and both served in the same regiment, suggesting they were friends who joined together. He also served in France and Flanders and was killed in action on 13 November 1916, five months before

Wilfred died. He is also listed on the Thiepval Memorial in France.

Frederick Charles Pearl: There are gravestones in the churchyard listing the deaths of the Pearl family back to the late-nineteenth century. Frederick was born in Elmsett in 1884 to Robert and Martha Pearl, who lived in The Street. He was Pte 201200 and served with the 4th Btn, Suffolk Regiment, and died on the Somme on 15 July 1916. He is also listed on the Thiepval Memorial in France.

Others who Died in the First World War
Several men from Elmsett who died in the First World War are not listed on the Elmsett Memorial.

The Commonwealth War Graves Commission also lists a Charles Smith as a native of Elmsett, Suffolk. Charles, who was awarded the Military Medal, was Rifleman 390851 in the London Regiment (Queen Victoria's Rifles). He died on 15 September 1918 and is commemorated in the Bronfay Farm Military Cemetery, Bray-sur-Somme.

The Naval and Military Press CDROM *Soldiers Died in the Great War* lists six men originally from Elmsett. They all served in France and Flanders.

Reginald Bernard Cousins enlisted in Ipswich and was Cpl 40997 (formerly 1239) Suffolk (Cyclist), 7th Btn, Suffolk Regiment. He died on 20 November 1917.

Horace Gant, Pte 18495, 2nd Btn, Suffolk Regiment, died on 12 July 1916.

Ernest Hiskey, Pte 8271, 12th Btn, Suffolk Regiment, was killed in action on 24 March 1918.

Ernest Albert Edward Leek, Pte 16432, 10th Btn, Essex Regiment, was killed in action on 1 July 1916.

Thomas Edward Parker, L/Cpl 15566, 9th Btn, Prince of Wales's Own (West Yorkshire Regiment), was killed in action on 10 October 1917.

William John Ratcliffe, Pte G/8129, 2nd Btn, Duke of Cambridge's Own (Middlesex Regiment), was killed in action on 23 October 1916.

Memories of the War Years
Today it is hard to imagine how quiet the countryside was at the time of the First World War. Traffic was mainly horse-drawn and certainly there were no cars in Elmsett. The sky was empty of anything flying but birds and farming was done by men, not machines.

Sybil (Billie) Ladbrook (1907–97) remembered lying awake on a hot summer night when she was about eight years old and hearing the dull thud of gunfire in Flanders some 100 miles away.

Reg Barber (1902–99): *Boys on the farm always wanted to go to the plough, myself included. War opened the door of opportunity for many of us, as when all the 18-year olds were called up the youngsters got their chance. We did all the horse work on the farm. I was hardly man enough to put the collar over the horse's head when I first started. An elderly man did all*

the feeding of the horses. We were hardly paid anything until we were 21. As soon as my brother Sidney reached the age of 18 he had to go, but thank God he was kept this side of the Channel. There were terrible times for everyone. Many of the men who returned from the war were unable to carry on their usual work, so there had to be changes all round.

Two Elmsett residents spoke of their childhood memories of the First World War during interviews recorded in 1988.

Cecil Barber (1904–94): *During the First World War the Attendance Officer came into school just before the harvest holidays and told us if any of the boys could get themselves a job on a farm during the holidays they need not come back to school in September. Several of us boys got jobs, so didn't go back to school. I was put in the stockyard with the stockman. I was taught how to milk cows, how to use the separator to separate the milk from the cream and how to make butter in the churns. I was taught all this at a very early age as the Boss said 'you must learn all this, boy, in case they take my stockman into the army'. But luckily that didn't happen.*

Pauline Watkins (née Wyartt) (born 1912): *I remember the First World War although I was only two when it started. We had Women's Land Army girls, nicknamed 'Hay Balers', who lived in the house with us. My parents had three at the time. They helped to bale up the hay, which was all done by hand in those days. They came from some way away and stayed with us all the time. I can remember that Hadleigh had an aerodrome, it had been a private airfield before the war and was in the Pond Hall Road area. The Germans tried to bomb it. (There were Zeppelins over Hadleigh.) I remember being with my Mum and Dad, wrapped in a blanket, walking up the road. We met the Skippings, who lived at Rhodd's Farm and worked for Mr Robert Turner, and we watched the searchlights playing above the airfield.*

Sam Harvey VC (1881–1960) used to do the odd day's work for the Cooper family at Manor Farm but never really recovered from the injuries he received during the First World War. His citation reads:

On 29 September 1915 in the 'Big Willie' trench near Hohensoller Redoubt, France, during a heavy bombing attack, more bombs were urgently needed and Pte Harvey volunteered to fetch them. The communication trench was blocked with wounded and reinforcements and he went backwards and forwards across open land under intense fire and succeeded in bringing thirty boxes before he was wounded in the head. It was largely owing to his cool bravery in supplying bombs that the enemy was eventually driven back.

Herbert Barber with his prize greyhound in about 1920. He lost his hand and most of his right arm in the First World War.

His head injuries left him with an inability to settle. He lived in Princes Hall on the Whatfield Road, a row of thatched cottages that were a type of almshouse. He tended to drink heavily, but he did attend a dinner, hosted by the Prince of Wales, to honour all holders of the Victoria Cross in 1931 or 1932. He was affectionately known as 'Monkey Harvey' due to his slight build and his ability to shin up a walnut tree and knock the nuts off.

He died in Ipswich where, in the year 2000, a ceremony was held and he was given a fitting memorial in the town. Members of the Cooper family attended the ceremony.

Reg Barber, writing at the age of 92: *I have started some memories of the 1914–18 War, living through it all and seeing our men leaving home one after the other. It hurts me to think of it all. Some never returned, others came home with their limbs off. One brother came home with one arm lost, the other full of shrapnel. I cannot write any more, you will probably read it in some future history book… Coming to the end of this week (November 1993) and thinking of Remembrance Sunday. I did not realise this would come into my memory – the poppies. Thousands of people, including myself, will find it hard to hold back the tears, having lived through the horror of two world wars. Facing the horrors of the guns. No one looked forward to the postman's knock. There was the strain on mothers' faces, on many wives and sweethearts. This Sunday, God willing, I shall wear my poppy. But in the Services of Remembrance held all around the country at war memorials I do not like to hear that 'men gave their lives for their country'. They were compelled to face death – they had no choice.*

The Second World War (1939–45)

Although none of the villagers who left to fight in the Second World War was lost in action, the village played its full part in the war effort and ten villagers died as a result of enemy action.

The village was the base for a searchlight battery which was part of the defences for Wattisham airfield. The 7th (City of London) Btn, Royal

The Street, c.1935, showing The Row, which took a direct hit from a stray German bomb.

Alfred Hiskey outside his cottage in The Row in 1938. He left Elmsett during the depression and found work at a brewery in the Midlands, but returned home in old age.

Artillery, manned them. Some of the men were billeted in huts at Ladbrooks' Mill, where one searchlight was situated, and there was another at Clouds Meadows close to Elmsett Church.

There were two bombing raids on Elmsett, although in both cases the planes were probably aiming for nearby Wattisham airfield.

The people killed in the second bombing raid were: Emma Barber, Mary Ann Carter, Anna Churchyard, Elizabeth Dodd, Alfred Hiskey, Alice Taylor, William Taylor, Violet Taylor, Michael Taylor and Edwin Taylor

Eight houses known as The Row, four of them brick and four lath and plaster with thatched roofs were destroyed. The brick houses were demolished; the thatched cottages survived the blast but were destroyed in the subsequent fire.

House 1: Both residents in this house were killed – **Alfred Hiskey**, who was in his 80s, had farmed Mill Farm in Elmsett, where he not only butchered and sold his own meat but also sold bread and groceries from the farmhouse! **Alice Taylor**, housekeeper to Alfred, was in her 70s at the time of her death.

House 2: **Joe Barber** was badly injured but subsequently moved to Flowton Road in Elmsett and later married widow Louise Haywood; **Emma Barber**, Joe's wife, who was in her 60s or 70s, died. **Mary Carter**, who, ironically, had come to live with her brother to escape being bombed in Ipswich, also died.

House 3: **Elizabeth Dodd**, a widow in her 90s who occupied this house, was killed Not much is known about her as she had moved into the village not long before the tragedy.

House 4: The entire **Taylor family** was killed in this house – **William**, his wife **Violet**, who was originally from London, and their two young children, **Michael** and **Edwin**.

House 5: **Anna Churchyard**, a widow in her 90s, was killed. Although she was from the village, her only relative was a daughter living in Kent.

House 6: The four occupants of this house survived the bombing. They were **Herbert (Jot) Hiskey**, his wife **Emily**, who was injured, and two evacuees, **Marina** and **June Lyons**, from Bethnal Green.

House 7: **Cyril Wyartt**, who drove a cattle transporter and his wife **Annie** (née Rampling) occupied this house with three of their four daughters – **June**, aged 6; **Yvonne**, who was a toddler, and the baby, **Hazel**. All of them were uninjured. Their eldest daughter, **Pearl**, aged eight, was staying with her grandparents in Bildeston. Cyril was convinced that William (Bill) Taylor had had a premonition of the coming tragedy. That spring, as they worked together on their allotments, he often spoke of his fears for the future and his feeling that something dreadful was about to happen to them all.

House 8: **Bill Steward** and his wife **Laura** occupied this house. They both escaped unharmed.

Although some people were killed others had near misses.

Taffy Skippings: *My brother and I used to share the same bed and when the bang woke us up we found that the picture of General Gordon which hung on the wall was between us on the bed. My mum told me that she and dad had heard it coming and Dad had said 'This beggar's going to get us'. Luckily we got away with it.*

Memories of enemy action in the village
Cuthbert Lambert recalled the night of 9 January 1941:

We all turned out when we were straddled by HEs. (bombs) at Lost Farm, Offton, and a string of incendiaries was dropped at Red House Farm. We were holding an evening service in our chapel at the time. The fires burned several corn stacks awaiting the thresher which also caught fire, but it was saved I think. I shall always remember the picture of the traction engine being driven from the flames by a man apparently wearing his best suit and a bowler hat. I never heard who he was. (Subsequently Cuthbert was told it was Harold Cooper who also saved the threshing machine.) A fire appliance arrived from Hadleigh in time to save the buildings, but I believe the stacks had to be abandoned to the flames.

Harold Cooper also remembered this incident and described the action he took to save the threshing machine:

Incendiary bombs were dropped in a line along the farmyard setting everything on fire – stacks, sheds, machinery. It was the middle of winter and we had to break ice to get water. Pigs which had been let out of the sheds were running around everywhere just yards from the burning building.

After the fire blitz at Red House Farm earlier that year a system of fire watching had been established during the hours of darkness.

Cuthbert Lambert: *On 12 May 1941 came the bomb which demolished the row of cottages in the 'Street'. We helped to recover the bodies. That was certainly a night to remember. Strangely, just two days later we heard that Rudolph Hess, Hitler's deputy, had landed a plane in Scotland, apparently on some sort of peace mission.*

Four men were on duty at the Reading Room that night, Edwin Westren, 24 at the time, and Reg Martin, had taken the early shift from dusk until 12.30a.m. Bill Wilding and a Mr Hill (a London evacuee billeting officer) covered from 12.30a.m. until dawn. The changeover took place as usual and for a time they stood talking in the roadway before the two who were going off duty rode off homewards on their bicycles.

At a little before 1.00a.m. the two Elmsett searchlights reached into the sky and, with uncanny accuracy, caught and held a German plane in their crossbeams. Knowing they were trapped the German pilot and his crew released a 500-pound bomb in order to escape.

Edwin Westren: *It was an oppressive night, with brilliant moonlight. A German plane had been in the area for some time, and at about 1.00a.m. it was caught in the beam of the searchlight at the bottom of Church Hill. Almost at once the bomb fell. Reg and I threw ourselves to the ground as the explosion came.*

The two lucky men escaped unscathed, but found themselves enmeshed in a mass of telephone wires brought down by the blast. Edwin rushed into the garden of the nearest cottage:

I was confronted with the thatched roof tilted over, the eaves resting on the ground, and the head of a small girl emerging through the thatch somewhere in the middle. I climbed up and lifted the girl out and took her along to the Rose and Crown.

She was one of the evacuees from Bethnal Green in London, who had been sent to Suffolk for safety. By the time he ran back to the bombed cottages a lot more villagers and some troops from the searchlight battery had arrived and were tugging at the rubble in a desperate race for survivors, because by now the thatch was alight and the flames were spreading rapidly.

Newly thatched cottages in The Row in the 1920s.

Telephone links were cut off, so 16-year-old **John Rouse** set off on his bike to alert the fire and rescue services in Hadleigh, four miles away. His valiant effort turned out to be unnecessary as a village shopkeeper, **Cliff Hiskey**, set out in his van and arrived there first. They were not to know that both their journeys were unnecessary because the Cooper's telephone at Manor Farm, half a mile across the fields, was still connected to the outside world.

As the survivors struggled or were helped from the ruins they were taken to the Rose and Crown, where Mrs Pearl had everything in hand, in spite of having her windows blown in and floors awash with beer and broken glass.

Edwin Westren: *She was marvellously cool and calm, and was soon dishing out cups of tea all round. Many remember seeing Joe Barber walk there covered in white plaster dust from head to foot but not seriously injured (his wife and sister were killed). Charlie Taylor was there looking grey and dazed but hardly hurt at all, although his mother had been killed.*

Others had miraculous escapes. The Wyartt family struggled out uninjured except for Cyril's cut feet.

Elizabeth Wyartt: *There was a large hole in the roof after the explosion. We wrapped the children and ourselves in blankets and went out into the garden. My husband went back to try and rescue some of our possessions but only managed to save my sewing machine – which I still have.*

Her daughter **June Skippings** (née Wyartt), who in later years married Taffy Skippings, one of the boys who survived the bomb, remembers the incident vividly: 'The stairs were covered in straw from the roof, and we slipped as we made our escape.'

Bill Steward and his crippled wife were unscathed, but Mrs Steward had problems with her feet and could only walk with special boots. They had gone to bed as usual, only to be woken by the tremendous explosion, their little cottage tilting over on its side and flames shooting up around them.

Bill helped his wife into her special boots and they were able to escape. Jot Hiskey and his wife also managed to escape, although Mrs Hiskey had a serious gash in her leg. She was taken to the casualty station in Hadleigh with Joe Barber, whose injury required hospital treatment.

The dead were identified by Frank and Gerald Barber and then removed to the Rectory Coach House. From there the coffins were taken the next day to the church to await a joint funeral service.

Edwin remembers the courage and fortitude of the survivors, most of whom had lost all their possessions and only had the clothes they stood up in:

Poor old Mrs Steward walked further that night than she had done in years. She and her husband went to the home of the Ladbrook family at Laurel Cottage, as did the Wyartt family. Bill Steward was soon chatting quite cheerfully to Mrs Ladbrook. Indeed his chief concern seemed to be that he had lost his life insurance policy in the fire. Clothes and shoes were found for Jot Hiskey, who had been found dazed in the road wearing only a shirt, a raincoat and a pair of wellingtons soon after the explosion – he was reunited with his wife, whom he had lost in the confusion. They and the two London evacuee children they were caring for were also taken to Laurel Cottage.

Aubrey Barber: *Recalling the night the bomb fell on Elmsett Street is painful and remains so for a lifetime. My memory is of saying goodnight to my Grandad (Alfred Hiskey) and his housekeeper (Alice Taylor) after evening service at the Methodist Chapel, then walking home in the usual way not knowing what the next few hours was to bring. That night I was woken by the explosion and after a short while heard my father say, 'It's the Street'. Then he and my brother Gerald went to see what had happened and to help with the rescue work. I remember being really frightened and was soon to hear that my Grandad, his housekeeper and two aunts had all been killed, while another aunt and uncle were injured. One of my aunts had moved out of Ipswich into the village to escape any bombing in the town and sadly became one of the victims that night. Two evacuees from Bethnal Green fortunately escaped injury. The Methodist Chapel was only a short distance from where the bomb fell and needed extensive repairs. If my memory serves me right, the Reading Room was used for Sunday services until repair work was finished.*

My memory of the immediate aftermath is blank. I recall the talk of a German plane caught in the searchlights. We had got to know the men who manned the Searchlight Battery, one of them rented accommodation in the village and he, his wife and daughter lived amongst us. All shared in the grief. This event was a huge blow, not only for my family, but also for the village as a whole. The population was 150 and everyone knew everybody else. I did a daily milk

round along with my brother Victor and sister Vera; we used to cycle with the milk cans on our handlebars measuring milk into the waiting milk jugs on the doorsteps. We knew all our customers quite intimately and the bombing was the topic of conversation. The shock was shared by all. I really missed my Grandad, just being able to call in and particularly the Saturday night family gatherings with him and the Taylor family (who were all killed) playing whist, dominoes, etc. The aladdin oil lamps lighting the room alongside the glow of the fire – a regular occurrence for families in those days – and a memory that I really treasure.

The parish organiser responsible for air-raid precautions and civil defence, was Percy Cooper from Manor Farm. **Janet Cooper** was living with her parents and brothers, and remembers the night, and of going next day into St Peter's Church, where all the coffins were lined up:

I remember my father coming in at about 4.30a.m. with a list of the dead. I held a lamp for him as he reported to his headquarters in Hadleigh – on the only phone still in order. In those days we were a real village where everyone was known to everybody else, so the impact of the bomb was that much greater.

Edwin Westren: *When daylight came nothing remained of The Row except one chimneystack. Bill Taylor's strange foreboding had been fully justified. Neither he, his wife, his two small sons nor his mother were among the survivors. The only living thing to survive from the Taylor household was the children's pet rabbit, which was found alive and well in its hutch in the rubble next day. Mrs Carter had not found the safety she had expected in Elmsett – she too was dead.*

Next day various officials came – the relieving officer and the billeting officer and also Sir Charles and Lady Rowley from Hadleigh, who brought clothing and other essentials from the Red Cross and the Women's Voluntary Service. The Wyartt family still remember the kindness shown by the Salvation Army. A consignment of children's clothes was also received from Ipswich High School.

Most of the houses in the immediate vicinity of The Row sustained damage from the blast, chiefly windows and doors blown in and roofs stripped, but only the Skippings family had to leave their home until repairs were completed.

The chapel was severely damaged, as was the Reading Room some distance away. The beautiful elm trees on the rectory meadow opposite The Row were never the same again and after the war they were all felled. The site of the disaster remained derelict for several years. Eventually two houses and two bungalows were built there.

Harold Cooper, Percy Cooper, Ken Gibbons, who had recently joined the Air Force, and Janet Cooper, 1942. Farmers and agricultural workers were not enlisted, but Ken's brother Hugh ran the farm with their father during the war.

Harold Cooper remembers seeing the R101 airship passing over Elmsett, and also recalled watching a Spitfire crash near to Barney Wyartt's on the boundary of the village. The pilot was not

Members of Comrades of the City of London Battalion, who manned the searchlight battery, presenting a plaque of their insignia in 1991 in memory of those who died in The Row in 1941. It hangs in the Village Hall. Left to right: ?, John Walker, Aubrey Barber, Harry Shortland, ?, ?, Col Pearce.

injured, but Barney took him in and gave him a strong drink of whisky. The Spitfire was taken away and salvaged, but not before some inquisitive village boys had been to look at the wreck. Jim Steward remembers climbing into the cockpit and looking at the controls. He thought this was in 1941.

In the spring of 1940 a ship en route for Norway was diverted to Ipswich docks. On board were two big crawler tractors which were confiscated by the Ministry of Agriculture. Harold was sent to drive them to the north of the county, where they were used to drain an airfield. The land was waterlogged and very boggy and the mole-draining job lasted about a year. From the accounts we have been able to obtain it seems to show that nearly everyone, even in

A street party, 8 May 1995, to commemorate the 50th anniversary of VE Day.

On the Cooper's horse, 1941, evacuees (right to left) Florrie Mills, Rennie Mills and Peggy Keeler all from Bethnal Green.

a small village like Elmsett, was involved in some way in the war effort and deeply affected by the consequences of war.

An emotional reunion was held in the village on 12 May 1991 when former evacuees and searchlight operators joined the survivors of the wartime bomb which fell on The Row in a memorial service at St Peter's Church, where a wreath was laid in memory of the ten people who died on 12 May 1941. In a packed Village Hall, over 150 people gathered to look at old photographs of the village before and after it was bombed. The occasion was organised by Aubrey and Ellen Barber. Surviving members of the City of London 7th Btn, some in their late 80s, presented the villagers with a plaque of their battalion badge for the Village Hall.

Evacuees

Elmsett's war effort started early on when, as was reported in the *Elmsett Recorder*:

About 50 London children from the East End (Bethnal Green) with their teachers and helpers arrived in the village during the evening of Friday,1 September 1939, two days before the outbreak of war. Householders were paid 10s.6d. for the first child and 8s.6d. per head for any others.

Percy Cooper, the parish organiser, was responsible for selecting destinations for the evacuees.

Rupert Cooper: *My father was involved in sorting out where the evacuees were going to stay. Some people*

refused to take them, so the police were involved and they had to go to the homes with the children. Nearly everyone had an evacuee. You could be taken to court if you refused, and that usually persuaded them. Mother had three girls – I can remember them well – and they were with us for two years.

When the blitz started in September 1940 more children arrived, this time some of them with their mothers. Most of the children soon settled well into the unfamiliar surroundings, and attended the village school with the local children.

Joy Sillitoe (née Barber): *The ones with us broke everything in sight – we had no toys left at all. My grandmother in Aldham had a family called Spicer, and there were five or six of them. It was quite hard work for her. My mother found it hard work too as she had three children of her own – I was the eldest at about five.*

The adults were more difficult to cope with. A few settled happily in the village but others could not stand the isolation, lack of shops, cinemas, etc., and returned to London to face the bombing rather than stay in the country. During the period of the 'Phoney War' a slow drift back to London took place, but with the worsening situation after September 1940, this stopped. Many of the evacuees had been bombed out, losing all their possessions and having only the clothes they were wearing. The arrival of the flying bombs and V2 rockets in June 1944 brought another wave of evacuees, grown-ups and children, and somehow they were fitted in with local families. By the Christmas of that year the end of the war was in sight and the evacuees began to return home.

The Home Guard

Few agricultural workers went into the Forces. The Germans were sinking many of the ships bringing food to Britain and the Government put pressure on farmers to produce more food. This meant that farmers and farm workers were exempt from conscription and even those who wanted to join up were prevented from doing so. They did, however, join the Home Guard.

In Elmsett the Home Guard used to meet outside the Rose and Crown pub on Sunday mornings and evenings. In the winter they met in the Reading Room. The shooting range was at Chelsworth and gas-mask training at Raydon. The Elmsett guard was led first by Alf Pearl and then by Stan Roxburgh, who had served in the First World War. Stan used to work for the Coopers at Manor Farm.

Fred Holder: *Stan was the officer and he knew what he was doing. He kept us all under control, but he was a good mate.*

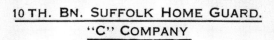

10 TH. BN. SUFFOLK HOME GUARD.
"C" COMPANY

This is to certify that

Pte. F. Holder

was a member of the

No. 5 Platoon

·300 Rifle team which won

Inter-Platoon
Runners-up Cup

at Hadleigh Range, Oct. 8th. 1944.

J.W. Wilson · Major.,

O.C. "C" Coy, 10th. Bn. Suffolk Home Guard.

Victor Barber in Home Guard uniform, 1942.

Fred Holder's certificate – an accompanying letter reads 'It was found impossible to obtain any miniature cups or medals for the winners… I hope the enclosed certificate will help to remind you of a very exciting and interesting match and of the part you played of which you have every reason to be proud.' Others in the team were Sgt J. Eggleston, Cpl K. Gibbons, Cpl V. Barber, Pte F. Holder, Pte S. Green, Cpl R. Barber, Cpl H.F. Gibbons, L/C R. Leeks and Pte S.R. Green.

Harold Cooper: *I was in the Home Guard from the start. There were 12 of us. We were not called out much, but we were keen and enthusiastic. I fired at a German plane once, but didn't bring it down! The German plane came over very low at dusk so as to avoid the ack-ack guns. They were flying very low, at about 30 feet.*

Because of the near proximity of Wattisham airfield there was constant fear of German parachutists, and one of the jobs the Home Guard had to do was to check the church tower. It was never a popular job – no lights could be used and the last ladder was a vertical climb. The unfortunate man on watch had to go through a trapdoor at the top and invariably a bat would fly out just as he reached the top and scare the living daylights out of him!

Rupert Cooper: *I was seventeen when war broke out and was involved in the Home Guard because I was working in agriculture and so was not called up. I was involved in night work when I should have been in bed. When the invasion was thought to be imminent, I can remember coming in from work at eight o'clock at night, getting changed and then going on Home Guard duty till the next morning, and then going to work the next day after breakfast. We were based at the Rectory and I used to go round with a chap called Jack Malster, nick-named 'Bodger'. We worked in pairs. We had our rifles strapped to our bicycles and to start with we had five rounds of ammunition. We rode round the village and into Aldham and on to Whatfield so we were riding around all night. We had one or two nights on duty each week.*

Percy Cooper at Manor Farm had new tractors and also bought bulldozers for mole-draining the heavy clay soil. These were driven by Alfred Dickens, Jack Bradbrook and Les Stockings, who worked for the Coopers for 50 years and also did contract work for other farmers in the area.

Rupert Cooper: *Jack Bradbrook was a good chap. One day we had an urgent call from the opencast coal mines in Rotherham, so the bulldozers were requisitioned and* sent up to extract coal. Jack went too. Unfortunately when they started checking up on the men working, drivers of bulldozers were not exempt from military service, unlike farm workers, so Jack was called up and sadly we lost him from the farm.

The Searchlight Battery

There were two searchlight batteries in the village, manned by the City of London 7th Btn. One was situated at the mill and the other at the bottom of the hill below the church. **Jean Leeks** remembers soldiers being in the village.

Land Army Girls

Many farms had Land Army girls to help with the work. One of these, Rose Smith, married one of the men from the searchlight battery, Harry McClelland. Rose was billeted with Victor Barber and his wife Flo at the old Mill Farm, and worked on Ladbrook's farm.

Reg Barber: *The horses became the delight of everyone who worked near them. The girls brushed them down morning and evening. Full praise was due to those girls. On one occasion one asked me how I knew when the horse needed to go to the toilet! I said when one is constantly working with them one notices all their different movements, and the horse would start showing a walk a bit wide. She was amused, as us horsemen kept a special whistle to blow at such times.*

Joy Sillitoe: *We had some lovely land girls, Rose lives in Harwich now and still keeps in touch with my mother.*

Taffy Skippings remembers the Land Army girls:
Greta Smith worked at Wood Farm for Ronnie Robinson, milking cows and working on the farm and delivering milk round part of the village. She lived at Whatfield, as did her sister Eva who worked at Ladbrook's farm. Other girls lodged in the village. Joyce Spurling stayed the longest – she worked at Gate Farm. On Sunday nights the village lads used to go to church. When we came out we went out the back, down to the Offton Lime Burners pub. Whichever land girls were here at the time used to come with us.

Prisoners of War

A number of Italian prisoners of war were housed at Barham Workhouse and delivered to various farms in the area by truck every day. Leslie Wilding drove the truck for three or four years and dropped them off each day at different jobs as they were needed. Farmers had to pay the War Agricultural Committee to have these men to work on their farms.

Rupert Cooper: *They used to make toys in their spare time in the evenings and they sold them. One of the toys I remember was made from a ten-inch square of wooden board. It had a hen in the middle, and around*

about some little chickens. When you pulled the string the chickens pecked at the board. Another one was a ladder with a man on it that went down rung by rung. If you gave the men a two-inch piece of perspex they'd bring you a couple of cigarette lighters the next day. The Italians didn't work as well as the Germans we had working for us later in the war, but we were glad to have them.

Later in the war Percy Cooper bought a farm in Bricett. It was in a very poor state, much of it overgrown and poorly drained. He had over 100 German prisoners working there every day for a year.

Rupert Cooper: *They came by lorry every day, five lorries with 20 men in each. The hedges were 20 feet high and ten yards wide. They cut every hedge and they cleared every ditch and cut every piece of wood up, and did it all by hand. It was the last big contract they did because the War Agricultural Committee had underestimated the work and they lost money on it.*

An Anderson shelter used to make a bridge over the stream in 1950 and still there in 2005! These small corrugated iron air-raid shelters were a familiar sight in many gardens during the Second World War. They were partly buried in the ground and covered with earth to protect the occupants from explosions.

Rationing

Petrol was the first item to be rationed in 1939, then in 1940 food rationing was introduced and ration cards, specifying where the food was to be bought, were issued.

Janet Cooper: *We had bees and were allowed extra sugar to feed them. Farm workers were allowed extra cheese. Meat was scarce, but we had chickens, milk and eggs.*

Pauline Watkins: *We were very fortunate – we kept hens and pigs and didn't feel some of the hardships. Village people weren't too poorly off either, because they produced some of their own food.*

Margaret Watkins: *Mother had to get her groceries from Hadleigh, but sweet coupons could be used anywhere, so we used to go to Mr Hiskey's shop for ours. They were put into a little three-cornered paper bag.*

Brian Hiskey remembered picking rose hips from the hedgerows and taking them into school for collection. Rose-hip syrup was an important source of vitamin C when fruit was in short supply.

The Elmsett Community

Inevitably, when the Second World War became a real threat there were people who did not wish to fight. In 1938 the situation in Germany was dominating the news; peace movements were being established and many communities were being set up. Several of these were small rural groups with a few acres of land where self-sufficient vegetarians grew their own food. The Elmsett Community was one such group.

In the East End of London members of the Fellowship of Reconciliation met at a centre known as Kingdom Hall. People from all over the United

The chapel at the Elmsett Community, 1946.

Edmund Ward relaxes at Bushy Ley, 1947 – literature, poetry and music were an essential part of life at the commune.

Kingdom met to talk about what they were doing and there was an attempt to unite these organisations into a group called Community in Britain. After some searching, the leader of this organisation, Edmund Cocksage, discovered Nova Scotia Farm in Elmsett. It had 16 acres of good land, a small three bedroomed cottage and a shepherd's hut. The ten founding members who arrived at the farm were regular church attenders and thus were accepted by villagers in Elmsett, if somewhat cautiously at first. The village had changed little over the centuries and the influx of young men and a few young women living together, wearing odd clothes and singing hymns in the fields was thought to be somewhat amusing. They were probably not aware that the whole community was based on love – not physical love, but the love of one human being for another. Poetry and music were important aspects of their lives.

When war was declared the community opened its doors to pacifists and conscientious objectors. Life was hard for the members, who had very little money and most of whom, from comfortable urban homes, were unused to the harsh agricultural life. They found the early rising difficult, especially in the bitter cold winter weather; the punishing physical labour was a great challenge and the basic diet of vegetables and home made bread, whilst satisfying, was repetitious.

Cuthbert Lambert, who still lives in the house, writes of his memories of those days: *Down the ages people have been drawn together to form small self-supporting communities, for one reason or another, because of religious persecution or a desire to spread a particular message, as with the early Christians.*

The community in Elmsett had its beginnings in a conference in East London in 1938 organised by a group of Christian Socialists alarmed at the prospect of another war-to-end-wars. Wishing to opt out of involvement, they agreed to form a group based on agriculture and where everything was owned in common, except for small personal items.

I don't know how Elmsett was chosen as a place to start except that two local farmers involved in the ongoing 'Tithe Wars' offered advice. They were Philip Butler, a Quaker in Needham Market, and Charles Westren of Elmsett Hall. They knew that Nova Scotia Farm had fallen vacant as a result of the death of the owner, Mr Tipple. Farming advice and machinery were offered in exchange for labour. This worked well enough for a time. Local labour became short as more men were called up or volunteered for the services and any of us who had any skills at all were in great demand. I had joined in 1940, having worked in Ipswich for six years as a 'wireless mechanic', so people were always asking me to 'come and look' at their old radios.

I had been called up with the very first batch of 'militiamen' before the war but had registered as a conscientious objector and was granted exemption.

Cuthbert Lambert repairing the tractor at Bushy Ley, 1947.

Cuthbert Lambert sharpening a hoe at Bushy Ley, 1947.

Cuthbert Lambert with children, residents and visitors to the community in 1947.

I had taken a great interest in comparative religion and was profoundly influenced by the writings and example of such minds as Mahatma Gandhi and Rabindranath Tagore, so Pacifism as a creed came naturally. I did, though, apply to the Friends Ambulance Unit, who were then taking volunteers to work in Finland at the start of the Russo-Finnish war. However, they were only taking members of the Society of Friends at that time, so I joined the Community to comply with the terms of my exemption, farming being one option, until training for the FAU could commence.

I became involved with the aims of the community and decided to stay. Over the next few years we must have been visited by many hundreds of people, some for just a day, others for weeks or months. Although somewhat isolated by being outside the village, we did put on Nativity Plays and organised a village fête. We shared firewatching duties and forward planning for the event of invasion or evacuation.

In 1944 we were asked by the National Provisional Council for Mental Health if we would take on patients invalided out of the forces for psychiatric reasons.

There seemed to be no sort of provision for some of them. None of us had any training in this field but we coped as best we could and some quite interesting experiences resulted. In the night, one poor chap took an overdose and while some people tried to get emetics into him, I was sent up to the village phone box to call a doctor. A curious argument ensued when I had to admit I had come out without any money. The operator seemed disinclined to believe me but relented eventually and put me through to a Bildeston doctor who, on being told the facts said I 'should let the silly beggar get on with it!' He then suggested I should get someone with a car to take him to hospital, but he wasn't going to come out himself. When I said the only car owner I knew was at 'The Hall', he indicated that he happened to know he was not fit to drive that night! He would call an ambulance himself. It seemed a very long time later that a brilliantly lit ambulance appeared out of the blackout and a very groggy patient was removed to hospital. One of us had to stay at the hospital all next day to make sure he didn't fall asleep as this could prove fatal.

With the number of patients we were taking, we were running out of sleeping accommodation so we put out an appeal in the East Anglian *for huts. They didn't charge us for this but strangely, we didn't receive a single reply. The situation was eased shortly afterwards when we were able to buy the big cookhouse hut from the searchlight unit on the Rookery Road. By the end of 1946 most of the members had decided to do other things, mostly humanitarian or other worthwhile work – teaching, the church or social services – but I wanted to stay on and re-form a community. I was able to buy the farm with the help of two remarkable ladies who had been great friends of the community. One was Clare*

Carting hay at Bushy Ley in 1947 – Alan Ablon leading the horse Bessie. On the left is the searchlight battery hut which was previously sited near to the church. It was used by the community for living accommodation after the war.

Cuthbert Lambert used to make a rough frame for a straw shelter. As the corn was threshed the straw was thrown onto the frame to make a covering – the shelter would last for one or two years. 1947.

Cameron, the editor of the Buddhist Society Magazine, *and Ruth Troward, who had a cottage in Hadleigh Road. Clare continued to produce the magazine from here, attracting several people with a view to joining us. We changed the name Nova Scotia to Bushy Ley for this fresh start, the name of a field in the area* which sounded nicely traditional. We had always aimed to farm organically and in 1948 we ceased to use artificial fertilisers completely. Crops did suffer for a time until we were able to build up the natural fertility of the soil and became one of the first organic farms in the country.

We didn't succeed in actual communal living again but we did attract many interested and interesting people. Some came as paying guests, some TB patients who wished to pursue Nature Cure treatment, some young offenders on probation and some farm pupils. There were also several unmarried mothers. Though not all at the same time!

I married one of the earlier members of the community in 1948 and we had a daughter. Ruth Troward was, I understand, the first civilian allowed back into Germany after the war, where she had taught music 20 years earlier. She suffered considerable hardship working among refugees and in a school for the blind.

Clare Cameron had to return to London to nurse her parents until they died. Ruth came to live with us briefly in 1969 but became very frail and had to go into a home. Both Clare and Ruth died about 20 years ago. When I retired in 1980, the farm was taken over by my daughter Catherine and her husband John Thoroughgood, who continue with the tradition of organic farming.

St Peter's Church.

St Peter's Church interior, showing box pews, c.1900.

Left: *The Norman door of St Peter's Church.*

✦ CHAPTER 3 ✦

Places of Worship

St Peter's Church

The oldest building in Elmsett, St Peter's Church, is a fine flintstone building which can be dated back to the twelfth century, but in addition to its mention in the Domesday Book there is strong physical evidence that a church stood on this site several centuries earlier. The most convincing of these is a piece of stone in the porch floor. It is not local stone but a very hard type of limestone, so must have been brought from abroad or from the West Country. The distinctive shape of this stone leaves no doubt that it was originally a Saxon grave cover, reused as paving.

In his *History of St Peter's Church* Allan Mountfield suggests that the early window heads are indicative of a Saxon method of construction, and favours a date of about 1050 for the nave. Whether the impressive broad ship-like nave was built in late Saxon times, or after the Norman Conquest remains open to conjecture

In 1997 the church underwent extensive restoration work, and detailed reports were drawn up for English Heritage by Dr Oliver Rackham, Corpus Christi College, Cambridge, and by Dr R.D. Carr, Suffolk County Council Archaeological Service. Dr Rackham's examination of the roof structure revealed that the present tiled roof is fourteenth century, and that it replaced an earlier structure. It was certainly thatched, as evidence of this can be seen on the east wall of the tower. The tower is later than the arch in the west end of the church, probably built in the thirteenth century, and Dr Carr suggests that the chancel also dates from this period.

Dr Rackham dates the porch from the thirteenth century also, saying:

The timber framed porch… with deeply moulded cruck-style arch and original barge boards, in remarkable condition despite 700 years of exposure to the rain. The doorway replaced an earlier Norman arch into which fitted a Norman door, with the earliest tongue-and-groove boards known to me, re-used in the Early English doorway, which it does not fit.

Inside St Peter's can be found a Norman/Early English font of Purbeck marble. Two altar boards bearing the Lord's Prayer, the Nicene Creed and the Ten Commandments are eighteenth century, and a Table of Affinity seventeenth century. A hinged board painted with the arms of Queen Anne, dated 1758, has an incomplete emblem of the Prince of

Wales on its reverse. A hatchment (funerary device) of unknown origin is thought to be eighteenth century; it bears the motto of Viscount Ranelagh and the corrupted coat of arms of a family whose surname was Jones. The memorials in the chancel are mostly to former rectors, with the exception of one showing Edward Sherland wearing a long black gown and ruff, kneeling at a desk on a red cushion with gold tassels.

By today's standards St Peter's is an unpretentious building standing in isolation away from the centre of the present village, but a thousand years ago it must have been an imposing building, standing as it does on the highest ground in the area. Today the impression of light and space gives it a quiet dignity and simple beauty which **Christine Ladbrook**, remembering her first visit nearly a century ago, expressed so eloquently:

It was a hot sunny morning in early summer. I was about six years old. I was sent out by Mother to entertain her friend Auntie Lil, who was staying with us, while she cooked the dinner. We were going to look at the church. First we had to walk to the village to fetch the key. Then we walked back. The unmetalled road was hot and glaring in the bright sunlight. We climbed over the white stile into the churchyard and walked up the gravel path. On either side were graves almost hidden in the grass, which would be mown with a scythe. I remember the ox-eye daisies growing in the long grass. We stepped down into the porch and Auntie Lil unlocked the heavy oak door and we went down another four broad steps into the nave. It was cool and dim. The bright light was filtered through the diamond-paned glass of the East window. It was very still. Not just quiet – still. Neither of us spoke. The old box pews were still in place, but I don't remember noticing them. I only remember the stillness, the holiness. We stood there in awe for a few minutes. Presently we turned and went out again into the hot bright sunshine. I have never forgotten that day.

The Ladbrooks were at that time Nonconformists and did not attend St Peter's, but went by pony and trap to the Baptist chapel in Somersham.

Church Bells

Although out of sight to the casual visitor the bell frame is of great historical interest. It is a high-sided type of which only three remain in Suffolk.

It probably dates from the fifteenth century and was designed for four bells, which it carried in 1553. None of the original bells remain, and the frame is now too weak to support a ring of four, so in 2003 a sound bell was sold. The proceeds from this were used to build a new frame and the 1636 Miles Grange bell, which had a 27-inch crack in it, was re-cast with a facsimile of the original engraving. In 2005 Rachel Hitchcock and John Ladbrooke donated a second bell in memory of their aunts, Sybil and Christine Ladbrook. The children from the school were able to attend the hanging of this bell.

Emily Greenfield (aged seven): *Once we went to St Peter's Church to see the new bell. At the church the bell was on the grass. It had a code on it. Both the bells in Elmsett have got the code. The new bell had lots of decorations which were grapes and berries. We watched it go up.*

Elmsett Charities

Glanville's Gift (or gift of the Revd Richard Glanville)

Richard Glanville gave in 1667:

… one small piece of land which he had purchased from John Dubbell of Elmsett upon condition that the Rector of Elmsett for the time being shall upon Christmas Day in every year distribute to six of the aged poor of the said Parish six pennyworth of bread each…

Richard Glanville was rector and lord of the manor of Elmsett, Somersham and Offton in the middle of the seventeenth century. The piece of land purchased by him and given to the church was a small woody grove adjoining Newlands. Rent from this land provided the income for the endowment. This grove is listed in the terriers, which give descriptions of Glebe lands from 1705 onwards. In 1770 it is stated that the grove was 'stubbed' by the late rector, Mr Haynes, and added to Newlands. In 1777:

… this grove does not appear, but according to the best information the present rector can obtain from the ancient inhabitants of this parish the said grove had been stubbed and laid to the contiguous piece of copy-hold land mentioned as belonging to Mr Coe (Revd Moses Coe) which by the executors or representatives of Mr Coe was sold to Mr Gregory Russel of Elmsett in whose use and possession it now remains.

A conveyance of Glebe lands dated 1 February 1921 states that Newlands was sold with three other pieces by Revd C.E. Scratchley to Mr A.E. Ladbrook.

In 1965 Ken Gibbons, churchwarden at the time, tried unsuccessfully to find what had become of the charity. Subsequent searches have also failed to reveal what became of the funds.

Moses Coe Charity

In his will Revd Moses Coe, Rector of Elmsett 1686 until his death in 1725, bequeathed the sum of £15:

… the interest thereof to be distributed among such poor of the Parish who constantly attend the Church service and the Sacrament of the Lord's Supper and the interest of the other five pounds to be paid to such poor children of the Parish as shall make the best responses when examined in the church catechism…

Moses Coe died in 1726 but his legacy was not received until 1736, when Mr William Mitchell of Lavenham, one of the executors of the will, paid £21.5s.6d. to the rector, Mr Hopton Haynes, and the churchwardens and overseers of the parish. The odd sum of 5s.6d. distributed complied with the terms of Mr Coe's will.

The parish records show a distribution of bread to the poor at Christmas in 1769 but from 1773 there was also a distribution of money. In this year ten recipients received amounts ranging from 1–2s. Further distributions were made in 1786 and 1855. One of the people who received a loaf in 1769 was James Aves, and in each of the years recorded a member of the Aves family received either bread or

Left: Revd Scratchley, Rector of Elmsett 1912–24, described by Fred Holder as 'a tall, frail looking man who was driven to church in his carriage by his groom, Golden Frost.'

cash, culminating in 1786 when Ste. Aves's wife received 2s. and Widow Aves received 1s.6d. From *Kelly's Directory* of 1912:

... the sum of money, with interest now amounts to £30 which has been placed by the parish under the control of the Charity Commissioners who have invested it in the funds...

In 2005 the charity was wound up and the sum of £76 was given to the school to purchase books.

Lord Bishop Andrewes' Charity
Bishop Lancelot Andrewes (1555–1626) owned land in Elmsett, Somersham and Offton. Bishop of Chichester (1605), Ely (1609) and Winchester (1619), he was one of the most learned men of his time. He was Royal Chaplain to Elizabeth I, James I and Charles I, and in 1611 headed the committee of scholars which produced the King James Bible,

Rectors and Patrons of St Peter's, Elmsett

1305	Gilbert de Helmyngham	Lady Joan de Boun
1305	William de Rydlesworth	Lady Joan de Boun
1306	John de Boun	Lady Joan de Boun
1318	Thomas de Somersham	Sir John de Boun
1340	Richard Aytrop	Sir William de Boun, Earl of Northampton
1341	Dominus Henry Broun	Sir William de Boun, Earl of Northampton
1361	John de Haytefield	Sir Humfrey Bohun
1370	Thomas Atte Ook	Sir Humfrey de Bohun, Earl of Hereford
1383	Richard Chubbe	Lady Johanna Bohun, Countess of Hereford & Essex
1405	John Warrok	Lady Johanna, Countess of Hereford, Essex & Northampton
1417	John Jepe	Lady Johanna, Countess of Hereford, Essex & Northampton
1436	Richard Aleyn	Katherine, Queen of England
1460	Thomas Beanfitz	The King of England
1480	Thomas Dolett	Queen Elizabeth
1507	Nicholas Hawmby	The King of England
1528	Robert Bossall	Katherine, Queen of England
1572	William Boyse	Queen Elizabeth (Duchy of Lancaster)
1588	William Tampon	Queen Elizabeth (Duchy of Lancaster)
1597	George Carter	Queen Elizabeth (Duchy of Lancaster)
1617	William Sympson	not known
1649	Richard Glanvile	Sir William Dayley, Knight
1668	John Glanvile	Richard Glanvile de Elmsett
1669	John Crane	Joseph Crane
1686	Moses Coe	Stephen Coe de Alpheton
1727	Hopton Haynes	Clare College, Cambridge
1766	William Talbot	Clare College, Cambridge
1812	Edward Twentyman	Clare College, Cambridge
1816	John Short Hewett	Clare College, Cambridge
1817	James Speare	Clare College, Cambridge
1850	James Burdakin	Clare College, Cambridge
1852	William Hardman Molyneux	Clare College, Cambridge
1864	Thomas Barber	Clare College, Cambridge
1912	Edward Scratchley	Clare College, Cambridge
1926	Christopher Beevor Haslewood	Clare College, Cambridge
1941	John Smyth	Clare College, Cambridge
1946	Thomas Robert Browne	Clare College, Cambridge
1957	Albert Scott	Clare College, Cambridge
1965	Frank Cyril Hodgkinson	The Bishop of St Edmundsbury & Ipswich
1969	Henry Alexander Tait	The Bishop of St Edmundsbury & Ipswich
1976	Geoffrey David Jeremy Walsh	The Bishop of St Edmundsbury & Ipswich
1981	Herbert Gerald Harrison	The Bishop of St Edmundsbury & Ipswich
1989	William James Sands	The Bishop of St Edmundsbury & Ipswich
1993	Ian Andrew Wilson	The Bishop of St Edmundsbury & Ipswich
2003	Janet Mary Simpson	The Bishop of St Edmundsbury & Ipswich

possibly contributing more work than others. In his will, dated 1626, he left the sum of £4,000 to be laid out by his executor to provide an income to be distributed in accordance with his bequest. Local people were not direct beneficiaries of this charity, but as the largest landowner in Elmsett for nearly 300 years, the Lord Bishop Andrewes' Charity provided employment for many workers. For most of that time the Stearn family were tenants. The estate, consisting of Elmsett Hall Farm, Church Farm Homestead, Lucy Wood Cottages, Lucy Wood and Elmsett Park Wood was sold at auction in August 1920 to Mr John Westren, the tenant.

The Family Welfare Association now administers the charity.

The Churchwarden's Accounts
In the Suffolk Record Office is a tattered and stained book recording the churchwarden's accounts from 1530 to 1663. It is a valuable source of information because the parish records prior to 1684 are missing.

From pre-Reformation days Elmsett owned a few neat (or cattle) which were chiefly let to parishioners and the rent was used to relieve the poor, chiefly in the form of loads of fuel. Most of the entries concern transactions regarding these cattle and the parishioners who hired them, and the names of the poor, the churchwardens and overseers. At the beginning of the seventeenth century Revd George Carter kept these accounts in his very neat handwriting, and also annotated the earlier accounts. He wrote:

... the townspeople purchased 4 cows with their town-stocke Anno 24 of the Queen's 1581 and 1582. The casting of 2 bells swallowed up 3 cows as appeareth by the accounts of 1595 and 1599.

John Bois (1561–1643)

In Shoberl's *Description of the County of Suffolk 1821* Elmsett is described as 'the native place of John Boyse – an eminent scholar and divine who was born here in 1560.' Son of a rector of the parish, and former curate, he was '... himself a great proficient in Greek and Hebrew languages'.

He was the son of a Protestant convert who fled to Suffolk for refuge in the reign of Queen Mary and married a local gentlewoman, Mirabel Pooly. John was born on 4 January 1561 and brought up in the Old Rectory in Elmsett. He walked into Hadleigh to school every day, a distance of five miles. He could read the Hebrew Bible at the age of five, and later was educated at St John's College, Cambridge, where he acquired the reputation of being the first Greek scholar of his time. He was elected as a Fellow in 1580, and held the post of Greek lecturer from 1584–95.

He was appointed as one of the Cambridge translators when King James ordered a new Bible (the 1604 edition), and was a member of the Board of Revision, receiving 30s. a week paid by the Stationers' Company. In 1615 he became a Prebendary of Ely Cathedral. Several other scholarly works were published, some posthumously. Shoberl states that on the death of his father John succeeded him in the rectory, but his name does not appear on the list of

St Peter's Church, drawn, etched and printed by Henry Davy, 1847.

rectors of the parish (see page 29). He spent his last years in Ely and died in 1643.

Revd George Carter, Rector of Elmsett (1596-1649), was subject to sequestration in the 1640's. The villagers were apparently very unhappy with some aspect of his conduct. The cause of this situation is unclear, but in 1646 an ecclesiastical court found him guilty. He was not removed from his office, however, and continued as rector until his death. The matter came to the attention of the iconoclast William Dowsing, who visited Elmsett in 1642. One suggestion is that he was responsible for the financial support of his curate, Revd W. Sympson, and was failing in this. Revd Carter was also in charge of Whatfield, and it is there that he is buried.

Revd William Talbot (1720–1811) was rector from 1766 until his death. In his will he instructed his executors to:

… place a marble tablet… where it may be most easily seen… and my beloved parishioners to be unceasing in their prayer. I earnestly beg… they will read the inscription every time they go into church so that I may be as useful to them when I am dead as I have endeavoured to be in my life time, and that one speaking to them as it were from the dead, they may repent…

The tablet is in the chancel where, as he also instructed, it is kept '… free from injury and… in a perfectly legible state'.

Revd James Speare, rector from 1817 to 1850, would appear not to have been so popular. In 1817, the year he arrived in Elmsett, he fell out with the Stearns at Elmsett Hall when they took issue with him over the removal of a stile and the blocking off of the footpath across the Glebe, which led directly to the church. Revd Speare wrote to their landlords, the Bishop Andrew's Charity, to inform them that the land was not being farmed properly. Inspectors were sent and they found everything in order, but the Stearns, a deeply religious family, stopped going to St Peter's, and went instead to Flowton Church. He paid to girls, who remained at their place of service for one year, a gratuity of 10s. Up to five girls benefited but in 1837 it is recorded that '… in consequence of Sarah Mower being in the family way and dismissed from service Rector withheld reward.'

The Poor House

This was situated by Cobbs Bridge on the northern boundary of the parish. At a meeting of parishioners in September 1770 an agreement was made:

… that £5 be allowed for each calendar month to a Master or Governor, who will engage to support and maintain the poor of the said Parish who are unable to support themselves.
1. That an apothecary shall be engaged at the expense of

the said Parish, to attend and take care of the said poor.
2. That the poor shall be supplied with new clothing at the expense of the Parish, and the mending where necessary shall be done at the Governor's expense.
3. That the fuel shall be supplied by the Governor
4. That all furniture, beds, kitchen utensils, needful for the poor shall be supplied by the Parish.

In October 1770 Dorcas Garood was appointed Governor and Manager of the Poor House for one year. She put her cross on the agreement in the presence of rector William Talbot, churchwardens Edmund Stearn and Robert Whimper and G. Russell, J. Mash and S. Vince. At the same time it was agreed that a boiler, mash tub, two beer vessels and a powdering tub should be provided.

The following year, 1771, the churchwardens decided to '… borrow from Mr Coe's Benefaction £21 for repairing the Poor House.' Interest of 5 per cent was to be paid on this loan.

Dorcas continued as Governor until 1777, but in 1773 Mr G. Russell had to be paid for 'curing the scald heads of Sarah Gentry's 2 boys.' This obviously highlighted the need for formal arrangements to be made for the care of the Poor House inhabitants, and in that year an agreement was made with George Parsons of Hadleigh and Henry Moor of Offton '… to take proper care of the sick on a payment of £2.10s.' These gentlemen were, however, allowed to charge extra for smallpox or infectious distemper, but a separate agreement would be needed if they had 'cancerous or scruphulos (sic) cases'. In 1777 Mr D'Oyley was to be paid half a guinea (10s.6d.) per patient with smallpox, a guinea and a half (£1.11s.6d.) for an arm and a guinea (£1.1s.) for a leg. Although the record does not specify, this was possibly for amputation.

In 1775 Dorcas handed over responsibility to Robert Smith, with Jeffery Southgate taking over the following year.

Memories of Former Rectors of Elmsett

Revd Harry Tait, rector from 1969 to 1975, wrote in the newsletter of his thoughts on his final walk around the village:

… this landscape hasn't changed in centuries. The church standing as it has stood for near a thousand years, towering over the lost graves of many smiths and ploughmen, a symbol of the eternity of God in the midst of change…

Revd Jeremy and Cynthia Walsh
We moved into the Rectory in the spring of 1976. We had never before lived in such a grand house. It was a very cold and draughty house in the winter. We used to shut up the drawing-room, and often the study too, making the dining-room into a family room. The hall was big enough to take a table tennis table. Upstairs,

the small bedroom over the garage, our daughter Helen's room, was the coldest room of all. It was lucky for us that our predecessors, Harry and Mary Tait, were great D-I-Y people, and they had done a lot of work on the house, leaving it in very good shape for us. One day we saw an elderly lady standing at the end of the drive, looking at the house. It turned out that she had been a parlour maid shortly before the war, when a large staff looked after the rectory. There was a resident house-keeper and housemaid, a village woman who came in to do the washing and a gardener who lived over the stables. The lady told us that she went in daily from her home just over the road. She arrived each morning at 6.45a.m. and went home at 9.45p.m. at night. She had a half-day off each week, and every other Sunday after-noon. When she was working on a Sunday she was allowed time off to go to Evensong at St Peter's. By 1976 things were rather different! It really was a lovely family home, and in many ways we were sad when a suitable alternative house in the village came on the market unexpectedly in 1979, and it was time for the old house to be sold. Just writing about it has brought back lots of happy memories.

Revd Gerald Harrison was rector from 1981 to 1988, when further changes in the role of the rector were being introduced.

In recent years fewer and fewer vicars are actually working in a truly rural village. Basically villages aren't rural any more. Hardly any of the residents work on the land, many have jobs in nearby towns, and many are retired. Because there are fewer vicars to spread around most country clergy are now vicars of rural villages, but are not in the villages – only a small minority actually have a resident vicar. Theoretically, the job is the same; that is to be there for God, as a pastor, a councillor, as a priest among priests. Practically it can't be done. The most hard-working vicar cannot be here, there and everywhere all the time. These changes were going on during our seven years at Elmsett Rectory, but I have never thought of those years as being anything but happy ones. It was good to be involved in many of the village activities, of which there were plenty, Elmsett being full of enterprising and willing people. The annual pantomime was a particular pleasure. It was especially good that in a village with two Christian places of worship, St Peter's (a gem of a church) and the Methodist Church I felt as happy and accepted in one as in the other. Since we left the changes have gathered pace and the present incumbent now has five village churches, as opposed to three when we were there.

Kneelers at St Peter's

Muriel Cook was the instigator of the kneelers at St Peter's. Few churches had kneelers in the early 1970s. Muriel headed a committee who decided on the colour scheme (brick red, yellow, black and white

Dedication of the church kneelers, 1974. Left to right: Revd H. Tait, Gwen Ransom, Muriel Cook, Cissie Holder, Brian Hiskey, Bishop Leslie Brown, Lily Holder, Alan Woods, Grace Woods.

tapestry wool) and designs which linked Biblical stories, festivals, village history and village life together, and also the badges of village organisations. The volunteer workers made their own designs up, but for those whose artistic skills were limited Muriel provided designs which she made herself. Woe betide anyone whose work was slipshod. It was hard to escape the beady eyes of an ex-headmistress whose standards were always high. Bishop Brown dedicated the kneelers in 1974.

The Village Sunday School

Reg Barber: *Most children attended Sunday school, and this was run by a farmer and his wife, Mr and Mrs Ladbrook, in one large room of their house, Laurel Cottage Farm. There was a harmonium played by Mrs Ladbrook and the hymns were sung from the Golden Bells hymn book. Once during the year we were trained to sing special hymns and the oldest children learnt recitations and dialogue. It was for the Sunday-school anniversary. This was held once a year at Elmsett Chapel. The teachers had a heart and they gave up their Sunday afternoons. Once a year they arranged an outing to Felixstowe. This was most exciting as we were taken to Ipswich Station by two horses drawing the miller's wagon. That was a treat in itself. There we were put on a train to Felixstowe and you may just guess the excitement. We should otherwise never have gone there until we went to work and had enough money to pay for the trip ourselves.*

Ellen Barber (née Robinson) moved into Elmsett in

The scale model of a Gilbert Islands fishing boat, used to collect the pennies from the Sunday-school children.

1946 with her parents. She was invited to help with the village Sunday school. She describes it:

It was held at the little library attached to Laurel Cottage, the home of Mrs Ernest Ladbrook and her daughters, Sybil and Christine. Miss Mervyn Hiskey, who attended the Methodist Church with me, was also helping.

It was a tiny room, very full of children and helpers. There was an emphasis on helping missionary work and the family had links with the Gilbert Islands, which was of interest. Mrs Ladbrook took the older children into her home for the lessons, the younger ones stayed and enjoyed Bible stories and activities, and this is the group I was involved with. Mervyn and I used to play the little harmonium which had pedals to pump air into the bellows. An annual activity was the National Scripture Union Examinations. All Sunday schools in the area

The village Sunday-school children in 1909. Back left: Mr Ernest Ladbrook with Jack; back right: Mrs Ladbrook with Sybil.

Sunday-school outing to Dovercourt, 1931.

St Peter's Sunday school, 1968. Left to right, back row: David Turner, Brian Skippings, Miss Sybil Ladbrook, ?, Helen Green, Angela Skippings, Muriel Fayers, Miss Christine Ladbrook; middle row: Philip Turner, Richard Turner, ?, Pauline Green, ?, Rosemary Butcher, ?, Cynthia Green, Barbara Skippings; front row: ?, Andrew Barber, Keith Barber, Clive Kemp, Jackie Kemp, Mary Skippings.

met annually in Ipswich, where a shield was presented to the one with the best results. To get the name of your Sunday school engraved on this was a real honour. Of course there was the Sunday-school treat, a special day and probably the only one in the year when many people went to the coast, or had a day out. It was a memorable time, which I look back on with great affection and I know Mervyn does as well. Mrs Ladbrook was a lady of great sincerity, charm and warmth and it rubbed off on us all.

Alfie Holder: *For the outing we used to go on a bus of sorts – a Model T Ford. When we got to a hill we all had to get out and walk as the bus could not go up with people in it.*

This era came to an end when the Misses Sybil and Christine joined St Peter's Church in the village. They felt that the Sunday school was remote from the places of worship, and the children should be encouraged to attend either St Peter's or the Methodist Church, and thereby find a 'spiritual home'.

The Methodist Church

After the Act of Uniformity in 1662 anyone who adhered to any form of religion other than the established Church was referred to as 'a dissenter'. Methodism originated as part of the Church of England revival (c.1729), led by John Wesley; in 1791 the movement separated and the Methodist Church was established. East Anglia was a thriving centre for this new form of religious worship. Jonathon Scott, the Superintendent of the Hadleigh circuit, missioned Elmsett in about 1830 and by the late 1840s a group of people from the village began meeting in a cottage.

A gentleman named Thomas Fenning then built a small chapel which he let at a cost of £3 per year for use as a meeting-place. During 1856/57 there was quite a revival of religion and the chapel became too small. The group decided to buy the site from Mr

The Old Chapel in 1958.

Fenning at a cost of £5. Jonathon Scott, realising that a few poor people would find it difficult to fund the building of a chapel, organised a tea meeting. After the tea he introduced a printed card to those assembled and suggested that each person take one and say how much he or she would try to collect. The money was to be brought together on Good Friday (2 April 1857). Promises to the value of £30 were made and by 2 April £40 had been raised. The building was put out to tender, the lowest of £96 was accepted and the foundations were laid on 1 June 1858. On Saturday, 1 August 1858 Jonathon Scott opened the chapel. The place was crowded, and the collection realised a further £40. The total cost of the building was £139.10s.4½d.

In 1926 a porch was erected in memory of one who, although never a member, was a lifelong friend of the chapel – Mr William Ladbrook. Shortly before the Second World War electric light was installed to replace the oil lamps. On 12 May 1941 the German bomb that fell on the cottages less than 100 yards away seriously damaged the chapel. The ceiling fell, the windows were blown in and plaster was torn from the walls. The building was repaired and reopened for worship on 31 August that year.

The chapel continued to thrive during the war years, hosting the annual village Sunday-school anniversary. The Wesley Guild met there on a Wednesday evening for many years. Various quiz evenings were held and at least once a month a social evening was held. As time passed the chapel began to show the effects of the wartime blast and large cracks could be seen in the walls. It was very difficult to warm the place in the winter and in 1958 it was decided that instead of continually patching up the place a new building project would be started. The minister at that time was Revd Kenneth Renouf. A centenary celebration was held for the old building with a 'Great Rally'. Revd Irvonwy Morgan from the London Mission came to speak, and the idea of a new Methodist Church in the village was formed.

It was not until 1962 that the new church could be built. Mr Arthur Barber and Mr Jack Ladbrook laid the Foundation Stone. The new church opened in November 1962, at which time Revd John Bolton was the minister. At the opening the church stewards walked from the old chapel carrying the Bible, the Holy Communion tray and glasses.

A number of initiatives took place in the early years of the new church. The Girls' Life Brigade was set up and later on a Boys' Brigade. Still later came the Ranger Boys for the younger boys of the village, and the Women's Fellowship (now the Women's Network), which had started in 1952, flourished. All these activities are still running.

A Methodist Church Sunday school began after the village Sunday school ceased, and this also runs today under the leadership of Alison Gillies with a band of helpers. The Methodist Church, situated in

Laying the foundation stone of the new Methodist Church, 1962. Left to right, foreground: Revd Clifford Lever, Revd John Bolton, Jack Ladbrook, Arthur Barber, David Hatcher, Bernard Sadler, ?; others in picture: Arthur Clouting, Madge Skippings, Eric Bowell, Susan Barber, Bill Beaumont, Percy Buckle, Lewis Melton, Mrs Melton, Jessie Barber, Flo Barber, Marion Barber, Ken Kemp, Betty Kemp, Miss Foster, Myrtle Whatling, Margaret Bowell, Ada Clarke, Phillis Clarke, Herbert Clarke, Connie Chenery.

The Methodist Church before the alterations, 1998.

the centre of the village, continued to thrive, and in 1995 it was decided once again to embark on a building project – this time an extension to the existing premises. The minister, Revd Elizabeth Bellamy, was very strong in her encouragement, and the project went ahead. She took on the task of applying for, and obtaining grants, but the members still had the monumental task of raising thousands of pounds.

After several years of fund raising with flower festivals, gift days, Christmas tree and scarecrow festivals, plant sales and the monthly luncheon club, enough money had been raised to start the alterations. The church now has an extended worship area, two new classrooms and a completely new kitchen area. Facilities include access for the disabled, toilets, storage facilities and a comfortable vestry for visiting speakers. The church itself, while still needing new chairs, really does look good.

Joy Sillitoe, the writer of this piece, ends: *It is now the beginning of 2005, and we hope that this year will be the year we can clear our debts, but it would never surprise me if someone comes up with yet another wonderful idea, and so off we will go again raising more money.*

Revd Elizabeth Bellamy was the Methodist minister from 1995 to 2004. She writes:

It was a dark December teatime when I first visited Elmsett and the Methodist Church was lit up against the darkness, glowing hospitality. Inside, the Elmsett Methodists were gathered in what I came to know as typical mode – round the tea trolley. They were waiting to check out whether I'd do as their next minister, or not. First impressions? A relaxed, informal, all-age group, chatting happily and unfazed by my late arrival, but determined to have their say in the decision making of their church. I was immediately made aware of the ongoing exploration of how to improve and enlarge the 1960s

The Methodist Church in 2005.

the old chapel were not very convenient, but they made use of what was available.

Ellen recalls how it all began:

The Sunday school followed a similar pattern as previously, including the summer outing and the Scripture exam, and we continued to have the Sunday-school anniversary

building, and this was to dominate my thinking and time for the next nine years, but we did it and raised the money. Other things also featured regularly in my diary, including school assemblies once a month until the children became eco-sensitive and insisted I should not burn fossil fuel to make a special journey from Ipswich just for them. Music and talented young musicians were a feature of the life and worship of the church. Yet these memories of activities and events within a lively church are but a background against which the people stand out.

Methodist Church Sunday School

After the Misses Ladbrook stopped having the Sunday school at Laurel Cottage, Ellen Barber helped to start one in the Methodist Church. The facilities in

every year. For this, children learnt recitations, songs, etc., and came dressed in their best clothes, often new for the occasion. Every child took part – even if it just was taking up the collection or handing out books. A special preacher, well suited for children's activities, commented on the recitations, monologues and songs with encouragement. These Sunday-school anniversaries were a big event and people used to travel around the villages to attend them. The collections were always for the Sunday-school funds – the annual outing was funded this way. The time came when the old chapel in The Street was no longer viable. It was basic, with fixed pews, a pulpit and a pedal organ. A large tortoise stove, which burnt coke, was lit each week and protected by a guard – it got very hot. Mr Jack Ladbrook offered to give some land in the centre of the village, and his offer was accepted, so the fund raising began.

Winners of the Ipswich and District Scripture Exam Shield from the Methodist Church Sunday school, 1968. Left to right, back row: Susan Cox, Paul Patterson, Frazer Moyes, ?, Scott Lawrence, Anne Sillitoe; front row: Mandy Lawrence, Wendy Grimwade, Jane Sillitoe, Valerie Dunnett, Alison Barber, Audrey Dunnett.

The Quaker Burial Ground

In 1674, just over 20 years after the birth of the Quaker movement in the north-west of England, a piece of land measuring approximately 30 yards by 20 yards was given by Mary Wright, widow of John Wright of Elmsett:

... to be used by the people of God called Quakers to inter the dead bodies of their friends, children and servants and all other sober people that at times desire to bury or be buried there.

This piece of land was in the corner of a field called Baker's Meadow in Whatfield Road and was reached by an entrance in 'Cooue Lane' (Cow Lane), later known as Snakes Lane. Access was allowed for horses and carts and other carriages.

There are records of only four burials, although it is thought more took place and the records have been lost. The names of the four are: Joseph Burrows of Copdock (died 26 September 1698, interred 28 September); John Grimwood of Bramford (died 15 April 1712, interred 17 April); Francis Woods of Needham Market (died 21 March 1752, interred 24 March); William Ward of Needham Market (died 19 August 1754, interred 22 August).

Before moving to Copdock Joseph Burrows (Burrose or Burroughs) was a tenant farmer in Elmsett and Quaker meetings were held in his house. The whereabouts of this house is not known, but there is a record of his having been fined £20 for holding a meeting there on 22 May 1670. To pay this fine he had '... taken from him seaven cowes and two heifers worth twenty six pounds.'

From the early-nineteenth century, after the plot had ceased to be used as a burial ground, it was rented out with various conditions as to how it should be used. In 1843 an application was made '... to hire the Elmsett burial ground for the purpose of building a place of worship for the Primitive Methodists...', but this idea came to nothing. A record of a hiring agreement dated eighteenth day of the twelfth month 1846 states that the burial ground was rented out to John Hobert at 18s. (90p) per annum:

... to be paid on the 11th day of the 10th month to the trustees on condition of not breaking up the same to a greater depth than 2 feet and not using it for any other purpose than as a garden or to feed cattle... that a new bank be made and a new gate fixed in the fence next the lane at the expense of the said John Hobert, and provided the whole of the fences be hereafter kept clean and neatly clipt an allowance of 4/- per annum shall be made for the same.

At one time the land was used as an orchard and then the trees were removed and a garden made and planted with potatoes. A further reference, dated 16 January 1917, shows '... a piece of land at Elmsett formerly used as Burial Ground...' was rented out for 4s. (20p) paid yearly. The tenant was J.H. Barber. Eventually the burial ground was added to the Chequers Park mobile home site, and the money from the sale of the land was used to help repair and redecorate the Quaker meeting-house at Leiston in Suffolk. In January 1972 Grace Hammond (formerly Woods), who wrote this section, and her two children moved into a mobile home on this plot and were told of a regulation forbidding digging below a depth of two feet; topsoil was brought in so that a new garden could be made. However, from time to time coffin nails were found whilst digging and planting.

Quakers intending to marry

It appears from records that a number of people attended the meetings in Elmsett and when they wished to marry permission was asked at the monthly meetings in Sudbury. Some extracts taken from the Sudbury Minute Book are listed below, in their original format.

1674	*Nathanaell Sherife of nedham and Mary Wright of Elmsett*
1677	*William Locket of felsham belonging to Ratlesdon meeting and Elizabeth Rand of Emset meeting*
1677	*thomas Chisnall of elldam in the county of Suffolk belonging to emseed meeting and ann Cooke of polsted belonging to boxford meeting*
1678	*thomas Rosuer of emsed and mary baker of the same touen*
1679	*John Woods of Elmsed and ann plantin of ald*
1686	*William Swaites of mildenhall and Hannah Wood of Elmset*
1687	*william hils and mary Field both of Elmset*
1691	*Josiph Burrough of Elmset and Sarah Wellch of stoke by nayland*
1693	*Josiph Chisnall of Elmset declaring his inten shon of takeing of debrah wood of coulchester*
1695	*John Squrill of Ringsell and Elizabeth Greenwood of Elmsit*

There are several variations on the spelling of Elmsett; *nedham* refers to Needham Market; *elldam* and *ald* to Aldham; and *Ringsell* to Ringshall.

❖ CHAPTER 4 ❖

The Agricultural Landscape

An Overview
by Miles Hitchcock Brown

The earliest agricultural record we have of Elmsett, as given in the Domesday Book, has been explained in Chapter 1. It lists the manor as six carucates (see the glossary on page 12) and 40 acres – approximately 640–700 acres. The size of the manor was therefore considerably smaller than today's parish; this apparent anomaly can be accounted for by the number of villagers cultivating land to the extent of around 1,000 acres, with the Church probably farming a further 65 acres. The total brings us much closer to the present-day acreage of the parish, around 2,000 acres. It is also certain that in medieval times Elmsett was heavily wooded, with the remains of three ancient woods, Borley Wood, Elmsett Park Wood and Lucy Wood, all surviving until recent

Ancient pollard oak behind Red House Farm. Evan Hitchcock Brown, aged 3, gives scale.

times. A fourth wood of which very little is known, namely Bringe (or Bridge) Wood, the location of which cannot be pinpointed, was grubbed out around the year 1600. (Incidentally, the Abbott of Bury's chartalary of 1442 mentions an Elmsetewode (217 acres) and Liuenzewode (149 acres), supposedly at Long Melford.)

The classic English manor in the twelfth century fell into two portions; the lord's 'demesne', which was land under his immediate control, and tenanted land. Slaves would have worked full time on the demesne, which usually included a manor house surrounded by fields larger than those of other land-holders. Unusually, Elmsett Manor Farm is some distance from the present village, as is the church, possibly an indication that either the village or the manor house (or both) have relocated for reasons unknown to us. It seems reasonable to assume that Church Farm would have been the site of the original manor house, being closer to the church as well as to the village which supplied the labour force. Tenanted land was held part freely (freeholders) and part in villeinage (villagers). Freeholders paid their dues to their lord mainly in cash rents, but might owe some labour at certain times of the year.

The villein's land was held entirely at the lord's will and passed from father to son. On taking over a tenancy he paid an entry fine; when his daughter married he paid a merchet tax; and when he died a heriot tax. Petty fines issued by the manor court plagued his working life. If ejected or denied succession he had no legal redress. He also paid a money rent and sent men to work on the demesne a few days a week at busy periods. The church took a tithe (one tenth) of his produce and shared in the death duties, often taking the family's best beast. The medieval villein evolved into the customary tenants, or copyholders, in later centuries, and several farms in Elmsett comprised both copyhold and freehold land up until the 1800s. One example of this is Red House Farm, as in the early-nineteenth century it comprised 37 acres freehold and 21 acres copyhold.

A classic model of a medieval farming system comprised areas of open field in which the tenants farmed their allocated strips of land. However, in Elmsett it is difficult to discern if such a system ever existed and, if so, where. It is generally accepted amongst historians that in the heavy clay lands of Suffolk the field patterns were set at a very early date. Many of the manors in this area predate the Norman Conquest and it is possible that many of the field

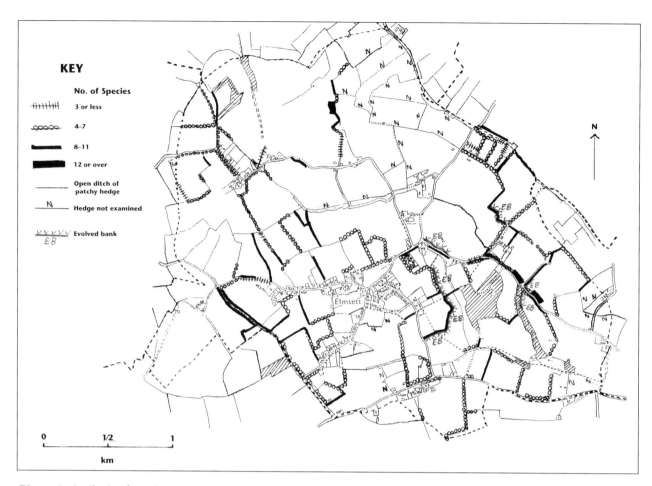

KEY

	No. of Species
⊬⊬⊬⊬	3 or less
ᴏᴏᴏᴏᴏ	4–7
▬▬▬	8–11
████	12 or over
———	Open ditch of patchy hedge
—N—	Hedge not examined
∨∨∨∨∨ EB	Evolved bank

0   1/2   1
km

Figure 1: Analysis of species composition of hedges for dating purposes.

Evolved bank.

patterns identified during the 1840s may also predate this time. The names of 'Vesey' and 'Lott', who owned and farmed Red House and Hill farms respectively in the sixteenth and nineteenth centuries, come from long-standing land-owning 'yeoman' farming names in North Essex and South Suffolk. The evidence for the antiquity of Elmsett's farming landscape, if not documented, is evident all around us and can be seen in the irregular field patterns, high boundary banks and ancient woodland. Parliamentary enclosure of open fields in the late-eighteenth and early-nineteenth centuries in other parts of the country usually resulted in very regular rectangular field patterns, and hedges of limited plant species, typically hawthorn or blackthorn.

The results of a hedgerow survey of Elmsett in 1990 are displayed in Figure 1. A hedge can be dated by counting the number of tree species in a 30-yard length of hedge by a method devised by Dr Max Hooper and known as Hooper's Rule. As a general rule the age in years is equal to 100 years for each species found. Thus a ten species hedge can roughly be calculated to be 1,000 years old. Figure 1 shows that most hedges had between four and eight species, with some having over 12 and, according to the rule, this would make them extremely old. Elm trees with a circumference of up to 14 feet have been found in some of these hedges, indicating a great age.

Of Elmsett's three, if not four, small ancient woods, Lucy Wood, in the north of the parish, was recorded in a document dated about 1420, but it was grubbed out in 1964, when farmers were being encouraged to do this. Elmsett Park Wood has no proven documentation, but can be dated through field evidence as a medieval deer-park. It is encircled by a bank and ditch, which would have been dug originally to contain the deer. The flora is extremely rich and complex and huge coppice stools of ash, hornbeam and elm trees, which would take many centuries of felling and regrowth to reach such a size, are to be found. One final piece of field evidence

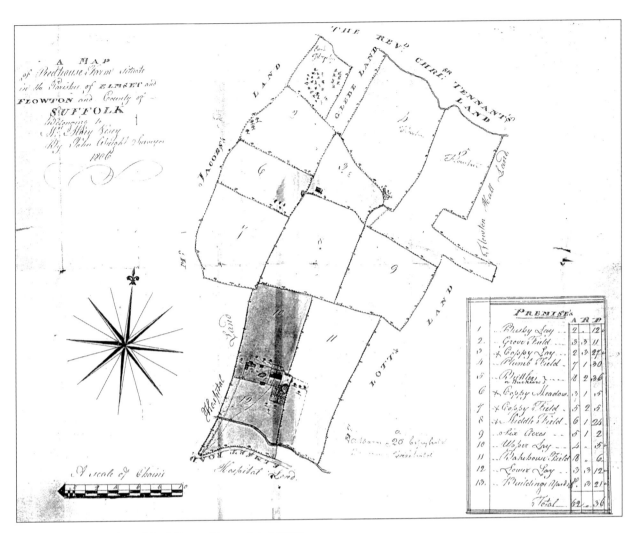

Figure 2a: Estate plan of Red House Farm, dated 1806.

points to the antiquity of some of Elmsett's field boundaries. Levels on either side of some boundaries vary greatly. Such features are named 'evolved banks' and occur after many centuries of ploughing by a field boundary which runs along a slope. The 'up' side of the boundary is forced to become higher than the 'down' slope over a long period of time. Variations in height depend on the level of cultivation and the fact that land on only one side of the boundary may have been ploughed. Some substantial 'evolved banks' are highlighted in Figure 1. It is curious that many of these more substantial banks are in the vicinity of Elmsett Park Wood. Could this be further evidence of a past larger wood causing the surrounding plough lands to form banks up to its perimeter?

Having attempted to account for the antiquity of many of Elmsett's fields, we can turn our attention to the changes that have taken place in the last 200 years. The earliest maps showing any detail of field patterns are estate plans for Red House Farm (Figure 2a) and Hill Farm, dated 1806 and 1819 respectively. There was little change on these farms until 1842, the date of the next detailed survey of our village – the parish Tithe Map (Figure 2b). It is often assumed that

hedgerow removal to create larger fields is a result of mechanisation of farming in the twentieth century. The comparison of the 1842 map (Figure 2b) with the Ordnance Survey map of 1884 (Figure 2c) shows that a number of boundaries have been removed and alterations made. Between the 1840s and the 1870s British farming enjoyed an interlude between the coming of free trade and the flood of cheap imported grain. The region's farms prospered and this period was characterised by widespread drainage of heavy clay land. Four plantations were also grubbed out, the largest being Highly Grove along Flowton Road. Elmsett Park Wood also lost part of its northern area and Poplar Hall Farm was incorporated into the parish. The flood of cheap imported grain resulted in the price of wheat falling by half and barley by a third. In an age when farmers still paid tithes and rents to the lord of the manor, the consequences were crippling, resulting in land being taken out of cultivation and farmers going bankrupt. During the First World War this was temporarily reversed, but thereafter decline set in again. By the 1930s foreign imports saw grain prices at levels unequalled since Tudor times. The Ordnance Survey map of 1921 reflects this state of affairs with virtually no changes

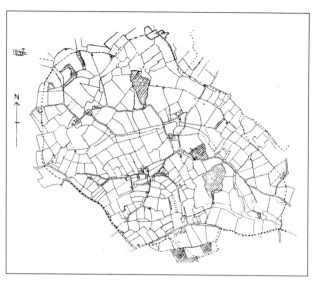

Figure 2b: The 1842 Tithe Map.

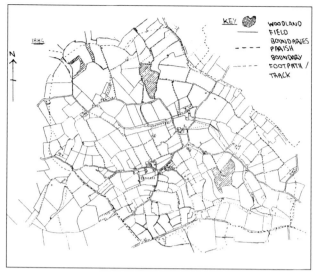

Figure 2c: The 1884 Ordnance Survey map.

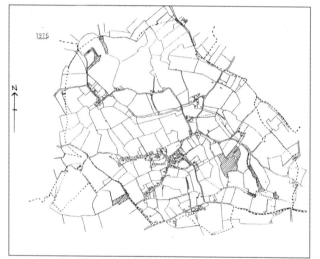

Figure 2d: The 1976 Ordnance Survey map.

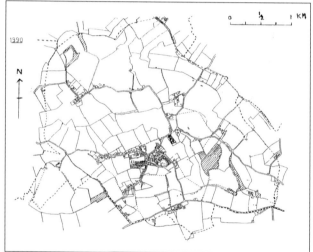

Figure 2e: The 1990 Ordnance Survey map.

in the landscape in the previous 40 years. The 1930s depression left many farm buildings derelict and thousands of acres of Suffolk's heavy land reverted to thorn bushes. Post 1945 was characterised by an influx of new landowners and farm amalgamations.

Between 1958 and 1964 over 6,700 government farm improvement applications were approved in Suffolk, at a cost of over £58,000,000. Between 1939 and 1963 over 1,000 Suffolk farms were lost or amalgamated into larger farms. Farm labour was reduced by about 17,500 workers between 1939 and 1971. These figures serve as examples of the accelerating intensification of agriculture, which was mainly due to increased mechanisation. Comparison of the 1884 Ordnance Survey map with Figure 2d, dated 1976, shows that a large number of hedges have been lost, including those to the west of Lucy Wood (in the 1940s) and the wood itself. Figure 2e serves to illustrate the loss of field boundaries in this 14-year period. However, the 2005 Ordnance Survey map of Elmsett differs very little from this map,

indicating that changes have slowed down.

Figures 3a and 3b show how farm amalgamation has occurred between 1842 and 2004. In 1842 there were 23 main landowners in Elmsett, very often with fields dispersed across the parish (a remnant of medieval pre-enclosure fields, maybe). Many of these farms were the property of a larger non-resident farmer, but were actually worked by an undertenant occupier. At this time many of these farms still comprised copyhold lands, thus rents were paid to the lord and tithes to the Church. At least two of the sites of former farms have now entirely vanished, namely Bone or Bourne Farm at No. 11 on the plan, and Slough Farm at No. 19. Another outlying site, which had already disappeared by 1884, was Daisy Cottage (or Daisy Hall), which was situated in the field between Red House Farm and Bushy Ley Farm. Table 1 is a summary of the Ministry of Agriculture's annual census returns for selected years in Elmsett. It is interesting to note the number of sheep and other livestock before 1952 and the corresponding acreage

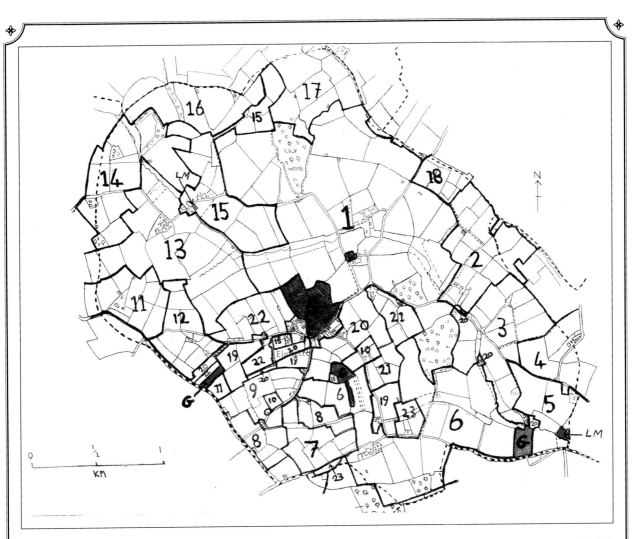

Figure 3a: Land ownership in 1842. Each number represents an individual landowner. Dark areas marked G belong to the church. L.M. belongs to the lord of the manor.

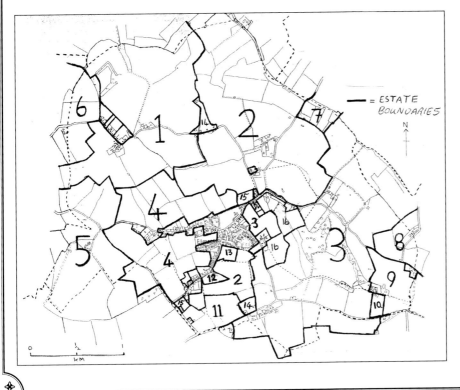

Figure 3b: Land ownership in 2004. Each number represents an individual landowner.

Selected Ministry of Agriculture Returns for Elmsett

	1866	1910	1935	1951	1970	1986
Wheat	223	394	554	347	446	2060
Barley	200	391	289	575	922	335
Oats	28	175	55	101	53	5
Peas/Beans for feed	65	151	208	71	194	173
Sugar beet	0	0	86	181	81	0
Oil seed rape	0	11	0	0	0	132
Potatoes	2	0	0.5	1	6	7.5
Turnips & Mangolds	84	120	27	6	1	0
Vetches/Lucerne	52	40	52	0	0	0
Veg – human consumption	0	0	0	32	0	0
Fallow	63	122	239	27	23	2.5
Rough grazing				15	13	37.5
Temporary grass	120	215	153	226	70	20
Permanent grass	103	323	360	165	115	.
TOTAL	**940**	**1942**	**2023.5**	**1747**	**1924**	**2772.5**
Total Cattle	63	152	171	169	278	113
Total pigs	316	577	772	625	2234	3997
Total sheep	659	1777	1262	0	0	0
Horses for work		100	51	10		
Total horses		114	60	10		
Poultry			6605	6336	4895	600
Farmers/Directors					13	18
Full-time men			57	51	20	14
Full-time women			0	4	1	0
Part-time men			11	6	1	0
Part-time women			3	3	7	13
TOTAL PEOPLE IN FARMING			**71**	**64**	**42**	**45**

Table 1.

of grazing and crops such as vetches, lucerne and mangles for animal fodder. Notice also how the number of work horses drops from 100 in 1910 to none in 1970, with a corresponding decrease in full-time farm workers (see table, above).

Field Names

The study of field names and their changes and corruptions can also give a fascinating insight into the history of the village. The origins of the majority of field names are lost in the mists of time. Many are self-explanatory, for example 'Four Acres' or 'Ten Acres', although occasionally the name bears no correlation to the real acreage because the name stays despite the boundary changes. Many other fields appear to bear the name of a past tenant, such as 'Sawyers', 'Buggs Meadow', 'Joe Roses', 'Webbs', 'Long Johns' and 'Makespears'. Curiously many of these occur in the centre of the village.

There is documentary evidence of the use of people's names, for example 'Stubbs Hill' derived from John Stubbins (from Hitcham), copyhold tenant of eight acres until 1795. Even in more recent times this practice continues, so that we have 'Cecil's Bit'

from Cecil Barber, who rented and farmed this field in the 1940s and '50s. We also have 'Waspie's Bit' after Harold Waspe, who farmed Wall Farm in the 1950s, and 'Goodie's Bit', after the man whose bungalow adjoined this field. With time these names may have become corrupted, so that 'Mother Gerard's' became 'Garards', and is now the site of Garrards Road. Some self-explanatory names include 'Mill Field', 'Stackyard Field', 'Gravel Pit' and 'Barn Field'. Others are derived from prominent trees, thus we have 'Plum Tree', 'Crab Field', 'Timbertop Ley', Walnut Tree Piece', 'Poplar Meadow', 'Willow Field', 'Grove Field' and 'Park Field'. The fact that the latter has the same name on the 1811 map shows that the wood was known as a former deer park nearly 200 years ago.

The 1842 Tithe Map also shows other common field names. Thus we have many named 'Home Field' adjacent to farm buildings, as well as 'Backhouse', 'Bakehouse' and 'Buckhouse' fields. The backhouse of a farmhouse was the storeroom and often contained brewing equipment. There are many fields containing the word 'Ley' or 'Lay', for example 'Bushy Ley' and 'Coppy Lay'. A ley is a piece of land which is pasture for a number of years

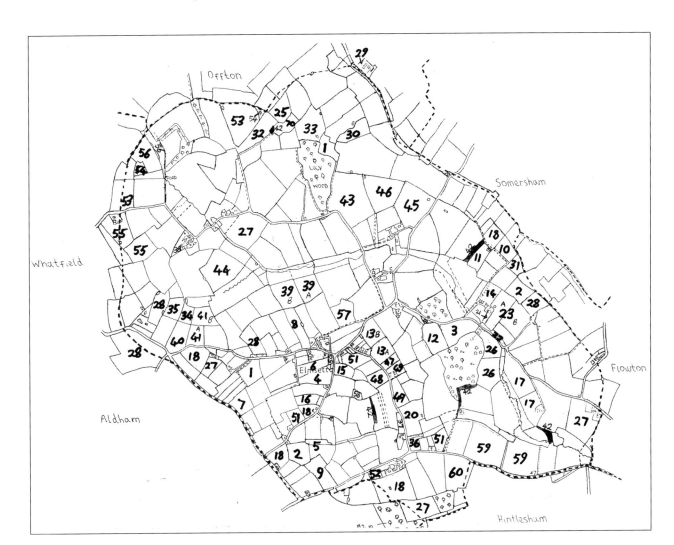

Figure 4: Based on the 1842 Tithe Map. Key to field names. 1. Four Acres; 2. Six Acres; 3. Nine Acres; 4. Sawyers; 5. Buggs Meadow; 6. Joe Roses; 7. Webbs; 8. Long Johns; 9. Makespears; 10. Taylor's Ley; 11. Stubb Hill; 12. Cecil's Bit (Little Park Field);13. Waspie's Bit (A: Stackyard Field, B: Chapel Field); 14. Goodie's Bit (The Ley); 15. Mother Gerards (Garrards); 16. Mill Field; 17. Gravel Pit; 18. Barn Field; 19. Grove Field; 20. Crab Field; 21. Walnut Tree Piece; 22. Poplar Meadow; 23. Willow Field (A: Hogshead Field, B: Barn Field); 24. Grove Field; 25. Timbertop Ley; 26. Park Field; 27. Home Fields; 28. Backhouse Fields; 29. The Ley; 30. Bushy Ley; 31. Coppy Lay; 32. Rumble's Lay; 33. Rushey Ley; 34. Moses Pightle; 35. Grimwade Pightle; 36. Dock Pightle; 37. Home Pightle; 38. Pightle; 39. A: First Cossocks, B: Second Cossocks; 40. Further Cassucks; 41. A: Upper Cassucks, B: Lower Cassucks; 42. Queech x 4; 43. Long Cobbs; 44. Water Cobbs; 45. Sparrow Cobbs; 46. Hunting Cobbs; 47. Potash Field; 48. Potash Pightle; 49. Great and Little Potash Fields; 50. Stocks Knowl; 51. Shop Field x 2; 52. Stew Pond Piece; 53. Kiln Field; 54. Kiln Grove; 55. Flax Ley; 56. Brakey Close; 57. Wood Field; 58. Lost Piece; 59. Brookets (Brookins); 60. Garlands (Garlans).

before being ploughed for a while and then put back to pasture. There are several 'pightles', for example 'Moses Pightle' or 'Grimwade Pightle'. A pightle is a small enclosure of land, often triangular in shape and usually near a dwelling. One curious field name for which no interpretation can be traced is 'Cossocks' or 'Cassucks'. We also have 'Upper Cassocks' and 'Further Cassocks'. On the map there are five 'Queeches', a name derived from the Germanic 'Queck', meaning brushwood, an area left uncut either because it was a small plantation or was full of bushes. There were numerous 'Cobbs', for example 'Hunting Cobbs' and 'Sparrow Cobbs'. Again the meaning is lost, but could refer to cobnuts, cob horses or the straw and clay building material used in the

past. The reference to 'Potash' in field names could be a reference to efforts to improve the fertility of the soil with wood ash. The field on which the Methodist Church now stands was known as 'Stocks Knowl', presumably the site of the village stocks. There are also three 'Shop' fields. Near to Gate Farm was 'Stew Pond Piece', an area of pasture with a reference to a pond stocked with fish.

Two 'Kiln' fields and 'Kiln Grove' fields are a reminder of the medieval pottery kilns of which we have documented archaeological evidence of large finds of pottery shards. 'Flax Ley' likewise was probably where flax, used for making cloth, was a past crop. Near to this is a 'Brakey Close'. A brake was either a hook used for uprooting and tearing up grassland or a robust harrow for breaking up heavy land. One curiously named field with an oddly undulating boundary is 'Wood Field', with no evidence of past woodland present but possibly the site of the elusive Bringe Wood. Whatever its past, this field is shortly to be planted with trees and will become Elmsett's Community Woodland, thanks to the generosity of the landowner, James Buckle. Finally, someone had a wry sense of humour in naming one field 'Lost Piece'. It is surrounded on all sides by land belonging to other farmers!

It is incredible that in 150 years many of the field names have remained the same, despite changes in ownership. Some minor corruptions have occurred – 'Brookins' is now 'Brookets' and 'Garlans' has become 'Garlands'. One can only wonder how old some of Elmsett's field names can really be.

The market town of Hadleigh, four miles from Elmsett, had a large and well-organised smuggling band in the late 1700s, and a corner of Cossocks Field, once known as 'Smugglers Hole', indicates that Elmsett was once part of its overall operations. Leonard Thompson, in his book *Smugglers of the Suffolk Coast*, quotes an escapade attributed to the Hadleigh Gang where an informant gave information to the local Preventative Officer about a run. The gang managed to move 300 casks and hide them in a vault accessed by a trapdoor and covered with a muckheap. The name of the field corner seems to indicate that Elmsett had a similar hiding place.

Elmsett Park Wood
by Richard Hitchcock

Elmsett Park Wood, extending to 22 acres, is of irregular shape and has both historical and scientific interest. In designating the wood a Site of Special Scientific Interest (SSSI), the Nature Conservancy described the wood as '... the best remaining hunting park in the county after the Bradfield Woods...', with '... diverse tree, shrub and herb flora strongly indicative of ancient woodland.' The Turner family, who farmed at Gate Farm, Elmsett, owned it. They used the wood for firewood in the home and faggots for the brick oven and for private sporting. They allowed Edwin Westren to survey the wood when he assisted Francis Simpson compile his *Flora of Suffolk*. Edwin remembered a small natural clearing of about half an acre. In 1947 the Turners sold the wood to William 'Whoopy' Steward of Ipswich.

Ralph Turner: *I remember Mr Steward bought it with the intention of extracting firewood. He had a big firewood round with two or three old lorries and two or three men cutting all through the wood. He also sold pea-sticks to the public from his house in Sproughton. Mr Steward had always been a dealer of a kind. I believe he had rights to a large quantity of drums from the plastics factory (and wooden tobacco drums which he had*

Aerial view of Park Wood, 1968, showing the clearing where the breaker's yard was established.

obtained before the war). Drums were the thing I remember most... they were stored in a relatively small area – certainly less than an acre, approximately where the breakers are now, near the entrance to the wood.

Mr Steward started to use this small natural clearing for his trading business. This grew until the early 1960s, when a few old cars were seen amongst the drums in the clearing along the sides of the tracks. In about 1968 a Mr Crompton started working on some of these old cars and in 1971 he was granted temporary planning permission for limited activity on the site. In 1972 A & M Dismantlers took over the whole wood. They already operated other scrapyards and they proceeded to concentrate their business in Park Wood and built up a large car dismantling operation selling car parts to the public. In 1974 they obtained planning permission for the business to operate in the original enlarged clearing of about one and a half acres with conditions regarding stacking height, the burning of oil and tree planting. This permission was surprising in a wood that was an SSSI with a tree preservation order.

Then followed a great deal more activity in the wood and the business outgrew the original site. More trees were cut down until the area extended to about four acres. Opposition was building up in the village. The Parish Council was particularly concerned, as were the Hitchcocks, who farmed around the wood. When A & M Dismantlers applied for permission to enlarge this area in March 1981, Babergh District Council refused and issued an enforcement notice to make them comply with the 1974 permission. A & M appealed against this enforcement notice and the whole matter went to a public enquiry in October 1981.

The barrister representing Babergh District Council and solicitors engaged by Messrs Hitchcocks and Bates (from nearby Hill Farm) were to present evidence of non-compliance. At the request of the Suffolk Trust for Nature Conservation (STNC) Dr Oliver Rackham, research officer in the Botany School of the University of Cambridge, attended the enquiry. He contributed important scientific evidence obtained during his study of the site of the age, flora and fauna of the wood. Many people sent sworn affidavits of their evidence of non-compliance, and aerial photographs of the wood clearly showed the gradual destruction of the ancient woodland. As a result of the inspector's decision the dismantlers had to restrict their activities to the original site area and comply with further conditions. Consequently, their business was too restricted and they let the yard to another operator.

In 1984 Hitchcock Farms Ltd bought the whole of the wood, with a sitting tenant in the scrapyard and, under the auspices of Geoffrey Swain (then Chief Planning Officer for Babergh DC), they marked a clearly defined area for the scrap business, which has since remained within this area of about three-quarters of an acre. In 1989 the dismantlers were granted permanent permission by Babergh DC. Hitchcock Farms have financed the installation of facilities for the treatment and storage of hazardous fluids and other waste to the satisfaction of the Environment Agency. Dr Rackham's report still makes interesting reading 25 years later. His detailed report outlined the importance of ancient woods:

… they are the product of centuries of conservation in the past and are supremely important for the future… they are a link with the human activities of past centuries and with prehistoric wildwood… they have a continuity that plantations and recent woods lack… they are by definition irreplaceable, and in Suffolk they are all uniquely different…

The list of 109 species of flowering plants and ferns, trees and shrubs, compiled by Dr Rackham was remarkably similar to that of Edwin Westren's findings 30 years earlier. Dr Rackham considered the number to be exceptional for the size of the wood. He also stated that apart from a small boundary change, the wood contained no evidence that its character had been changed (e.g. by tree planting) for the last 200 years.

Jenny Barnes: *Park Wood, when we came to the village was well organised. Mr Pryke, a very old man, was employed to do the coppicing. He was a next door neighbour, and every day at about midday Mrs Pryke would stand on her doorstep and blow a whistle two or three times to call him home for dinner! The coppiced wood was used for bean poles, clothes-line posts, pegs and pea sticks. Villagers were permitted to walk there — the floor was covered in a wonderful variety of wild flowers all through the year. We always found the first primroses there, and these were used for Easter decorations in the church. We would often come across a hedgehog coming out of hibernation and snuffling in the dry leaves. In about 1970 part of Park Wood became a breaker's yard almost overnight. The Parish Council*

was unaware of it until it was too late to stop it. I was deputy chairman of the Parish Council at the time and remember the enquiry taking place.

Brenda Woods (née Hiskey): *We used to play in Lucy Wood and Park Wood which was known as The Park. In spring we picked primroses, tied them in bundles, and took them into Ipswich. We used to go on the bus with our mother on a Saturday morning. We sold the primroses to a flower shop to earn a bit of pocket money. On Sundays families would go to Park Wood to walk and play.*

Elmsett's Highways

The medieval road routes remain today exactly where they were, and most would have had names. Access for carts and wagons to every farm and homestead was needed and, not surprisingly, many of the petty court cases were concerned with road offences. Broken gates and blocked ditches were the commonest complaints in the seventeenth century. One of these was noted in the Elmsett Parish Records:

Rev Moses Coe, on behalf of the parishioners, took to court at Bury St Edmunds at Michaelmas 1696, Edmund Stearn, the tenant of Elmsett Hall, for failing to maintain the 'Greate Gate' leading to the highway to Somersham to the grave danger and disquiet of the inhabitants of the said Parish. The Rector was granted an injunction requiring Edmund Stearn to repair and maintain the 'Greate Gate'.

The highways were part of the common land of the manor and had definite boundaries. Major diversions were rare and usually required permission from the king. Where a wide verge occurred between the road and the boundary (a hedge or ditch) a farmer sometimes extended his frontage, or a small-holding was set up, but these transgressions would have been dealt with in the courts. Women and children were paid by farmers to pick up stones from the fields and these were stacked in heaps by the roads to

The Maltings and village pond after the retaining wall was built to prevent flooding, c.1950s.

Road men in Hadleigh Road in 1948. Left to right: *Jot Hiskey, Herbert (Tyke) Clarke, Bob Taylor.*

be used to mend holes. A team of road menders maintained the roads, which were not tarred until 1928. After this they kept the edges in good repair and filled any potholes that developed.

Road Names

The road now known as Manor Road used to be called Rookery Road. Flowton Road was called Ipswich Road until the development occurred in the present Ipswich Road in the 1960s. Locally, a grass track off Whatfield Road near the green was called Snakes Lane and, further along, the bend at the top of Cornhatches was known as Primrose Corner. Primroses still grow there in abundance.

Christine Ladbrook was born in 1911, and lived in Elmsett all her life. Her description of the roads in Elmsett is taken from a recording made in the 1980s:

You may be surprised to hear that roads in the village were much narrower in our childhood. The hedges were in the same place but the grass verges on either side of the roads were much wider. There used to be a little beaten path on the verges where people walked to keep out of the way of the traffic. They were covered with wildflowers. The roads were not metalled and Flowton Road was gated; they were very, very muddy in winter and dusty in summer. In the winter there were deep ruts. There were three flocks of sheep in the village and they used to make the roads very messy when they were herded from one field to another. We didn't have wellington boots in those days – we had laced up boot galoshes. There was no public transport so most people had bicycles. We went to Ipswich in a wagonette drawn by a bay horse called Polly, and it used to take an hour. On the flat the horse went at a

good spanking pace but she had to walk up and down the hills as we hadn't got a brake on the wagonette. Another method of journeying to Ipswich was made by Mr Arthur Skippings, who twice a week used to take a horse van loaded with flour from the mill to shops in Ipswich. There was also a carrier's cart in the village which belonged to Mr Pearl, landlord of the Rose and Crown. During the First World War he was called up and his wife was too nervous to drive the carrier's cart, so her friend, Thirza Clarke, used to drive it for her. As soon as the roads were dried up in spring, about March, children's tops and hoops came out. Some had wooden hoops, some iron, which they bowled along the road. We also used to go for walks with our skipping ropes. Another thing the children did was to make dust houses – I can remember them in The Street. Children also had quite a lot of jobs to do, like fetching milk from the Hall or Gate Farm, or water from the pump. They used the footpaths across the fields to shorten the journey.

Elm Trees
by Matthew Hitchcock

Elmsett means 'the settlement in the elm' – and this it was until the late 1960s, when disaster struck in the form of Dutch Elm Disease. This disease usually started at the top of the tree, turning the leaves brown and dead in early summer and by late summer or the next year the whole tree was dead.

In the 1970s I remember them dying by the dozen every summer, year after year. There were probably hundreds on our farm at this time and so thousands in the whole parish. Some were huge trees, perhaps 100–150 years old, but most were

English elms on the southern parish boundary. One of the few stands left in the county, the trees have been listed as Heritage Trees by Suffolk County Council.

under 70, as there had been heavy felling for timber in the First World War.

Trees that had died from the disease were dangerous and so had to be cut down – winter was the time on the farm for this job. Chainsaws had just come onto the market and they were heavy, unwieldy machines with petrol engines that took ages to start, and so we were worn out from pulling on the starter cord before work could even begin! To fell a large tree we cut a 'snotch' or 'jaw' out of the trunk about two feet from the ground and then from the other side of the trunk we started cutting straight through horizontally until the saw met the snotch and the tree fell. This was the theory, but sometimes the tree would twist or rock back and jam the saw. So the safest method was to tie a rope high up the tree and pull it over as the saw reached the snotch. A tractor or two men usually did the pulling. The tractor method could be a bit dodgy as the rope could break when pulled too hard or too soon by the tractor, and this could leave the tree wobbling precariously with no one sure if it would fall in the right direction!

Initially the idea was to burn the cut wood as soon as possible to stop the disease from spreading. This kills the elm bark beetle, which lives under the bark and is the culprit for transferring the fungus from tree to tree. It was, however, a vain attempt, as the disease spread too rapidly. Hard winters slow the disease and fungicides injected into the trees also have their role to play in saving the elms. We tried using fungicides on several important large trees, especially the avenue of English elms on the southern

parish boundary which do still survive, but this was expensive with no guarantee of success. We hired a petrol generator and ran a large drill to bore several inches into the trunk. We would drill a circle of holes half an inch in diameter round the trunk and push the fungicide powder into the holes, which were then sealed with a plug of clay.

Of the several varieties of elms in our village the wych elm has proved the most resistant to the disease, and several trees still survive. The English elm reproduces by suckers, and although the mother tree may die, the suckers will survive for ten to 15 years, and then may succumb to the disease. Elm trees and hedges were everywhere, including roadsides.

The trees I most remember were the ones that held rooks' nests – a rookery may consist of two or three nests, but more often has 20 or more, even as many as 50. The nests would be built 40 – 50 feet high in the trees and were made of a mass of twigs woven tightly together in a huge bundle, able to withstand very high winds and rain. Mid-February would be the time to see the rooks gathering in the trees to begin building nests or repairing old ones. Rooks would 'caw' constantly at one another at this time. It was loud and would continue throughout the day. Discarded twigs and the rooks' droppings littered the ground. The young would be ready to fly early in May, just when the leaves were appearing on the trees, which helped to hide the fledglings from predators. The worms and grubs they fed on were plentiful in May, unless there was a drought and the ground was hard, when many would die of starvation. There was a rookery in the Old Rectory garden, which was filmed in the 1960s by cameramen on scaffolding built up in the trees. There are rookeries at Gate Farm and at Bushy Ley Farm, but the one I remember most vividly was the one down our drive at Red House Farm, which had at least 50 nests. I remember having to cut the diseased trees down in 1972, which was very sad. Nearly every farm with a cattle yard and a few elms nearby had a rook's nest. In pollarded elms jackdaws and owls used the holes for nesting – one such behind Red House Farm with ivy all over it also housed a fox snuggled in the ivy about eight feet up – my mother and I both saw it. More recently, hybrid varieties of elm, hopefully disease resistant, have been raised. We have planted some on the farm to help keep elms in Elmsett, so perhaps our grandchildren may see the rookeries high in the elm trees again…

Products and Harvest from the Woods and Hedgerows

Traditionally, trees of a wood fall into two types – timber trees and the underwood. In order to allow timber trees to grow to maturity the underwood is managed by coppicing, which allows the trees to regrow or sucker. This also opens up glades of light, and the timber tree seedlings grow to replace any mature trees that have been harvested. The wood yields two products: the trunks provide timber, which is used for buildings; coppicing provides wood which is used for fencing, logs, poles, posts and for other specialised purposes, in addition to its main purpose, prior to central heating, as fuel, but there were many other by-products.

Hazel Broaches
These were an important product from the coppicing. Hazel sticks, 18 inches long and sharpened at both ends, were twisted in the middle and bent over like hairpins. They were used in thatching.

Hurdles
These were important on the farm, especially for making folds for the sheep and blocking gaps in hedges.

Reg Barber: Father made hurdles or wattle gates at home. He needed many tools for the job. The large ends of the poles were cut to the length required. Skill was needed to split the poles in two on his splitting rack… a cleaving axe was used for this (an L-shaped tool with a handle about a foot long and a sharp tapering blade *of a similar length). This was knocked into the pole by a wooden mallet and pressed up and down the pole, which may have had to be turned a bit, and there were the two ends of the hurdle. From thence… the bars were fitted into the poles and any ends that may have come through cut off, and a piece of wood was nailed from the top bar through the centre to the bottom bar. This kept the hurdle square.*

Tools
Many agricultural tools would have been made from the coppiced ash or elm wood. Straight handles could be selected from the growing wood and left to season for a year or two. Handles for scythes had to be shaped, and this was done by steaming and bending before leaving them to season. Axe handles had to be cut from a much larger piece of wood, usually about ten inches thick.

Pegs
Clothes peg making was always an important source of income for the gypsies. They were made from willow and bound with tin from old tin cans. Gypsies also made tent pegs from hazel.

Bark
Harold Cooper: *… Jimmy Johnson used to collect pieces of bark in sacks. He would take it from fallen trees and branches, especially from oak trees. He then took this into Ipswich to sell to the fishmongers for them to use in their smokeries.*

Faggots
Sticks were tied into bundles or faggots and sold to butchers, bakers and other tradesmen for fuel. Farm labourers would often have a length of hedge allocated to them from which they were able to cut wood for fires. Fred Holder continued to take wood from his allocated hedge, but as he got older he was more than happy to stop for a chat and often accepted help with carrying his firewood home.

Food from the Hedgerows
Nutting was a regular activity in the autumn. The hedgerow has often been referred to as 'Nature's larder', and not without reason. The fruit was used for jam and winemaking and some fruits, such as plums, could be preserved in jars for the winter months.

Harold Cooper: *My father shook the nuts from the trees for the children to collect. Walnut trees produced a valuable crop, so the trees tended to be in gardens or orchards. Those growing in fields belonged to the landowner and the walnuts were not there for the taking.*

CHAPTER 5

Farming

Memories of Farming

The Harvest

Before any form of mechanisation was developed the corn was cut by sickle and, as farms increased in size and employed more labour, by teams of men with scythes. Later, when the fields were cut with horse-drawn binders, there would be someone to drive the horses, someone to work the binder and a harvest gang of anything up to 12 men to make up the sheaves. They would have five or six pieces of straw in their hands and would weave it to tie round a sheaf. Such was the height of the corn that it came right up to the horses' nostrils. Harvesting would start on the outside of each field and work in towards the centre. Once a small area of standing corn was left in the centre of the field the rabbits would start to run from it. Boys and young men would chase them with sticks to kill them as an extra source of food. The corn, which was cut a couple of weeks earlier than when cut by combine, continued to ripen in the shocks. It was then at the mercy of the weather until it was ready for stacking. It was a skilled job to make a wheat stack, which was then thatched.

Cecil Barber: *My dad was a thatcher and I used to go to the farms and houses where he was thatching. I had*

John Waspe, 86, demonstrating the use of a sickle at the 'From Sickle to Satellite' demonstration, 1998.

(PHOTOGRAPH: ROGER SMITH)

John Waspe making straw bands for tying sheaves of wheat or oats cut by sickle, 1998. (PHOTOGRAPH: ROGER SMITH)

John Waspe demonstrating flailing corn at the 'From Sickle to Satellite' demonstration in 1998.

Team scything demonstration, 1998.

to dampen the straw ready for him to use. He used to thatch haystacks and straw stacks and also he used to truss clover stacks and I had to help him with that.

Christine Ladbrook: Small boys used to ride the middle horse on the binder. They used to drive the harvest wagon from the field to the stack because all

the sheaves were stacked before they were thrashed. The binder would bind them into sheaves and they would stand in the fields for several days until they were quite dry and then they would be pitched onto these big wagons and stacked. It was quite a skilled job both loading and stacking the sheaves and they would make lovely wheat stacks... they would

Harvesting gang at Turner's farm, 1920s. Left to right: Bill Warren, George Barber, George Warren, John Leary, ? Taylor, ?, Roly Clarke, George Cobbold, Frank Scott, ?, Bill Holder.

Cutting corn with a binder at Bushy Ley in 1947.

Reapers shocking corn, 1950s.

Reapers resting, 1950s.

be beautifully thatched with a little knob on the top to look nice.

Many children were involved in the harvest. They used to take food to their fathers in the fields and at half past four the whole family would have what was called 'beaver' in the field – a picnic of food and drinks, usually bottled tea or home-brewed beer. The men would continue working until dusk. One sheaf was always left in the field after loading was finished. The field would then be raked and cleared, this work

Threshing in 1953.

being done by women and youngsters. Only after this were the gleaners allowed into the field. The signal that the last sheaf had been removed was the gleaning bell. It was rung at 8.00a.m. and 6.00p.m. between which hours people were allowed to collect any remaining corn to feed to their chickens.

Fred Holder: *The only time we went into Ipswich was when Father got his £5 harvest bonus. The whole family used to go in Jimmy Johnson's lorry until the buses were available.*

The £5 bonus was a lot of money – wages would have been about 28s. (£1.40) a week. Victor Barber had a threshing machine powered by a Field Marshall tractor which he hired out to other farmers.

Flo Barber: *The stack would have to be threshed with the threshing tackle to separate the corn from the straw. There would be a man on the stack throwing sheaves onto the drum, which would be turning all the time. Corn would then come out one end and the chaff the other. Someone would then stack the loose straw.*

On a good day about ten tons of grain could be threshed, keeping ten men occupied for the whole day. Today a combine can cut and thresh ten tons of grain in about 20 minutes. Such is the change. The machinery was very dangerous – many a man lost a hand or an arm in the workings. Rats and mice used to live in the stacks and caused lots of fun as the stacks were dismantled.

Elmsett's First Combine Harvester

Percy Cooper and his family had arrived at Manor Farm in Elmsett in 1906 from Cheshire. Following a visit by his Canadian cousins in the early 1930s, Percy became convinced that the only solution for the

The second combine harvester in Suffolk at Manor Farm, 1936, with John Cooper (standing at the wheel), *Harold Cooper* (driving the tractor) *and Percy Cooper* (on the lorry).

The restored Case combine. It was shown in full working order at Manor Farm in 1993.

The Cooper family with the original 1936 Case combine harvester, restored to full working order by Oliver Cooper and his son Xavier in 1996. Left to right: *Harold, Oliver, Rupert and John Cooper*

Children ride on the tractor at Bushy Ley in 1947 – before the days of Health and Safety regulations!

depressed state of agriculture in eastern England was rapid mechanisation – especially of the harvest. He purchased a Case Model 'Q' Prairie-type combine for just over £500 at the Suffolk Show in 1936. That year the show was held at Great Finborough on Friday and Saturday 5 and 6 June. Attendance over the two days was 14,360 and the admission was 3s. (15p) on

the first day and 2s. (10p) on the second day. The combine went from the show ground to the Royal Show at Bristol and was returned by rail to Hadleigh Station. From there a local haulage contractor (Jack Gray) towed it up to Manor Farm with a six-wheel Morris Commercial lorry. The lorry was loaded with ballast and towed the combine, with the header on its own transport trailer attached to the rear of the combine. Two Case engineers, Oscar Linquist and Johnny Parfitt, rode up from Hadleigh on top of the combine – Oscar Linquist staying for about a month to assemble and commission the machine. The combine replaced a process that included cutting the crop with a daisy wheel binder, stooking the sheaves, pitching the sheaves onto the wagons and making the corn stack, thatching the stack and then finally threshing the stack and putting the sacks of corn away in a barn. Combining reduced the 'man days' for this process to about a quarter and made the grain available on the same day that cutting took place. So revolutionary was the purchase of this Case combine in 1936 that upwards of 200 local visitors would come to watch it – some with great reservations – during its first few days at work. At one point the Red Cross made a collection among the spectators in aid of Ipswich Hospital. John and Harold Cooper were in their late teens when this combine

Dolly Barber (standing) *with Freddie and John* (in the pram), *1938. Their sister Monica is third right.*

was bought. John, the eldest, took charge of the combine and Harold drove the Lanz Bulldog tractor that towed it. Rupert Cooper, the youngest at 15, had the job of carting the grain back to the farm. The most wheat harvested in one day during those first years was 27 acres, yielding around 30 tonnes. This was done between 11.30a.m. and 9.30p.m. – a running average of three tonnes per hour. The Case combine was used until after the Second World War. The last time it was used was in 1958 – an extremely wet summer when the new combine, a Ransome 902, was unable to cut some 40 acres at Manor Farm. An International TD14 crawler was hooked to the front of the old Case to complete the year's harvest.

Rupert Cooper: *When father's cousin came over from Canada he said to him, 'You are never going to do any good at farming the way you are, growing corn with small fields; you'll never compete with us Americans and Canadians. You'll need to take your hedges out and make the fields bigger and get yourself a combine harvester.' We got on very well for the first few seasons. It was easy. I remember the Wadleys from Semer who were dairy farmers heard that father had a combine and they came up to the farm one day. They were little chaps and they wore porkpie hats. They said, 'How are you going to get it through your gates?' Father said that was easy and he widened all the gateways. The main thresher went through OK, and the table was carried on a couple of railway sleepers.*

The Case combine was stored on the farm for 35 years until Oliver, Rupert's son, decided to renovate it. Work began in 1987 and finished in 1993.

Everything was completely restored in the farm workshop and the machine was brought into full field working order. It was exhibited in 1995 at Manor Farm, where over 1,000 people turned out to see it working. In 1998 Oliver grew several acres of taller corn and ran a large demonstration of harvesting techniques called 'From Sickle to Satellite'. It was a hugely successful day, with people attending from all over East Anglia. A video of the same title, made by Old Pond Publishing at this event, has preserved a valuable record of over 100 years of harvesting techniques and equipment.

As mechanisation took over from horsepower the role children played also changed. If a child was strong enough to depress the clutch on the tractor they could drive in the fields.

Joy Sillitoe: *I cannot remember wet summers! During the harvest I used to drive the grey Ferguson tractor whilst the sheaves of corn were gathered. I was about ten. I had to go from shock to shock as the sheaves were thrown onto the trailer. Uncle Gerald (Barber) on the trailer used to complain because I jolted him occasionally.*

Richard Hitchcock has memories of the early days of combining: *Our first combine was an early 1950s silver-coloured German Claas. It was mounted on a pair of ex-aeroplane tyres and pulled by a Fordson tractor. It had a six-foot side-mounted cutter and an engine mounted on the top. The grain was collected in hessian sacks, hired for the purpose, which when filled had to be placed in a chute and dropped to the ground. It took two men to lift the heavy sacks into the trailer.*

Aerial crop spraying, 1974.

The next combine was a self-propelled Massey Harris 726 with a front-mounted cutter bar that could be raised and lowered, and a tank for the grain. The engine was mounted underneath, and sometimes caught fire when chaff accumulated on the exhaust manifold. Sacks of grain were still manhandled but in 1959 we bought three hydraulic tipping trailers for transferring the grain to the farm to be bagged. The sacks were discarded in 1964, when the grain was stored and transferred in bulk. Since then combines have got bigger and faster, trailers are larger and yields have increased.

In 1981 Robert Fison achieved a Hustler wheat crop of 11.46 tonnes per hectare, just over 0.16 lower than that listed in the *Guinness Book of Records*.

In recent years farming has developed to incorporate the use of satellites and the pinpoint accuracy of GPS (Global Positioning System).

Nick Bird: *Combine harvesters can now utilise GPS for basic position knowledge. Coupled with continuous yield monitoring, this information is merged to produce a map of a field showing the spatial variability of yield within it. The map can then be used, in tandem with the farmer's knowledge of the soil structure, to vary the next season's seed rates and fertiliser rates across the field automatically, with no need for operator input. The effect of weather conditions on the seed bed, bird and animal damage and slug activity can also be taken into account. A further use of GPS, using a precise correctional signal, allows centimetre accurate positioning of the tractor on the ground. This allows the tractor to self-steer precise working widths with no overlap enabling great improvements in efficiency and reduces operator fatigue considerably. Although possible now, driverless tractors are unlikely to be seen in Elmsett for the next two or three years!*

Other Crops

At the organically-farmed Bushy Ley a six-year rotation of crops is still followed. Other farmers use a 'change' crop in order to retain the fertility of the soil and the one used most widely is oil seed rape. Its use as a cooking oil has increased hugely in recent years and more might be grown if the government backs the use of bio-diesel products to replace the burning of fossil fuels. Linseed is a different form of the flax that was grown during the war to supply linen for

Workers with a load of peas in Webbs Field in 1930. Left to right: *Fred Holder, Wal Taylor, George Meadows, Hip Mower, Charlie Laflin.*

fire hoses and other necessary items. Linseed oil is used in many industrial products from lubricants to paints and putty. For a while the blue fields were seen again in summer, but a change in European Union regulations has almost eliminated the production of this crop. The other most widely used change crop grown in Elmsett is the field bean, which is used for animal feed. But in 2005 a large acreage in the parish was either fallow or in permanent set-aside.

Farm Workers

The Horseman

Many horsemen displayed what appeared to be magical powers, but in fact they simply had an instinctive understanding of and empathy with horses, often passed from father to son, as boys would assist with the horses from an early age. One Elmsett horseman was Flaky Cousins, who had uncanny control of horses. He was a stallion leader and would take stallions all over the area to breed. Fred and George Holder's father was a horseman at Gate Farm. He used to walk to work in the morning, plough his acre and then walk home again – covering about 14 miles on foot every day.

Reg Barber: *My job was as head horseman to a stable of ten horses. I had to be up to feed the horses at five o'clock each morning. Four other men turned up at the proper time, which was six o'clock in the summer and six-thirty in winter. My wages were one pound and six*

Shire horses at work, c.1935. The man on the left is possibly Reg Barber.

Edmund (Ted) Hiskey (1877–1960) working for the Turner family at Gate Farm in the 1930s.

Farm workers at Poplar Hall with Claude Westren (on the right).

Sheep shearing in the 1890s in Aldham barn, with the three Barber brothers, Frank (shearing), Joe (front right) and George Barber (back right). Back left is Ken Barber. The men are wearing the traditional calico smocks which were hand-stitched by mothers and wives. A shepherd's smock was embroidered with the symbols of his work – a crook and a lantern. The symbols on a horseman's smock were a whip, a head collar and a horse shoe.

shillings (£1.30p) for a seven-day week, but on Sundays the horses were just fed. Farm work was a full-time job the whole year through, and needed more skills than ever men were paid for. As head horseman I had to do the drilling of seeds – wheat, barley, beans, peas and oats. I had to know all the different cog wheels for different seeds, and also turn the barrel end to end for the different seeds to make sure they were spaced properly in the earth. All my horses responded to their names. They had a lovely bed of straw in winter and in summer they were turned out to pasture.

Ploughing was done in the winter months in those days. January was hard work for the horseman because this was probably the heaviest work the horses would do throughout the year. Even if the land was frozen too hard to be ploughed the horses were needed for other jobs – muck spreading was another January job.

Cecil Barber: *In my young days the head horseman had to get up at 5a.m. to feed his horses and clean his pair out so that he was ready when the other men came in to work to begin ploughing at 6.30a.m. His wage was 14s. (70p) a week. The cowman got 12s. (60p) and labourers anything between 10s. and 11s. (50p and 55p).*

In summer horses also had to be taken to the pond to drink. In winter, if the pond was frozen, water had to be carried for them in buckets.

Rupert Cooper: *We used to have a horse pond with elm trees round it – it was a big pond, about 50 yards across. Ponds were made for horses; they had stones at the bottom. There were no pumps and they used to take the horses to the water at the end of the day. They used to drink the water and roll in it to freshen up after pulling a binder – they got very dusty at harvest time.*

The Shepherd

Sheep were a valuable commodity on the farm in that they provided both meat and wool. They often grazed over large tracts of land and the shepherd seemed instinctively to know where each of his flock was.

Blanche Seager (née Hiskey): *My grandfather was a shepherd and used to drive his sheep to Layham which is about six miles away, the other side of Hadleigh.*

The shepherd was a man who enjoyed solitude and at lambing time would live in his shepherd's hut, often in bitter weather. He would have a stove for

Old shepherd's hut at Paigle Farm.

warmth and this was also essential for keeping orphan lambs warm. Sometimes a sheep that had lost her lamb could be persuaded to foster an orphan, but often the shepherd had to bottle feed it until it could be returned to the flock.

Reg Barber*: Father was a sheep shearer… to start with they would take off the large barn door. They placed bricks underneath, at each corner and half way along each side. This made a lovely smooth surface to work on… and they could put the shears underneath when changing sheep. I have often wondered if Father took the bricks with him from place to place. The money paid for each sheep was three pence. The men had a white overall on, as the sheep were greasy. They were washed from time to time. The fleece of wool was neatly folded, rolling up a band of wool to tie it together. Father was the leader, making all the arrangements. I should have mentioned that the male sheep, called Tups, were sheared for six-pence. Of course there were very few. Also that the barn door was rightly fixed when the shearing was finished.*

Cecil Barber*: After the sheep were shorn the fleece would be wrapped into what we called 'pockets' and taken off to the Ipswich Wool Growers to be processed.*

Taffy Skippings*: Quite a number of farmers used to keep sheep in the village. There was a dipping tank at Church Farm where I worked, and farmers used to bring their sheep for dipping each year.*

The Stockman
He was responsible for the bulls, cows and bullocks. He was concerned with milk yields, bringing on heifers which would join the dairy herd and fattening bullocks as fast as was possible for beef.

Alfie Holder*: I left school when I was 14 and went to work at Gate Farm for Mr Turner. My job was to help the stockman to look after the animals. The only water supply at that time was the huge horse pond, and I used to have to carry buckets and buckets of water from that pond to the animals and to the barn to mix up the animal food.*

Cecil Barber*: I used to have to go in early to get the cows milked and ready for the carter to take the milk into Ipswich. This went in milk churns by horse and cart. Cows had to be milked twice a day, 365 days of the year. No half day on Saturday, and no annual holiday. Good Friday you had to work until 1.00p.m. and by the time you had eaten your lunch it was 2.00p.m., and as you had no money in your pocket there was not much to do.*

Taffy Skippings*: When I worked at Church Farm I used to have to work on Saturday afternoon and Sundays milking the cows. We had about 20 cows, I think. We used to have to put the milk into churns and leave them on the side of the road for the lorry to collect.*

Joy Sillitoe*: I can remember as a small child taking my cup into the milking shed and my uncle milking the cow into the cup – something you would not be allowed to do now!*

Richard Hitchcock*: One of the first jobs we were taught was milking our two Jersey cows, Mary and Corinne. I remember sitting on a three-legged stool washing the cow's udders, then putting special cream on my hands which was soothing if the cow had sore or cracked teats. The milk was directed into a stainless steel bucket, which the cow would kick over if she was irritated. The milk was poured into shallow pans to cool and allow the cream to rise to the top. This was then skimmed off with a tool like a perforated plate. Sometimes we made butter, adding a little salt and then patting it into blocks.*

Arthur Barber had a herd of cows and used to deliver milk to the villagers. People who wanted milk used to leave a milk can at their gate.

The Fison Dairy Herd
In 1958, at Elmsett Hall, Fred Fison made the decision to start the Elmsett dairy herd. His son Robert showed a keen interest in dairy farming so a herd of 45 Friesian heifers was bought. Milk production began in December 1959. In the early 1960s they gave up the pigs and sugar beet and concentrated on grain and dairy farming. Their cattle were regular winners at shows throughout the area and one cow, Butler's Aleta, won an award for producing 50 tons of milk. She produced their prize-winning bull, Elmsett Firework, in 1964 and he went on to win many prestigious awards, although the Fisons were unable to retain the King George VI cup because their three wins were not consecutive. In order to become an accredited herd under the brucellosis eradication scheme they were unable to show cattle for two intervening years. On one occasion Firework seriously misbehaved himself at the Suffolk Show when his nose ring broke as his handler, Peter Theobold, tried to restrain him. The

Trophies won by the Fisons's bull 'Elmsett Firework',
1969. Left: *King George VI Trophy, Royal Norfolk Show;*
right: *Perpetual Challenge Trophy, Essex Show.*

'Elmsett Firework' at the Suffolk Show, 1969, with Peter
Theobald and Eric Fison leading the bull.

cause was the near proximity of a cow on heat;
Firework, not a bull to miss an opportunity, mounted
and served the cow, whose owner was not best
pleased! When Firework died in 1981 Robert planted
a horse chestnut tree over his grave. The herd eventually expanded to over 100 cows in milk and in 1972
17 were sold into the late Queen Mother's herd, but
in 1976 the herd was dispersed and replaced with
beef cattle.

Pigs

Most households kept a pig and often it became
something of a pet; it was kept near to the kitchen
door, where it would get fat on all the kitchen waste.
There is often a runt (or weak) piglet in a litter.

Doreen Ladbrook: *Our daughter, Naomi, loved the*
piglets and liked to look after the runt of the litter. We
would put it into a large tea chest with straw and news-
paper and she looked after it. One in particular used to
roll up in a rug on the floor and it also followed us
round the field when we went for a walk. Naomi and
the piglets became very fond of each other. We had four

at different times, and there were some real characters
amongst them.

It was a sad, but necessary day when it had to be
slaughtered. Unlike other meats, pork can be
preserved for consumption through the winter
months – cured hams and bacon keep for many
months if properly stored. Pigs were usually sent to
the village butcher for slaughter.

Reg Barber: *Father was also a slaughterer of pigs –*
only for the butcher. We had one butcher in our village.
I can well remember when he wanted a pig killed... one
of us boys had to go and tell the butcher to have the
copper hot at a certain time. This was very important
because as soon as the pig was killed it had to have all
the hair scraped off... the hot water was not put on all
at once but used as required to scrape off the hair bit by
bit. The tool used for this was called a squid. To
describe it, it had a wide blade about six inches long
and a short handle. The pressure used was not heavy
and of course no soap was used. The knife had to be
dipped repeatedly into the hot water to wash off the
hairs. Father would not leave as much as a little hair
on the pig.

Rachel Hitchcock: *I can well remember the day when*
the pig was killed, and how the meat arrived in large
baskets roughly jointed. Everyone in the house was
busy all day preparing the fresh pork for storage and
consumption. We seemed to live off pork for days. A
few days before the slaughter my mother visited a friend
to borrow earthenware bowls, large enough for a side of
bacon or a ham. She also bought the ingredients for
making sweet pickle for the bacon, and saltpetre for
rubbing on the pork before curing it. I remember the
delivery – the whole pig, with head, trotters and tail.
The trotters and tail and pieces of the head were cooked
and then the good pieces of meat were put into small
bowls to be made into brawn – only we called them 'pork
cheeses'. We usually had pig's fry (the skirt, as it was
called) on the first day which was made with apples,
onions, sage and pieces of bacon. The tongue was
cooked and pressed for eating cold. The bacon and hams
were prepared for pickling, a lengthy process. The joints
were soaked in syrupy liquid in the huge earthenware
bowls, and each day had to be turned and basted. One
of the more tedious jobs was cutting off the excess fat,
and then cutting it into half-inch cubes and putting it
in a large pan to be heated and melted. The liquid that
ran off was pure lard, which kept well, for cooking. The
remaining shrunken scraps were drained and were
dipped in salt. We called them 'scraps' and they were
far tastier than today's pork scratchings.

Robert Everett has a smallholding in Manor Road
and remembers when he used to herd his sows
through the village to The Maltings to visit the boar.
About a week before they were ready to be mated he

Corn ready to be transported to Ladbrooks' Mill in the 1920s. Verdun Green is with the horse. The traction engine would have been driving the threshing machine. The thatched barn in the background was at Church Farm – it was destroyed by fire in the early 1960s.

left them with Cecil Barber, who looked after them and put them to the boar. Another week after this Robert herded them home again. He usually had two or three ready at the same time. One on its own could be quite a handful on the road, especially if people left their garden gates open.

Disease has always been a problem with pigs.

Brian Hiskey: *There was a building in Whatfield Road where pigs farrowed. One day as I was going to school several men arrived and there was a strong smell of disinfectant in the air. When I got home I was told that all the pigs had been slaughtered, covered in quick lime and buried. I'm not sure if it was foot and mouth or swine fever.*

Jack Ladbrook standing on the haywain supervising the workers, c.1920.

Pinkie Meadows and Bob Green resting on their hoes, c.1935.

Later in life Brian worked for the Ladbrooks at Malting Farm, where for many years he looked after their large herd of pigs, firstly Wessex Saddlebacks, some of which were exhibited at agricultural shows, and later Landrace pigs, which produced a leaner meat. In the 1990s dealing with pigs became an increasing problem. When adjacent land was sold for a development of 26 houses in Sawyers the pig unit was not popular with the newcomers. Muck carting in the centre of the village was also becoming a problem, so in 1995 pig keeping at the Maltings ceased.

Richard Pryke ran a successful pig-breeding unit at Potash Farm for 30 years until the mid-1990s. His mother, Molly Skippings, had inherited the house prior to her marriage to Walter John Pryke, a baker from Hadleigh. The couple ran the smallholding together and lived there until their respective deaths. The house, where Richard still lives at the time of writing, has changed little over the last 70 years.

The Labourer

Many of the inhabitants of Elmsett are described in the records as 'Agricultural Labourer' – and his skills were generally manual ones. He would be expected to be able to drive a horse, no doubt always under the watchful eye of the horseman, thatch corn stacks, repair machinery and mend fences, gates and walls. In summer he worked tirelessly through long summer days haymaking then harvesting, and in winter threshing the corn. All this work involved a lot of lifting and carrying, so he had to be fit. Often

in cold and wet conditions, the labourer would have to clear ditches and coppice hedges, toiling through the daylight hours, January and February being the traditional months for this job.

Labourers usually started their working life as a farmer's boy.

Brian Hiskey: *When I started work at the Maltings Farm it was doing general farm work. There was still a house cow and one working horse, a Suffolk Punch, which I only worked with once to do a bit of rolling. I had to get someone to help me harness it because I couldn't get the collar over its head. My first job was to re-shock a field of oats after a stormy Sunday night – the shocks had blown all over Plumtree field. Arthur Meadows, known as Pinky, was an old man but he kept on going all day. I was shattered by four o'clock and glad to get home for my tea. I worked with poultry for a while. They were mostly Rhode Island Reds or Light Sussex and were kept in pens on Cassocks meadow. The chicken feed was kept in an old shepherd's hut, one probably used by my grandfather. He was Ladbrook's shepherd. Crops were also grown on Cassocks: potatoes one year, which were stored in a big clamp that caught fire. I looked after the pigs for most of the time that I was working. In the early days they were sold at market, but later most were sold by contract.*

The Backhouse (Back'us) Boy

These young boys started work in farmhouses when they were only eight or nine. There used to be keen competition to get a boy work in the farm kitchen: it was a warm, clean environment, they were well fed and slept in the farmhouse. They used to fetch and carry for the maids, they brought in wood and logs, lit the copper, collected eggs, etc. After a year or so as a back'us boy they became yard or stable boys.

Alfie Holder: *I was paid 9s.4d. (47p) when I first went to work (1931). Sometimes the farmer couldn't pay us all on a Saturday and we had to wait another week for our money. This did not happen very often, but there wasn't any unemployment in the village at that time – if you felt like changing your job you could always get another on another farm.*

Farming Memories 1950–2003
by Richard Hitchcock

Our grandfather bought Red House Farm in 1947 from Mr H. Gibbons and initially had a farm manager, Basil Wright, to run the farm. The Hitchcocks eventually moved to Elmsett in 1951 with three of us boys and a fourth – Matthew – arrived later. We had moved from West Row, where we had mains water and electricity, whereas here water had to be pumped from a well filled by a spring in the back garden and a diesel generator supplied a limited amount of electricity. This was only run in the evenings when daylight faded. In 1954 Father

Bill Osborne loading sugar beet, 1967.

Bill Osborne drilling sugar beet, 1968.

Bale carting in 1967.

Sows crossing the road to Gate Farm for their food, 1967.

Stubble burning in 1967.

Right: *Elmsett school children on a farm visit to the pig unit at Gate Farm in the 1980s. Richard Hitchcock is explaining the feed system in the Suffolk house.*

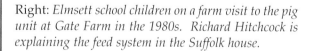

bought Gate Farm and, as he was continuing to work for Fison Fertilisers, John Chorley was brought in to manage it. When after a few years John left, Father managed both farms, until firstly me then my brother Robert finished agricultural college and joined him. Initially the stockmen were Dick Mayes at Red House and Walter Mowles, followed by Michael Page at Gate Farm. Our tractor drivers were Bill 'Beans' Osborne and 'Shrimpy' Green at Red House, with Felix and Jim Taylor at Gate Farm. After the two farms were amalgamated Felix and Jim did all the ploughing. At harvest Bill and Felix drove the combines while Jim carted corn – he often had trouble reversing the trailer up to the grain pit and there were shouts of 'whoa' when he got there!

Crops We grew barley, wheat, peas for animal feed and sugar beet. In the 1950s sugar beet needed a lot of hand work as the husk had more than one seed inside and the seedlings appeared as doubles and trebles. In order to produce a large beet each row had to be reduced to a single plant at nine inches spacing free of weeds. This backbreaking work was often done by casual labour on a piecework system, whereby payment was by the chain (22 yards). In the 1960s the pelleted seed was developed so that we could sow at the correct spacing and pre-emergence weed killers were developed to keep the weeds down. In the autumn/winter the beets were lifted and spun out of the ground by machine. The leaf tops had to be cut off by hand and left in the field. I remember Sam Clarke with a hessian sack tied round his waist and head down topping the rows of beet then throwing them into heaps. In November 1960 he was paid 3s.6d. (18p) per 100 yards. The heaps of beet were collected using a hand fork, with blobs on the end of the tines to prevent stabbing, and thrown onto a trailer to be taken to the clamp. From here they were again loaded by hand fork into a lorry to be taken to the Ipswich sugar beet factory. In 1960 we bought a harvester which lifted the beet and transferred into the trailer which was driven alongside. They were still tipped in the farmyard but we had a tractor-mounted elevator to load them into the lorry. As our land was so wet and heavy the fields would often turn into quagmires and ruin the soil structure so we ceased growing beet in 1981.

Straw The first bales I remember were more like a bundle and had to be picked up by pitchfork and tossed to a man in the trailer. To stack properly you needed to do the edges first and then fill in the middle. If the sides were straight and vertical the middle would take care of itself and the load wouldn't fall over. We bought a mechanised bale handler in 1961 – a sledge attached to the baler which collected blocks of 16 bales. These were then lifted in cages mounted on the front and back of the tractor and carried back to the farm, where they still had to be stacked by hand. Some bales were sold to Stramit Boards (a product used for building), but it took a lot of work and was not very profitable. Our next baler used a flat eight system and with the younger members of the family helping we were handling about 24,000 bales a year. Finally we used a contractor to make the high-density bales, equivalent to about 20 small ones. The handling of these was done by one man.

Robert Hitchcock remembers straw burning: In the 1970s and 80s this was common and often a spectacular sight in the late summer. As crop yields increased and livestock number declined it became the most common method of disposing of surplus straw. A good burn in the field was a perfect start to the preparation of a new seedbed, destroying unwanted seed and making subsequent cultivation simple and cheap. It needed a bit of thought and a great deal of care, as the fire could race across a field at frightening speed, sometimes jumping several metres of the firebreak. If the timing was right lighting the two opposite sides of the field would draw the flames to the middle and control would be maintained. As burning became more effective the incidents of fires out of control increased. Black clouds of smoke hanging over the countryside, together with accidental damage to hedges and trees, angered the public forcing the government ban on stubble and straw burning in 1987.

Richard Hitchcock ran the pig units: Soon after our first farrowing house was built at Gate Farm in 1962, swine fever came to Suffolk and our pigs were affected. After struggling to control it with anti-serum there was little improvement and the whole herd had to be slaughtered. We re-stocked with Wessex Saddleback gilts (young sows) at the end of that year. Electricity was installed at Gate Farm in 1964 and so we were able to move the feed mill from Red House Farm and install a mixer to make our own pig rations using a protein/vitamin/mineral concentrate mixed with our own ground wheat and barley. At this time the breeding and rearing of piglets was done at Gate Farm and the fattening at Red House Farm. The sows were kept outside in fields and were brought back across the road to feed in individual feeders. A fattening house was built in 1964 so we could run the whole pig enterprise from Gate Farm and rear pigs to a heavier weight. They were sold as heavy hogs and taken to the Harris Bacon factory in Ipswich. We built four sow yards in 1966 so sows could come off the field and be under cover. In the late 1960s we gave up mixing our own feed and bought pelleted pig feed from Ladbrooks' Mill.

As the herd expanded we needed more accommodation for pregnant sows and so sought advice from the Ministry of Agriculture, then offering 40 per cent grants. We planned open yards, but were steered towards tie stalls, where sows were tethered and their movement restricted, but management was easier. We could vaccinate and test for pregnancy without difficulty and each animal received the correct amount of food without bullying. A tie stall house was built in 1971 and was used for 20 years. This method is now banned in the UK. During this period more fattening accommodation was built and 24 covered yards for weaners. The redundant tie stall house was altered to farrowing accommodation as our herd continued to grow.

In 1990 we had a herd of 260 Landrace sows and ten

James Hitchcock with piglets in the pig unit at Gate Farm in the 1980s.

Large White boars, a total of 2,500 pigs – quite large for an indoor unit at that time. My son James managed the herd with three other people working full time. In 1991 we built a large strawed yard to house the pregnant sows, which were fed automatically by a computer-controlled feed system. Each sow wore a neck collar with a transponder attached so that the feed station could identify her and give her the correct amount of food. In 1993, after 30 years of continuous pig keeping, we had many sub-clinical diseases affecting the growth rate and breeding performance of our pigs. And because

of the additional cost of medication, our pigs had become unprofitable. The only solution was to sell all the pigs and disinfect the buildings. Within six weeks we were able to restock.

We decided, before re-stocking the herd, to work with a breeding company and produce gilts for outdoor units. So, in partnership with Rattlerow Farms, a Stradbroke-based breeding company, we restocked with Duroc boars and Landrace sows in order to produce the outdoor gilt called Landroc. This required very strict biosecurity and first class animal husbandry. We were successful in breeding some excellent gilts which were sent all over the country, with some being sold into Europe and America. Unfortunately, pig prices kept falling in the 1990s in spite of many campaigns to promote British pig meat. I remember my stint of looking after the sow in Parliament Square, the marches and supermarket promotions. It was hard to make a profit. There were more regulations to comply with and skilled labour was difficult to find, so in 2003 we reluctantly decided to sell all the pigs and close the unit. We decided to diversify and convert some of the buildings to let for workshops and general storage.

The average size of farms has changed dramatically since the beginning of the twentieth century. Of the 21 working farms in the parish in 1900, 15 have been absorbed to create five arable farms of a much larger acreage. Only Bushy Ley, the organic farm, has remained within its original boundaries.

Farms in Elmsett in 1900	In 2005
Boarded Barn Farm, Manor Road	Original buildings gone
Bone Farm, Whatfield Road	No evidence remains
Bushy Ley, Offton Road	Organic farm with a small beef herd
Chequers Farm, Whatfield Road	Two private dwellings
Church Farm, Manor Road	Private house. Building used by contract farmer
Coates Farm, Whatfield Road	Private house
Elm Farm, Whatfield Road	Private house
Elmsett Hall Farm, Offton Road	Arable farm
Gate Farm, Ipswich Road	Arable; buildings converted to storage units/workshops
Hill Farm, Flowton Road	Private house
Laurel Cottage Farm, Flowton Road	Private house, some buildings remain
Manor Farm, Manor Road	Arable farm
Mill Farm, Hadleigh Road	Private house, buildings remain
Moat Farm, Hadleigh Road	Private house
Old Barn Farm, Manor Road	Smallholding with pigs and cattle
Poplar House Farm, Whatfield Road	Arable farm/business centre/air field
Potash Farm, Ipswich Road	Private house, buildings remain
Red House Farm, Flowton Road	Arable farm
Rhodds Farm, Flowton Road	Pedigree sheep, buildings remain in use
Rookery Farm, Manor Road	Private house, some buildings remain
Wall Farm, Ipswich Road	Private house

CHAPTER 6

The Elmsett Tithe War

Standing in a prominent position across the road from St Peter's Church is a rare and defiant memorial commemorating the tithe seizure at Elmsett Hall in May 1932. Intentionally sited just across the lane from the entrance to the church, it is a reminder of the bitter war between Church and farmers at that time.

A tithe, as many people will know, was an ancient form of taxation levied on the produce of the soil for the benefit of the clergy. The word tithe means one tenth, and originally it was paid in kind, with every tenth calf, lamb, piglet or sheaf of corn given to the clergy. The 1836 Tithe Commutation Act converted it to a fixed cash payment known as the Tithe Rentcharge. Always a very contentious form of taxation, it caused much bad feeling in the farming community towards the Church, and this was exacerbated in the long depression, which overshadowed British agriculture from 1921 until the late 1930s. Among the hardest hit were those who had bought

The tithe memorial.

their holdings during the great land sale boom of 1918–21 when, in the atmosphere of optimism induced by the high prices of the First World War, perhaps six to eight million acres of land changed hands. Landlords were only too happy to sell farms to their tenants, thus divesting themselves of an asset which, through maintenance and taxation, was rapidly becoming more of a burden than a benefit. By the 1930s many of these new owners, burdened by the debt incurred in buying their farms, were then plunged into crisis due to the onset of the recession.

Farmers in East Anglia, a predominantly corn-growing area, were particularly hard hit during this acute agricultural depression; tithes were high and had no relation to income, but regardless of the farmer's hardship, the Church demanded payment in full. Protests were made, but the Church would not accept reduced payment and many farmers were simply unable to pay. The Suffolk Tithepayers' Association was established in 1931 under the chairmanship of A.G. Mobbs, with Makens Turner as vice chairman. It vowed to support all farmers refusing or unable to pay their tithe and the press reported subsequent events as the 'Tithe War'.

The incumbent at this time was the Revd Haslewood, who arrived in Elmsett in 1928 from a mining area in the north. Rupert and Janet Cooper, whose parents farmed at the neighbouring Manor Farm, remember him well. **Rupert Cooper**: 'I can remember the Revd Haslewood coming to Elmsett – people were afraid of him.'

Janet Cooper: *There was much bad feeling between the Revd Haslewood and the local farmers. He had come to Elmsett from a mining area, and had no understanding of rural Suffolk and the problems farmers were facing at that time.*

Elmsett Hall and Church Farm were both purchased by Charles Westren in 1920. His parents had been tenant farmers since 1882, when the farms were owned by the trustees of Bishop Andrew's Charity, a church charity established in 1625 for the benefit of the poor. Charles Westren was one of those who refused to pay his tithe and the bailiffs were sent in to impound cornstacks and furniture. As reported in local and national papers, on Monday, 2 May 1932, the authorities planned to make a surprise visit to Elmsett Hall, but had notified the police beforehand and word got back to the village. Lorries arrived at 6.30a.m. to remove the corn and, as no local haulier would touch goods impounded for tithe, they came from as far away as Cambridge (50 miles). The contractor's employees, having surprised Charles Westren, managed to load and cart away about a third of one stack before help arrived.

Neighbouring farmers were contacted by telephone and news of the happenings quickly spread. Sympathisers with Mr Westren soon began to assemble to protest and demonstrate against the action. The village school was closed and the children given a day's holiday; local farmers gave their employees a day off. Cars arrived every few minutes, bringing farmers from all parts of the county and from Norfolk and Essex.

The Cooper family at Manor Farm were close neighbours and when they heard the lorries arriving the women rang the church bells to alert villagers.

Janet Cooper: *Mother got into trouble for ringing the bells – she and her sister decided it would be the best way of letting people know there was something going on.*

Rupert Cooper: *Things got very heated that morning. I gather the Chief Constable of West Suffolk rang the Haslewoods and said, 'If you've got anywhere to go you'd better move out because we can't guarantee your safety,' and they went to spend the day in Hadleigh.*

With great ingenuity supporters disrupted the hauliers with a variety of actions – Charles Westren knew the law well and had his horses and carts going round and round, so drivers were frequently requested to move their lorries in order to let farm vehicles pass through.

Lily Holder was working at the Hall and remembered the event: *… it was very frightening at the time… trees were felled along the drive – magnificent elms, stacks were fired and my future husband was holding the bull on a leading rein ready to let it loose if the Bailiffs approached the Hall itself, where all the doors were barricaded. I wasn't married then, but I was ever so worried about him!*

Other obstructions included a trench being dug across the gateway leading into the farmyard, with the excuse of inspecting the underground pipe which carried water through the ditch on either side, thus making it impossible for the lorries to leave until the inspection was completed and the trench refilled. A tractor drew a large poultry house to the end of the drive where it met the highway, where farm workers removed its wheels for oiling and greasing. When the men began cutting the trees down and the hauliers saw their exit was being completely blocked, they feared for their safety and decided to withdraw their lorries, with much cheering from the large crowd.

The tithe memorial in 1936.

Scenes like this were repeated all over East Anglia. In April 1932, 273 non-payment cases were heard at Sudbury, and the revolt continued (even Sir Oswald Mosley's Blackshirts got in on the act) until the law regarding tithes changed in 1936. However, it was not until June 1976 that the victory of the anti-tithe movement became virtually complete, when Parliament was informed that from October 1977 the collection of this contentious tax would be suspended. The cost of gathering it had been too great.

Elmsett's tithe memorial is inscribed thus:

TO COMM'ERATE THE TITHE SEIZURE AT ELMSETT HALL OF FURNITURE INCLUDING A BABY'S BED & BLANKETS, HERD OF DAIRY COW, EIGHT CORN AND SEED STACKS VALUED AT £1200 FOR A TITHE VALUED AT £385.

Positioned opposite the entrance to the church, this monument is one of only two tithe memorials in Suffolk and, as Charles Westren intended, it is a bleak reminder of the harsh times in the 1930s. Ben Harvey, who was a builder, wheelwright, cabinet-maker, coffin maker and taxi driver, built it. In order to reinforce the memorial and to prevent it from being demolished, ploughshares and bits of iron were packed inside it.

Headlines concerning the Tithe incident, 1932.

The list of items seized on the inscription is some-what exaggerated!

Lily Holder: *Although Mr Westren stated on the tithe memorial that the baby's cot was seized, this was not the case, as we were barricaded into the Hall and nobody entered.*

Brian Hiskey: *Father worked at the Hall during the Tithe War. The memorial says that the cows were taken, but they heard that the Bailiffs were coming and father and Sid Barber ran the cows up to Priory Farm at Aldham.*

The event was widely reported in the press, with photographs of the angry crowd. Headlines included: 'Crowd Obstructs Removal of Seized Stacks' and 'Hauliers Abandon Difficult Task'. It was followed up in the *East Anglian Daily Times* with a bitter exchange of letters between Charles Westren and a Mr Cobbold.

Shortly after this event Mr Westren emigrated to New Zealand, but he returned for a brief time to see his solicitor in Ipswich about retaining the monument. When he sold the farm he retained the small piece of land on which the memorial stands. It is now the subject of a preservation order.

Makens Turner (1890–1978)

Makens was described as a 'gentleman farmer'. He was vice-chairman of the Suffolk Tithepayers' Association from its establishment in 1931, was a prominent member of the National Union of Farmers and usually spent three days of the week in London. In Elmsett he was also very active. He was a governor of both the school and the workhouse and, at the time of the tithe incident at Elmsett Hall, was a churchwarden at St Peter's and was on the Parish Council. After the incident he travelled to Bury

Makens Turner with his wife, Marjorie, in 1956.

St Edmunds and made representation to Bishop Whittingham, but returned to the village disgusted with the bishop's attitude. His support for the tithe-payers was unfailing, and he was instrumental in keeping the Tithepayers' Association active. He is buried in Elmsett churchyard.

Revd C.B. Haslewood (1872–1941)

The Revd Christopher Francis Beevor Haslewood was a dictatorial man who was not at all popular with the villagers. He had previously been the incumbent in the North East in a coal-mining town, and had little sympathy with those affected by the hardship caused by the depression in agriculture.

Fred Holder: *... he came down from Durham, and was a sturdy, rather serious, man. He must have been a scholar because sometimes he wore a mortar board.*

He was married to a doctor's daughter – they had no children. When they first came to Elmsett they were quite poor, and went everywhere on bicycles.

Opening the rectory fête, 1936. Left to right: *Mr A.E. Ladbrook, Mrs Maxwell (of Semer), Revd C.F.B. Haslewood, Mrs Haslewood.*

Cissie Holder (née Barber): *I remember his bicycle, it was a big, green, heavy Army type with a little wicker basket on the back.*

He benefited from the successive deaths of several wealthy aunts, the first about two years after his arrival in the village.

Rupert Cooper: *As the aunts died, he really went to town. He had a brand new Armstrong Siddeley Self Change every year. These aunts weren't married and he told my father they had left him about £50,000.*

He was totally unsympathetic towards farmers who could not pay their tithe. Rupert remembers him being invited to tea to try to persuade him to take less money.

Grandfather was put on to ask him, he said, 'We will give you 75% of the Tithe if you will accept it'. Revd H. said, 'No, I want it all.' They never had it all, although they went to a lot of trouble. I know we let part of the house at the front to a chap, and Revd H. tried to get the fellow's rent before it was paid to Father. The chap was very good – he gave Father two years' rent in advance, and said, 'That will sort the tithe out'.

After the Tithe War at the Hall the Revd Haslewood was severely reprimanded by the Bishop for allowing the women to enter the church and ring the bells.

Janet Cooper: *Revd Haslewood's reaction to the ringing of the bells was to lock up the church, almost unheard of in those days. My father had been church-warden, but he took a rest during the tithe war.*

The farmers' wives who had rung the bells were also reprimanded for their part in the events, and received a very severe letter from the Bishop.

Janet Cooper: *I remember my father telling me once there was a feeling that he [the Bishop] would have done better to have ignored the whole thing. By sending such letters he only added fuel to the fire. It made my mother very angry, but she wouldn't answer it – her sister was very worried and wrote an apologetic letter, but Mother wouldn't write.*

It seems that the Bishop was no more popular than the rector was!

Rupert Cooper: *The Bishop wasn't a nice man – his name was Whittingham, the Bishop of St Edmundsbury*

Cutting down a tree with which to block the road. The top branches, however, were tangled in those of the larger tree, and this prevented it from falling. (EADT PHOTO)

and Ipswich. I remember two children making a bit of a noise in the church – he got down from the pulpit and told their mother to take them out – not a very nice thing to do. He wasn't very considerate.

The Revd Haslewood, likewise, was not very tolerant of children. He objected strongly to the noise they made whilst playing on the village green, which is adjacent to the rectory, so in 1934 he bought a four-acre field just beyond the village boundary

which was gifted to the parish. The Deed of Gift, dated 20 October 1934, was made between the Revd Haslewood and the St Edmundsbury and Ipswich Diocese Board of Finance.

The terms of the Trust are put simply:

The Board will hold the property upon trust to permit the same to be used as a recreation sports and play ground for the Parish of Elmsett but no games shall be allowed thereon on any Sunday, Good Friday or Christmas Day. The Rector and Churchwardens shall be administrative Trustees...

The land was subsequently used as a sports field until the Rectory Meadow was purchased by the villagers in 1968, and the sports facilities were transferred there. Cycle speedway was a popular event there in 1976. Playground equipment was erected in 1977, and also later moved to the Rectory Meadow.

In 1993 part of the land was sold and a small estate of low-cost houses for purchase or rent was completed in 1994. This little community continues to house local people, several of them young, who grew up in the village, and attended the school to which their own children now go. The rest of the land remains a recreational and wildlife area, with a small grove of trees, planted in 1999. It is still known as Hazelwood – the spelling was changed for convenience.

A group of the saw and axe wielders, whose tree-felling exploits provided them with plenty of hard work. Judging by this picture, they all seem on good terms with each other. (EADT PHOTO)

Grass cutting in Laurel Cottage garden in the 1920s, with Cecil Barber pushing the mower, Frank Barber pulling.

A village outing in the 1950s. **Left to right:** *Dick Beaumont, ?, Alf Pearl, ?, ?, Robert Green, Stanley (Bob) Green.*

CHAPTER 7

The Village at Work

Up until the outbreak of the Second World War the work of the majority of the residents of the village was centred on agriculture and the land. There were farmers, farm managers, horsemen, stockmen, thatchers, hurdlemakers, toolmakers, a wheelwright and a blacksmith. Wages were poor and working hours were long.

Many people did several jobs to make ends meet. With its variety of trades and businesses the village was self-supporting. It had a mill, three shops, a public house, a brewery, a builder who was also the undertaker, a blacksmith and a butcher. Most of the employment was also within the village itself. Each farm employed between four and six men and the mill, at its peak, employed over 30, the majority being men, although women did work on packing the flour and other such jobs.

In the early part of the twentieth century it is difficult to find anyone who did not have more than one job:

Arthur Barber was a farmer, pork butcher and he had a milk round.

George Barber was a thatcher, hurdle maker, sheep shearer and carter.

Ben Harvey was a builder, coffin maker, cabinet maker and taxi driver.

Alfred Hiskey was a baker, pork butcher, shopkeeper and carrier.

Kate Hiskey only had the Widow's Allowance of £1.10s. (£1.50) a week so she did all sorts of work, including sugar beeting and working at the mill. She was also the school caretaker for over 20 years. This last job involved lighting the old tortoise stoves and, every Friday, scrubbing out the old bucket toilets and

Occupations as shown on census returns

Occupation	1861	1891	1901	Occupation	1861	1891	1901
Agricultural labourer	120	107	55	School Monitor			2
Ale/Beerhouse/Inn keeper	1	2	3	School Teacher			2
Bailiff			2	Shepherd			1
Beekeeper		1	1	Shopkeeper/Blacksmith			1
Blacksmith	1	1	1	Shopkeeper			1
Blacksmith assistant	2	2	2	Stockman (1 cow boy)			8
Butcher		1	2	Thatcher	1	3	1
Carter/Carrier		1	2	Thatcher's apprentice		2	
Clergyman/Rector	1	1	2	Thatcher/Hurdlemaker		2	1
Coachman			1	Tinsmith			1
Cordwainer (shoemaker)	2			Wheelwright	2	1	2
Farmer	12	9	6	Backhouse boy	1		
Farmer's son/assistant		2	6	Cook	1	1	1
Farmer + Dealer	1	1		Dairymaid	2	1	
Farmer + Engine man	1	1		Domestic servant	2		3
Farmer + Grocer	1			Draper's assistant		2	
Farmer + Miller	1	1	1	Dress maker		1	
Farmer + Publican	1			Housekeeper	3		2
Farmer + Shepherd		1		Housemaid	1	2	2
Gamekeeper		2		Laundress	1	1	1
Gardener	1			Mother's help			1
Horseman/Groom	3	2	21	Servant	2	2	
Maltster		1	1	Student		1	
Maltster's assistant		1	1				
Miller		3	1	Total workers	165	159	144
Miller/Maltster			2				
Miller journeyman			3	Number of males	229	227	204
Ratmen	1			Number of females	219	207	157
Roadman			1	Number of residents	448	434	361

The Rose and Crown Darts Team, 1932. Left to right, back row: *Frank Green, George Holder, Victor Barber, George Row, John Rouse, Robert Taylor, Alex Moore, Cyril Wyartt;* second row: *Herbert Hiskey, Alf Mower, Jim Taylor, Edmund Green, George Malster;* front row, sitting: *Tom Green, Jack Hiskey, Bill Osborne, Gerald Barber, Roger Leeks.*

burying the waste. She also had to spring clean the school once a year, scrubbing everywhere with cold water and cleaning the windows.

George Meadows was a beer retailer and carrier.

Arthur Robinson, who kept the Post Office, also kept cows on Manor Road and used to supply milk for the school children. It was collected by the school bus as it passed.

Bob Skippings was harness maker and repairer – he also mended shoes and cut men's hair.

The Rose and Crown

For nearly 200 years the Rose and Crown in Elmsett was in the hands of Mrs Pearl's family. The last landlady of the family, Elizabeth (Lizzie) Mary Pearl, lived in the pub for 72 years. Her husband, Alfred Pearl, served with the Royal Army Veterinary Corps in France in the First World War and took over the pub in 1922. He was partially paralysed in an accident and spent the latter years of his life upstairs bed-bound. Lizzie, a neat little woman, not only ran the pub single handed, but also looked after her husband for the last 21 years of her tenancy. Blanche Seager knew them well – her father, Jack Hiskey, shaved Mr Pearl three times a week and was Mrs Pearl's 'pot boy'.

Taffy Skippings: *I remember Alf Pearl. Bill Waspe, who lived at Wall Farm, broke his leg and Alf helped to look after his stock. One day he came along the fields at the back of Wall Farm getting a load of hay and he fell off and couldn't move. He told the old horse to go home*

The Rose and Crown in 1973.

and the horse arrived at the Rose and Crown and got stuck in the gateway. Bill Vince was at the pub at dinnertime and saw the horse arrive without Alf, so he went to look for him. He collected me and my old chap (Taffy's father) and Ben Harvey on the way. Alf was laying there on the ground. There was a hurdle there so we tested it to see if it would bear his weight and then we carried him home on it. He had broken his neck, they said. He lived a long time after that but he couldn't do anything for himself. His wife looked after him.

The late Simon Dewes, who wrote several books about Hadleigh, was a regular visitor to the Rose and Crown. He wrote of visiting the inn with his father, who was a doctor, recalling that Mr Pearl endured great pain but was always cheerful. The dazzling white sheets, which were changed three times a

Whatfield Road, c.1925, showing the rear of the Chequers Ale House (on the right).

week, the polished brass and the spotless utensils also impressed him. At this time there was no running water in the village – it all had to be carried from the pump on the corner of The Street. Likewise, the commode (a portable lavatory) had to be carried downstairs to be emptied. He remembered Mrs Pearl with great affection and continued to visit her for over 50 years. In old age she became bowed and shrunken, but remained cheerful and uncomplaining. When Lizzie died in 1966 Alf went into a home, where he stayed until his death in 1974. They are buried in Elmsett churchyard.

When men first entered the pub they had a sup from the 'communal pot'

Brian Hiskey: *My grandfather called in the Rose and Crown one night on his way home from the allotments with some visiting relatives from Birmingham. On seeing the locals with their beer and smoke-stained moustaches (from smoking clay pipes) they declined to sup from this communal pot.*

The Chequers Ale House

An ale house, brewery and farm, Chequers has a well-documented record of ownership from 1720 to 1824. At the beginning of the eighteenth century it was owned by Nathaniel Shreeve, who had three daughters, Mary who married ? Moore; Sarah, who married Isaac Duncan, and Martha, who married Mr ? Skinner (names illegible on original document). In 1720 Mary Moore and Sarah Duncan were each admitted to a moiety (half share) of the late Martha Skinner, and Mary Moore died soon after. In 1724 the moiety was transferred to Isaac Duncan. His will, dated 1744, left his moiety to his widow and in July 1749 she became sole copyhold tenant. The copyhold tenancy passed to George Roberts in 1776, and in 1790 was acquired by Benjamin Stearn when occupied by Robert Mirrington, possibly his maternal grandfather.

In 1839 it was listed in an advertisement of three lots for sale by auction: Lot 1 was a small farm comprising two dwellings, outbuildings and land. A map attached names it as Mr Benjamin Stearn's farm, formerly occupied by Robert William Mower. Lot 2 was the Chequers Public House, and gives the occupant as Anthony Shipp. Lot 3, a double cottage, was occupied by John Hiskey and William Hiskey.

At some point the owner was named Cobbold, and his tenant Orrise. At the end of the nineteenth century it was taken over by William and Mary Grimsey. Their granddaughter, Miriam Hawes, was told by her mother, Ellen, that she had to help her parents clean the pub, which was not always a pleasant job. If customers had walked more than two miles they were allowed to sit in the pub all day. It ceased being a pub in the early 1900s.

In 1928 Bert John Malster, a blacksmith, and his wife, Louisa Nellie, who had been living in a cottage on the green, bought it. When they moved in, a side room still contained pub seats and there were barrels in the cellar. A further conveyance in 1936 added more land to the original property. Bert and Louisa lived there until their deaths in 1952 and 1953 respectively.

Shops

The Butcher
The slaughterhouse was located at Mill Farm, where Cliff Hiskey had his business. Pigs were killed using a stun gun (humane killer) before the throat was cut. He and his wife butchered the carcasses and joints, and sausages, brawn and lard were sold to locals. He also sold a few groceries and bread.

In 1930 he bought two cottages in The Street for £200 and converted the front room of one into a shop. A small butcher's shop was built onto the side of the properties. He also provided a delivery service, sometimes as far as Burstall and Hintlesham.

The Street – Angelina's shop and the butcher's shop, c.1910.

Mervyn Beckett (née Hiskey): *In school holidays I often went with him on the delivery round – he was always very punctual. We used to go as far as Red Hill in Aldham, where we met Mr Budd, the baker from Hadleigh. The bread was transferred from his van to ours, and Father and I would take a break then and eat some warm crusty bread with a lump of cheese.*

Beef and lamb was delivered from Ipswich in a large wicker basket by Beestons bus on Thursdays. The

butchery business had to be closed when war broke out and new regulations were introduced.

Angelina's Sweet Shop

Cissie Holder remembers this little shop, which was just a room in a cottage. The area called the shop was just a curtained off part of the living-room where sweets and tobacco were sold.

Edie Leeks: *Boys used to go into the shop and ask Angelina for something which she kept out the back,*

The Street showing the shop, c.1950. The premises is still a shop and Post Office.

and while she was gone to get it they would fill their pockets with sweets.

Harold Cooper: *Angelina Kennington was a character and we loved her sweet shop. She would deal in farthings and halfpennies, and would sell only one sweet if that was all you could pay for.*

Elmsett Stores

Running a small grocery business in tandem with the butchery meant that Mr Hiskey still had the shop when the butchery closed. During the war rationing caused an additional workload, as forms and addi-

A shoe found behind the baker's oven in Fred Holder's cottage during renovations in 2002.

tional paperwork had to be sent to the Food Office in Hadleigh. Many foods, such as custard powder and syrup, although not on ration, were in short supply, and it caused great anxiety as to who should have them – who had had them last week, who the week before? Mrs Hiskey provided a small stock of haberdashery, a few drapery items and some women's necessities. At Christmas time she also sold fancy soaps and perfumes, boxed handkerchiefs and novelty chocolates. The Hiskeys retired and sold the business to Mr and Mrs Pizzey in 1949. In addition to the Post Office business the shop acquired an off-licence when Peter and Joan Waters owned it. Ron and Rosemary Venis introduced the lottery terminal during their tenure. It is still a thriving business, providing newspapers, both at the shop and through a delivery service, in addition to a large range of fresh fruit and vegetables, groceries and stationery. Elmsett is one of the few villages in the area to still have a thriving shop and Post Office service.

The Old Post Office

This shop, which closed in 1996, had been run as a grocery shop since the 1850s, when the house and adjoining store were bought and run by John Ladbrook. After his death the shop was taken over by his son, Alfred, whose widow and daughter continued to run it after he died in 1871. In 1887 the first Post Office came to Elmsett. Before this date the nearest one was in Ipswich, although there was a Money Order and Telegraph Office in Hadleigh. Thomas and Emily Cousins ran the business from

Mrs Robinson outside the Old Post Office, c.1935.

77

1895 until 1913, when Arthur Robinson and his wife took over and moved into the house.

Brian Hiskey: *In the 1940s Mr Robinson sold boots. An uncle of mine, Jack Hiskey, went into the shop wearing his old boots and came out with new ones on and proceeded to throw his old ones into the moat opposite. Some 50 years later when the moat was dredged one of the older residents enquired 'Did they find Jack's boots?'*

The Ladbrook family still owned the property and received rent until 1947, when the Post Office and shop were sold to Mrs Robinson. Within a year it had changed hands and, like many small village shops during the latter part of the twentieth century, saw many changes of ownership. Myrtle Gibbons, an Elmsett resident, was one of these. When she sold to John and Gloria Sherwood, the Post Office was transferred to Colin and Margaret Andrews in the other shop. The Sherwoods stayed for 11 years, during which time they combined a newspaper business with the groceries. Jeremy and Penny Lang ran it for four years, and Steven and Lesley Davies for six, but they finally closed the business in 1996.

Village Characters

Many of the people who provided the services in the village are still remembered, and many of the older residents made the same comments about them.

William (Bill) Pitt in 1956 – Elmsett's postman for 30 years.

Reuben Bains, a tinsmith who did soldering, '... mended Charlie's honey separator.'

Ben Harvey, builder and undertaker, 'always bought his wife a new hat or coat after every funeral.'

Smoker Mowles lost a leg in the First World War but could still climb a ladder. He worked on trees at Manor Farm, pollarding them.

Fred Rouse used to make ladders 'if you could wait long enough'!

Barney Wyartt lived just outside the village. He was a haulage contractor and always wore a huge watch, which apparently weighed two pounds.

Doctors

Dr Grainger used to hold a surgery once a week at the Reading Room. He had a very loud voice and when you went in to see him everyone sitting waiting their turn could hear.

Dr Muriel came up from Hadleigh on his bike until he was fairly old, when someone drove him in a motor.

Dr Newell 'was a very good family doctor for many years'.

Nurse Clunn lived at Elm Farm and used to deliver all the babies in the village.

Postmen

In the 1920s the postman was **Geoff Green**.

Fred Holder: *The younger postmen wore the military style peaked hat, but he wore a kind of coalscuttle hat – I suppose it had been a regulation hat before. Sometimes he rode a bike, and at other times he would have his horse and cart. He was very free with his whip if we should be near when he passed, and was not very popular with us boys.*

Bill Pitt, who lived in Elmsett with his wife and four daughters, was the last postman to deliver mail by bicycle. His day began at 4a.m, when he made his way to Semer to sort the post before setting out on his round of Semer, Whatfield and Elmsett. When he got to Elmsett he would stop off at home for his breakfast. After finishing his morning round he had to return to Semer by 2p.m. to start the second delivery of the day. It was a hard life; he covered 40 miles a day in all weathers. Christine Ladbrook recorded in her diary that on 22 February 1947 he tramped across the fields carrying his bicycle because the snow had made the roads impassable. His daughters, Sheila, Eileen, Sylvia and Carol, have many stories and very happy memories of him.

Sylvia Hiskey: *One day Dad slipped off his bicycle on an icy narrow road and fell under a bus which went right over the top without touching him. He was 25 years older than Mum and had served in the First*

Off to the smithy. Cuthbert Lambert driving a trap, 1947.

World War. He was shot but went back a second time. After the war he served in India for 10 years; he loved the country and said that he hadn't had a good cup of tea since he left there.

Carol Robinson: *One time when he was on his round he was shot at by a German plane which was returning from dropping bombs at Wattisham Air Field. He jumped into a ditch and lived to tell the tale.*

He was a very popular postman. Christmas day deliveries could take a long time because he would be offered a drink and mince pie at more than one house. He would return home pushing his bike, and in a very happy mood!

Brenda Woods: *On the morning of my 21st birthday Mr Pitt went out of his way to deliver my cards so that I could open them before I left for work at 7a.m.*

The Policeman

The village policemen, of which Mr Jarrold was one, traditionally lived at Wall Farm.

Fred Holder: *He had a military look and a waxed moustache, and always regarded us boys with suspicion, which was mutual. When the evenings were dark he would patrol very quietly in the shadows and woe betide if he caught you where he thought you shouldn't be. Being young then, I was not out late, but*

in regard to us kids, in daylight he would stop us on the slightest excuse.

After Mr Jarrold a Mr Rose was in Elmsett for a few years. Then Mr Dewey, considered a 'nice chap', who suffered a long illness and died fairly young, leaving a widow and young family. In the 1930s a purpose-built police house was built in Whatfield, and Elmsett lost its 'village bobby'.

The Maltster

Malt was produced at the Maltings Farm up until the early part of the twentieth century. The process involved steeping barley in water to encourage it to sprout and, when the growth appeared, spreading the grain evenly on the floor of the malting, where it was turned frequently by men using wooden shovels. The maltster had to judge when the barley had grown enough, and was able to control this by varying the depth of the spread. The grain was then 'cooked' by spreading it on the floor of the kiln, where a fire beneath heated the floor tiles and the hot air passed through the grain. The process completed, the grain was sieved to remove the rootlets (malt culms), which were a valuable food source for cattle and poultry.

Rupert Cooper: *People used to go down from the cottages to the Maltings to collect malt to brew their own beer. They used to have a day off to do this*

79

The village green and smithy in 1935.

brewing, as they had to cart a lot of water and heat it. The kiln was very high, but the other storage buildings were very low and it must have been hard to haul 16-stone sacks under the low ceilings.

The buildings were demolished in 1996.

The Blacksmith

Many older residents remember when Bert Malster was the blacksmith. He was a very big strong man, and his shop was on the green under the chestnut tree. He used to shoe the farm horses, repair farm implements and wheels.

Fred Holder: *I spent many happy hours in his workshop in the holidays. The way he put an iron tyre on a wheel was very clever and something never seen now. The wheel was bolted on an iron plate and the tyre heated to almost red hot. Then two men would pick it up with tongs, place it on the wheel and hammer it on. All the time another man would pour water on the wheel to control the burning. When finished it would stay tight for years.*

Later, when Bert Malster was living at the Chequers, he moved from the smithy on the green and did his work in an old barn at the farm. The blacksmith work stopped when he sold the farm. Two of Bert Malster's granddaughters, Hazel King and Gwen Horne, still live in the village.

The Wheelwright

Records show that there was a wheelwright in Elmsett in 1844 by the name of John Archer. Patrick Archer succeeded him for 30 years and then Alfred Archer from 1891. Alfred was still working at the time of the 1911 census, but the man still remembered is Ben Harvey, a multi-talented, happy man who always sang while he worked. He used to bowl his wheels from his workshop in The Street to the blacksmiths on the green, whistling as he went.

The Thatcher

In Suffolk long straw thatch was the traditional roofing material, and almost every farm labourer could turn his hand to thatching. The method was relatively simple, but over the years developed into a highly skilled craft.

Reg Barber describes one aspect of the work his father, George Barber, did: *He was a thatcher. This work I look upon as the farmer's bank. I will try to explain. In those years all the corn was stacked in different shapes in stack yards. Some were built round and finished with a pinnacle. There were square stacks and boat shaped stacks. The first yelum (layer) of straw was fixed with rods and broughters (broaches). The rods were cut down in winter, all lengths about the size of a thick walking stick. The broughters had to be shaped and twisted round, one length shorter than the*

Thatchers in the 1930s. Left to right: *David Lloyd, Harry Mayhew, Tom Beaumont, Fred Holder.*

other. They were placed to hold the rod on. They had to be pointing upwards with the short side upwards to keep the thatch of straw on. The payment for this work was by measurement. My father was paid by the square yard.

Taffy Skippings: *Once the thatcher left the farm while we were working, and he left two stacks, so I thatched them. George Barber gave me a few tips.*

The Harness-Maker

Bob Skippings is also well remembered. As well as making and repairing harnesses and boots, he also mended the canvases which carried corn up into the self-binders. This was usually an emergency job when they broke during harvest. Most farmers could not afford to keep a spare set in those days. His son, Taffy, used to deliver the repaired harnesses on his bike after school. If he was paid he had to give them 2d. for a stamp which had to go on the receipt.

The Carter

Arthur Skippings, grandfather of Taffy and Tony, worked for Ladbrooks' Mill. Twice a week he delivered flour and other mill product to Ipswich. He had a team of three horses, but only two were allowed into the town centre, so the trace horse was left at the Rose and Crown at the top of Bramford Road. In the early mornings, when the road was icy, he had to screw frost nails into the horseshoes.

Taffy and **Tony Skippings**: *... the sacks of flour weighed 20 stone. One day when he was delivering flour to a bakery in Ipswich he was asked to carry some sacks, which had been left by another person, up a ladder to the second floor. He was given sixpence for doing this. He liked a drink, and one day, when he was home early, his boss asked him if he had run out of money! He was always willing to do shopping for people in the village, even ladies' corsets. He didn't mind what he did so long as he got paid. At one time people got fed up with the Co-op meat, so next time he went he asked for it to be wrapped in plain paper, and they thought it was lovely meat. Once someone in Ipswich wanted a brace of rabbits so he took some that had been clean killed. But the man wanted ones that had been shot, so he took them home again, hung them on a hedge and shot them. When he took them back the man said they were just right!*

The Coalman

Fred Holder: *A Mr Charlie Leeks delivered coal. He had a pair of very well cared for Suffolk horses and a four-wheeled wagon. He always seemed a happy man, besides being a clean-looking coalman. When he finished his round he would adjourn to the pub to wet his whistle, but not before he had put nosebags on his*

Arthur Skippings on an Elmsett Mill delivery wagon in Commercial Road, Ipswich, c.1920. The Three Tuns public house is on the corner of Wolsey Street.

A lorry in Flowton Road, c.1920. Frank Barber is on the left.

horses. After a while he would come out and jog off to Hadleigh – in winter time he had lights front and back.

At the beginning of the twentieth century boys still went mainly into agriculture or worked at Ladbrooks' Mill and the girls went into service in the larger houses in the village and local area. This slowly changed and people started to get jobs further afield.

June Skippings: *I worked in Ipswich at Corders. I stayed with an aunt in Ipswich during the week and came home at weekends. I also worked at Marks & Spencers. I used to cycle to Burstall and leave my bike at a cottage there, then catch a bus into Ipswich. We only had a bus service in Elmsett on Tuesday, Thursday, Saturday and Sunday afternoons. They were no good for work* [this last point still applies in 2005].

Brenda Woods and **Sylvia Hiskey** told us:

When we left school there wasn't any work for us in the village – we had to go to Ipswich. We biked to Hintlesham to catch the bus and left our bikes at the George. It was a long day; we were away from the village for about 12 hours. Sometimes we stayed on in Ipswich to go to the pictures and caught the ten o'clock bus back, and then had to cycle home. One winter when it snowed we had to walk to Hintlesham. It was so deep we didn't know if we were in the fields or on the road. We were soaked.

Towards the End of the Century

During the latter part of the twentieth century there were big changes. Many smaller farms had been merged into larger units and mechanised, with far fewer employees. Some of them were run solely by the families which owned them. Only one shop and one pub remained, and employment was limited, with most people now working outside the village. The doctor no longer held a surgery in the village, and there was no nurse or policeman living and working in the village, although we still had a hairdresser. However, one or two new businesses had opened up.

The Village Garage

The village garage opened in the 1960s, finally closing in 1999. For most of the time it was run by Marty Page, dealing with servicing and repairs, with his father-in-law, 'Willum', doing the body work and spray painting. They also employed four other people. For a period the garage also sold tractors and combines and the suppliers used to send a helicopter to take the staff to repair tractors and combines in the fields.

Recent Occupational Changes in Elmsett
At the beginning of the twentieth century the majority of Elmsett residents worked in the village. The table below compares employment prospects and trades available during the last 30 years.

1975	Business/Trade	2005
1	Builder	1
1	Cabinet maker	1
4	Electrician	3
5	Farms: arable	5
1	Farm: organic	1
3	Farms: pig	
1	Garage	
1	Hairdresser	1
1	Mill (Flour/Provender)	
3	Plumber	4
1	Poplar Airfield	1
1	Poplar Print	
1	Poplar Toys	
1	Poplar Fitments	1
	Poplar Paintshop	1
1	Public House	1
2	Shops	1
4	Smallholdings	4
1	Thatcher	1
	Video/film unit	1

Hairdressing

It used to be said that Elmsett was a village with dozens of barbers but there was nowhere to get a hair cut! That is no longer the case. Lesley Woor has a small salon next door to the Post Office, and has been running her business successfully for 27 years.

Poplar Hall Group

Poplar Hall Farm came into the Gray family in 1967 and, although farming continued, Jack Gray had other interests. He had two large dairy herds at other farms near Hadleigh, where he also had a milk bottling plant and seven milk rounds in the town and the surrounding villages. He also owned several racehorses and the White Horse public house in Stone Street near Hadleigh.

In 1965 Jack's son, Tony, built a fish and chip shop, Gray's Takeaway, in Angel Street, Hadleigh, on the site of his father's birthplace, which remains in the family.

On Jack's death in 1967, Tony moved into the Poplar Hall Farm house with his wife Linda and family, and took over the running of the farm, which reared pigs for a while and grew cereals and also potatoes for use in the fish and chip shop. Tony did some major renovations to the house and, as the old farm buildings were in disrepair, he replaced them with modern steel-framed asbestos-clad buildings.

In 1977 he started to diversify, first into Poplar Toys, making high quality wooden toys, as an outlet for which he opened a shop in Hadleigh called Puss in Boots, run by his wife, Linda. Out of this the need then arose for screen-printing and Poplar Print was established. Wooden toys lost their popularity in favour of plastic, and competition affected all three businesses, causing the closure of Puss in Boots in 1985 and Poplar Print in 1998. Poplar continued with another line, making timber fittings for kitchens and hotel bathrooms, and retail shelving and display stands, for which computer numerical control has been installed. A well-equipped paint shop offers paints, lacquers and other hand finishes.

Tony took up flying and in 1969/70 established a landing strip which came to be used by aerial crop spraying companies and other local aviators. Lights, necessary for night flying, were installed in 1971 and maintenance of both resident and visitors' aircraft commenced in 1974. The business proceeded at a low key until 1997, when Ipswich Airport was closed and it was declared that its flying, training and parachute clubs would be transferred to Elmsett. This move was opposed by a number of local residents, who formed CREAD (Campaign to Resist Elmsett Airfield Development). After two public enquiries a voluntary agreement was reached with Babergh District Council to contain the number of aircraft movements and harmony was restored.

The agreement is maintained through the Elmsett Airfield Liaison Committee, which successfully monitors the voluntary noise abatement procedure and recommendations to pilots to minimise the impact of flying on the local community. In 1999 Poplar Aviation was sold and renamed, and Aero Anglia Ltd now offers aircraft maintenance there. Elmsett airfield has a good relationship with Wattisham airbase and adopted their Air Training Cadets in 2002. They also hold open days and dances, and raise money for charity.

Fashion Design

Miranda Cooper (née Holland), a well-known fashion designer, came to Elmsett in 1982. Her collections were already selling all over the world, and she soon set up a studio and workshop at Manor Farm to continue the production of her exclusive clothing and fashion accessories.

She employed several people, including Gloria Sherwood, also a trained designer, along with 200 outworkers doing sewing, embroidery, beading and knitting to provide the very individual items of clothing that were Miranda's special identity. Her flair for design and her love of gardening inspired her to start a new business in the 1990s, and she now designs and landscapes gardens all over England. She has designed several Mediterranean gardens in Greece.

Smallholdings

In 2006 there are four smallholdings in Elmsett. Robert Everett continues with his cattle and pigs at Lucy Wood Farm (previously known as Old Barn Farm) in Manor Road. Also in Manor Road Clifford Collins has a beef suckle herd, and in the past his animals have won awards at the Smithfield Show. Russell Goodchild runs an agricultural contracting business, grows potatoes and keeps hens. In Flowton Road at Rhodd's Farm, William and Susan Durrant breed and run a small flock of Suffolk sheep and frequently win prizes at local shows.

The table on page 83 compares employment prospects and trades during the last 30 years.
There has been a steady decline of businesses in Elmsett, but many residents now run small ones from their homes, e.g. accountancy, cycle maintenance, driving instruction, floristry, garden design, home and garden services, motor repair, paint spraying, taxi services, etc.

The History of Grain Milling

The earliest mechanism for grinding wheat and other corn was the quern (Swedish for the word mill – *kvarn*). A rounded hand-propelled upper stone was rotated against the grain in the concavity of the fixed stone. Such equipment was common to many households from long before the first century AD. Eventually the apparatus evolved and the upper stone was turned by a handle, easing the physical effort. The Egyptians, and later the Greeks and Romans, improved this process further by using animals, generally oxen, to turn the stone. Around 2,000 years ago, the dramatic change was made when water power was harnessed to drive a paddlewheel which turned the millstones.

The Romans undoubtedly brought water-mills to Britain, and at the time of Domesday there were 178 of these in Suffolk. Windmills were unknown till the twelfth century, when a brick base held the millstones and the upper part of the mill, made of wood and bearing the sails, rotated on a vertical post to face the wind, which in turn drove the millstones. They were known as post mills and in 1840 three were recorded in Elmsett.

All mills, until the Middle Ages, were under the ownership and control of the lord of the manor in which they lay. Everyone in the village was obliged to use this mill – they could use no other to grind their corn. In lieu of payment the miller took a percentage of the flour, some taking more than the permitted amount. The artful miller would be one who had one hand in the hopper and one hand in the sack, implying that he took twice what he should so that he had flour to sell to his customers.

With the loosening of manorial control as a result of the Black Death, the millers became lessees of the mills from the manors and operated on a commercial basis.

The original Elmsett Mill and outbuildings, c.1910. The miller's house is on the right.

At first rents were paid partly 'in kind', in the form of flour or sticks of eels. By 1438 the rent was paid in cash. Both wind and water-millers tended to have their mills away from the main village and to be of an independent nature. Rarely did farmers who replaced the manorial system own the mill nearest to them, for milling was not a straightforward job and required a proper apprenticeship. In the nineteenth century, three events changed the traditional pattern of milling of 600 years. First, by using steam power to drive the stones, the miller no longer had to rely on the vagaries of wind or water. Next, the availability of the abundant 'strong' wheat, which started to arrive in Britain from the North American Prairies in sailing ships, resulted in mills being established at major ports.

By 1900 most millers had installed the modern Hungarian system of roller flour milling. This method ground wheat between a series of metal rollers, which produced finer and whiter flour. Some mills started to specialise in biscuit flour, while also carrying on a small trade in bread flour to the numerous local bakers. Later, most millers ceased flour milling and adapted their mills to produce animal feeds. From the scurrilous millers of earlier days, the milling industry gradually became the most honest of any. It was a lifelong career for all who worked in it and nearly everyone who joined, in whatever manner, stayed with the job for life.

Ladbrooks' Mill
by Rachel Hitchcock (née Ladbrook)

John Ladbrook, an experienced stone miller who had learnt his trade at Bures mill, purchased a windmill, situated on high ground just off Whatfield Road, from the Stearn family in 1848. It prospered and in 1869 John's son, Alfred, erected a small brick mill with two pairs of stones. Later two further stones were added, powered by a steam engine. In 1895 John's other son, William, installed a roller mill, a newer method of flour milling, and the old stones were discarded. Further modernisation followed when a gas suction plant replaced the steam engine in 1904.

The business became W. Ladbrook & Son in 1891, when William's son, Ernest, joined the firm and became a partner. A gale damaged the old windmill in 1926 and the wooden structure and sails were taken down. Ernest replaced the gas plant with a crude oil engine in the 1930s and introduced the production of pig and poultry meal, a new line of business. A silo was built in 1936 and improvements were carried out to the buildings. Flour remained the most important product, and the production capacity was increased. The fourth generation of Ladbrooks to join was Jack, Ernest's son, and when he became managing director after his father's death in 1946, he was joined by Rex Barrett as mill manager and Kenneth Gibbons as sales manager. Modernisation continued and a grain dryer and machines for cleaning grain commercially and for seed were installed in 1944 and driven by electricity. An electrically driven direct-coupler impact grinder was installed for the provender department and the last pair of millstones was discarded.

Edie Leeks: *My father used to dress the stones that ground the flour. He used to cut the ridges in them*

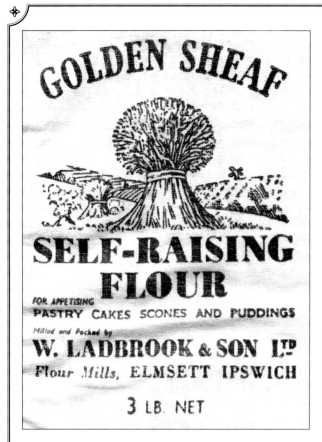

Ladbrooks' Mill flour bag

The mill in the late 1960s.

Aerial view of Elmsett Mill, 1962. The building on the right was destroyed in the fire in 1963.

At Ladbrooks' Mill annual dinner in the 1980s. Left to right: *George Laflin, who worked in the flour mill, John Ladbrook, Jack Ladbrook, George Holder, who worked in the feed mill and was also a driver.*

The round house (the base of a windmill) at Mill Farm in 1935. It was demolished in the 1980s.

when they wore smooth. There was just one engine room then.

The mill was now lit by electricity from the mains, replacing the diesel generator.

As the centenary of Ladbrooks' Mill approached in 1948 seven people were employed in sales and the offices, 17 in milling and transport and the mill owned three lorries. The centenary was celebrated by an outing by bus for all employees and their spouses to Great Yarmouth, where a meal was enjoyed at the Imperial Hotel. The employees presented the management with a clock, which was placed in the office, and Jack compiled a booklet entitled 'Souvenir of a Century'.

Flour from locally grown wheat was still the chief product, with half being dispatched to London and the rest bagged and sold locally under the brand names of 'Golden Sheaf Self-raising Flour' and 'Snowdrift Plain Flour'.

Cissie Holder: *After the war we moved the flour packing into a hut beside the flour mill. When I worked at the top of the mill where it was very cold I was never ill, but as soon as we moved into the hut I had numerous coughs and colds. The top of the mill was much more healthy.*

Taffy Skippings remembers the 1960s, when his wife June, Daphne Fayers and Lucy Clarke did the packing on a table which he now uses in his home.

The provender side of the business increased and balanced rations were made for pigs and poultry and sold in the neighbourhood and to farms throughout East Anglia. Following the advent of combine harvesters, the drying of grain from nearby farms became another important line of business. All grain for the production of both flour and animal feed was stored in the tall silo building, built in the 1950s and a local landmark.

The mill was very busy at harvest time. Formerly, grain was delivered in hessian sacks by tractor and trailer, but during the 1960s most farmers were changing to bulk deliveries. On reaching the mill the grain passed over an intake weigher on its journey by conveyor to the silo. Joy Sillitoe and Marion Brown, both of whom worked at the mill, remember the sampling of each load to test for moisture content before it was transferred to the silo. It was advantageous for the mill to buy in grain at the lower harvest-time price; delivering straight from the combine also benefited farmers with insufficient storage or drying facilities. The mill was progressively updated in the 1950s and '60s. A major introduction was a new building to house the cubing press, enabling the animal food to be made into pellets and cubes of varying sizes. A further building, with a large storage area and housing the new mixing plant for the manufacture and bagging up of the provender food, was opened at a special ceremony by the then local MP, the Rt Hon. John Hare.

In 1963 there was a serious fire which destroyed the entire flour mill, but it was rebuilt, designed for greater efficiency, and continued in operation until 1969. Biscuit flour was made and deliveries taken to Reading, London and Liverpool. For a time, the mill supplied flour to Suffolk schools' kitchens and special flour, which contained egg yolk colouring, was supplied to fish and chip shops in Suffolk. A system of three eight-hour shifts was introduced at this time.

John, Jack's son and the fifth generation of

Ladbrooks, joined the firm in the 1960s.

Seed corn dressing continued until the 1970s and also grain merchanting with malting barley. For a few years agro-chemical sprays and chemical fertilisers were stocked and sold to farmers.

Much of the commercial business took place at corn exchanges and Ladbrooks had a stand at the weekly markets in Ipswich and Bury St Edmunds. On Mondays Jack, wearing his dark suit and bowler hat, also attended Mark Lane in London, trading flour and malting barley. Corn exchanges were open when there was a livestock market in the town and merchants, millers and farmers traded their grain.

In the early 1960s there were over 20 independent mills in Suffolk alone and nationally there was gross over-production of flour. The Millers Mutual Association compensated those who voluntarily ceased production on condition that the milling machinery was disabled and removed from the premises. Ladbrooks took advantage of this in 1969, and so were able to install a new feed milling plant in the former flour mill. They subsequently became well known for animal feed, especially the pig food range. After the sudden death of Kenneth Gibbons in 1971, Eric Matthews was appointed nutritionist and sales director and later on Michael Grimwade, a long-standing employee, became a director and company secretary. Feed for pigs, cattle, horses, sheep, poultry and game was produced. The pig food range accounted for a large proportion of the tonnage and Ladbrooks became specialists in early weaning feed.

As the market increased, much of it was delivered in bulk to pig farms in East Anglia. In its heyday the mill had over 30 employees, most of whom lived in Elmsett, and at the end of the working day Whatfield Road was busy with cyclists riding home. During the 1970s a grass tennis court and an outdoor swimming pool were provided for employees and their families. The pool also served as a ready supply of water in case of fire. An annual staff dinner was held in a local hotel.

The animal feed business became very competitive in the late 1980s as the number of small and independent pig farmers fell, and Ladbrooks found competition with the large manufacturers increasingly difficult. When dried dog food gained popularity in the 1990s the firm, having first installed a coarse mix plant, diversified into this range. The brand Lively was introduced and, after a concerted advertising campaign, became established. It was sold throughout the UK and exported to France. It is still made in Suffolk. By the 1990s time was running out for small mills.

John Ladbrook: *In November 1994 we were approached by Dalgety, at that time one of the major animal feed manufacturers in the UK. They wanted to buy our name, the goodwill and our knowledge on the young pig diets. A condition of the sale, which was completed in March 1995, was to stop producing farm animal rations in Elmsett. This meant we had to make many people redundant because the dog food production required very few staff. I found this very upsetting, as my family had been the major employer for many years and I felt I was letting the village down. Several farmers wrote to me when this trade stopped to say how much they had valued our relationship. One told me he would not now be in business if his father had not received extended credit from my father when he lost a major part of his cereal crop in a severe July hailstorm one year.*

In 1995 an American company, 'Pretty Bird', which had established a presence in the UK selling exotic bird and reptile food, made us an offer for the mill site and buildings, where they planned to establish their European headquarters and where research and educational work would be carried out. They promised to employ many local people, and it was this promise in particular that attracted me to agreeing to the sale. Unfortunately they were severely under-funded and the expertise to make the venture a success was not forthcoming.

The business closed in 2002 and ended an era of milling and major employment in Elmsett.

June and **Taffy Skippings** both worked at the mill, and their house was situated in Mill Lane. In November 2003 June wrote the following article for the village newsletter:

Elmsett Mill, goodbye

To many people who have moved into Elmsett in recent years, the old mill site is referred to as an eyesore, but to us it is not thought of as such. To my husband, Taffy, it was his living for 48 years. Looking back I can only remember what a busy place it really was, providing employment for over 30 men and women. Taffy watched it grow and modernise; now sadly, we are watching it slowly taken to pieces. The grain store is still standing. It was busy with deliveries all the year round, but at harvest time it was really busy with tractors and trailers queuing down Mill Lane waiting to tip their corn. After the flour mill closed and it was made over into the provender mill the animal feed pellets were moved from building to building by conveyor belt and the noise was deafening. Some was sold in bags, but a large amount was sold in bulk and loading the lorries was noisy, too. Lorries, farm vehicles and cars were coming and going all the time. When everything was finally closed down, I missed the hum of the machinery, the smell of the manufacturing processes, the traffic. It was so quiet, sometimes eerie. No more noise means no work and that is sad, but out of sadness comes good and one day new houses will be built here, breathing new life into the old place again, and hopefully some new families will come and enjoy our village. So it's farewell old mill, and hello to a complete new life.

CHAPTER 8

Houses

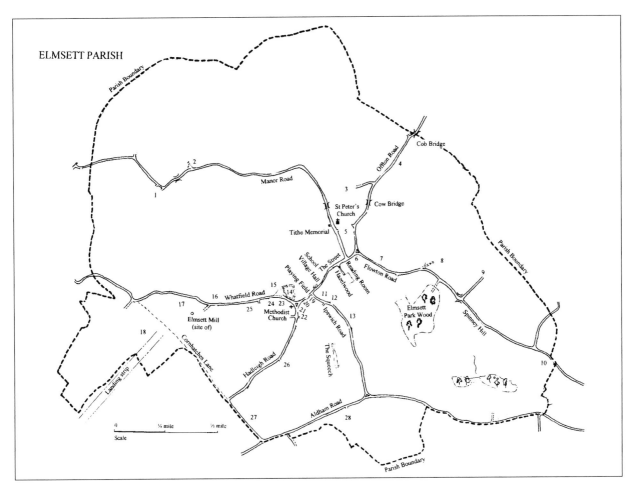

ELMSETT PARISH

Key: 1 Rookery Farm, 2 Manor Farm, 3 Elmsett Hall, 4 Bushy Ley, 5 Church Farm, 6 Laurel Cottage, 7 Thatched Cottage, 8 Red House Farm, 9 Hill Farm, 10 Rhodds Farm, 11 Tara Cottage, 12 Wall Farm, 13 Potash Farm, 14 Old Rectory, 15 Mannings, 16 Elm Farm, 17 Coates Farm, 18 Poplar Hall, 19 Wheelwrights, 20 Rose and Crown Inn, 21 Shop & PO, 22 Yew Tree Cottage, 23 Old Post Office, 24 The Maltings, 25 Chequers, 26 Mill Farm, 27 Eley's Cottage, 28 Gate Farm.

There are several medieval houses in Elmsett, but the expansion of the village did not begin until the first half of the nineteenth century, as can be seen from the numbers of inhabited houses detailed below:

1674	32	1901	76
1801	46	1951	105
1851	96	1981	227
1871	103	2002	292
1891	85	2005	320

Church Farm

This timber-framed sixteenth-century house is Grade II listed. The remains of a medieval moat surround it, suggesting there may have been an earlier structure on the site. Its having had three names clouds its history. For 300 years it was known as Elmsett Hall

until, early in the nineteenth century, it became Old Elmsett Hall. By the end of that century it had become Church Farm. Although none of the original windows survive, traces remain of the diamond-shaped mullions, as well as slots for the sliding shutters. The roof is of a crown post construction. Evidence that a seventeenth-century wing existed is confirmed from the lithograph overleaf, and also from the tithe map of 1842. The original owners are not known, but one suggestion is that it was Sir Edward Sherland, whose monument adorns the chancel wall in the church. Another suggestion is that there may have been an ecclesiastical connection – the setting up of the Bishop Andrewes' Charity on his death in 1626 gives credence to this, as does the acquisition of three farms in the area, including Elmsett Hall, by the trustees of the charity. One of the earliest recorded

An etching of St Peter's Church, 1812, showing Church Farm (on the left).

Eley's Cottage, c.1950.

occupants was Thomas Gardner Tenant, who was found guilty at Ipswich assizes in 1690 for failing to keep the cart track and bridge in good repair between the church and Somersham. In 1694 Edmund Stearn was the first of the family which was to remain there for almost 200 years. In 1735 the valuation of the land and buildings was assessed at £77. Towards the end of the eighteenth century, when the house was in need of considerable repair work, the Stearns built a new house on the rise to the north, and named it New Elmsett Hall. Part of the renovation to the Old Hall was the demolition of the wing. The extended Stearn family now occupied both houses. What part the trustees played in these developments is unclear, but they appear to have been good landlords. In 1860 they funded a range of new farm buildings adjacent to the Old Hall, and a plaque commemorated the completion in 1867. When the Stearn connection ended in 1882 John Westren became the tenant and this family stayed for almost 70 years. In 1920 the trustees of the charity sold their farm properties and John Westren bought the farm for £9,000. After the tithe incident Charles emigrated to New Zealand and the farm was sold to Fred Fison.

Coates Farm

This timber-framed house was probably built in the sixteenth century, as there is evidence of mullioned windows. Originally thatched, it was later roofed with peg tiles. At one time known as Skippings Farm, it was originally two cottages. Taffy Skippings remembers that his grandfather, Arthur Skippings, used to walk there to work from Baylham, some six miles away. Taffy lived in one of the cottages when he married June in 1956, and kept turkeys in his half of the orchard. Bob and Connie Green occupied the other cottage, which was converted into one home in 2000.

Eley's Cottage

How the cottage came to be known as 'Eley's Cottage' is not clear, but although nobody by the

name of Eley can be traced to the village, a small undated map in the County Record Office shows the 'Land in Elmsett in Mr Ely's occupation' as five fields around the cottage. A later bill of sale and map dated 1895 for 'Ely's Barn' shows the same fields, and the house as two cottages. Between the barn and cottages there was a large pond, filled in during the 1970s. The present owner, John Lee, has single-handedly, with proper regard for its medieval construction, restored the house and added a new wing in the same style using green oak and traditional timber joints and fastenings. The foundations of the barn have been uncovered in the garden.

Elm Farmhouse

This timber-framed, lime-plastered Grade II listed building is a sixteenth-century two-storey construction. It originally had a thatched roof with a ridge chimney, casement windows and a boarded door. In the 1930s it was altered internally to provide a small two-storey residence at one end consisting of two ground floor rooms and one upper room. George and Cissie Holder moved into this when they married in 1942. Arthur Meadows was living in the larger part of the house. In 1962 Brian and Sylvia Hiskey moved into this part. The Ladbrook family employed both George Holder and Brian Hiskey. Records show that in 1947 the house was sold to Jack Ladbrook, together with other properties and land in the area. It was sold in 1976, and some renovations took place. Sold again in 1983, the renovations were completed, including the thatch being replaced with clay tiles. In 1987 the acquisition of additional land enlarged the garden.

Elmsett Hall

The house, built in the 1790s by the Stearns, stands on high ground to the north of the village. Up until the early 1900s the annual toy fair was held nearby. There is a dropping well close to the house, which is now somewhere within an adjacent farm building. During the Stearns's tenure they became friendly

Elmsett Hall, 1965.

with Mrs Charlesworth of Flowton. She subsequently wrote a novel, *The Yeomen of England*, based on their life in Elmsett but using fictional characters to preserve their anonymity. There are descriptive passages in this novel which can readily be identified with Elmsett Hall and the surrounding area. (The present owner, Nick Bird, is very distantly related to Mrs Charlesworth.) The Westren family bought the Hall in 1920 and in 1932 it was at the centre of the Elmsett tithe incident.

Gate Farm

A large horse pond and short drive separate the house from the road and farm buildings. Partially moated, the brick-built Victorian-fronted house has a prominent porch with a balustrade balcony above. The Victorian conservatory was rebuilt in the 1970s. The back of the house is probably sixteenth century, and is timber framed. Several utility buildings in a poor state of repair were demolished in the early 1960s. In 1885 Robert Turner, listed as a farmer, surveyor and rate collector in *White's Directory*, lived at Gate Farm, which was then owned by Miss E. Lott. Robert Turner bought it in 1921. In 1955 it was sold to John Hitchcock and has remained in the family.

Gate Farm, 1908.

Hill Farmhouse

Hill Farmhouse is approached by a steep drive from Flowton Road. A Grade II listed house, it is described as sixteenth to seventeenth century, timber framed, with exposed timbers on the north side and sham timbers on the east. The roof is tiled, with a central ridge chimneystack. It has a mullioned window above the modern porch; the added wing is also modern. In 1885 farmer and overseer William Garnham lived there, and in 1924 the Pryke family moved in.

Eva Osborne (née Pryke) described the house in her book *Eva's Story*:

It was a large farmhouse with a peal oven like bakers use. Father had to heat the oven with faggots, the bread being put at the back, cakes in front, always a rice pudding right near the oven door. Oh that delicious bread, none like it today. There was water for washing and scrubbing, as there was a horse pond. For drinking water we had to go down the hill to a meadow where there was a spring. Water was ice cold on a summer's day. It was a drag to take it home, as the hill was very steep.

In 1939 the house was condemned, and Walter and Anna Pryke moved into a council house. Eva remembers that the house sold for £20. It was obviously restored, because the occupants were named as Mr and Mrs Steward.

Laurel Cottage

A Grade II listed building, this former timber-framed farmhouse dates from the sixteenth century and has an early-nineteenth-century frontage added to give it an attractive Georgian appearance. It was advertised for sale in 1819 as 'The Delightful Residence and Estate of Mr Thomas Canham' with a further description:

The Mansion is supplied with excellent water; is pleasantly situated near the great road of which it commands

Laurel Cottage, 1980.

The Maltings, c.1925.

a lively view, for a considerable distance, in the midst of the most interesting rural scenery... the estate is remarkably well timbered, skirted behind by a fine screen of woods, and has ever afforded an unobstructed liberty to sport over a thousand acres.

The barn to the east of the house is thought to be seventeenth century and is Grade II listed. It is timber framed and weather-boarded with a thatched roof and gabled entrance bay on the south side. It has been extensively repaired and the internal timbers replaced with English oak.

The Maltings

This large brick-built farmhouse facing the green is mainly Victorian, with evidence of a much earlier core of an uncertain date. It was bought by John Ladbrook in 1860 and remained in the family until 1996. In the early 1900s an extension was built as a mill office and remained in use as such until 1940. A conservatory was added which incorporated the front entrance, but this is no longer there. The actual malt-house and outbuildings which were to the rear of the house were demolished in the 1990s. The property has been extended and has had major renovations, including the addition of distinctive white railings on the front boundary. Adjacent to the house is a large horse pond, which overflows in very wet weather, flooding the road. In severe winters village children used to skate and slide on the ice.

Mannings

Formerly two dwellings, this seventeenth-century thatched cottage is situated on the green, where it was originally known as the Blacksmith's Cottages, approached by little bridges over a deep ditch. The forge was close by, beside a large chestnut tree which is still standing. Although converted into one house, the building retains many earlier features, including the eyebrow windows. The name 'Mannings' is thought to have come from an earlier large house of the same name, which had the second highest window tax in the village. The present owners have

One of the Blacksmith's Cottages (now part of Mannings) on the green, c.1930. The dilapidated state was due to the landlord's lack of maintenance.

Mannings, 2002.   (PHOTOGRAPH: ALAN NEWMAN)

created a beautiful garden and the church summer fête held there overspills onto the village green.

Manor Farm House

Originally a large L-shaped timber-framed house built in the sixteenth century, Manor Farm House was probably moated. Only part of the original house remains, 20 or more rooms having been taken down in a state of disrepair about 200 years ago. The early-Victorian frontage, erected according to the fashion of the time, incorporated extensions to the property. A large conservatory fell victim to the 1987 hurricane. Janet Cooper remembers shelves all around it for her mother's geraniums, and a blue-flowered plumbago growing up the wall. There are few existing records of Elmsett Manor, although it was advertised for sale in 1830 with 95 acres, which were let for the annual rent of £120. Only offers in excess of £3,000 would be considered. It has

Manor Farm House in the early 1900's, with members of the Newman family, occupants at the time.

Poplar Hall, drawn by Lynn Ulph.

belonged to the Cooper family since 1906 and Oliver has lived there since 1969. His wife, Miranda, has created a garden which won the East Anglian Large Gardens Award in 1997, and for several years it was opened under the National Gardens Scheme.

The Old Rectory

The house has a Tudor core dating back to around 1530, a Queen Anne-style front and a Georgian drawing-room built onto the back. The moat is older than the house and has been dated back 800–900 years, giving an indication of a former house or settlement on the site. It is thought that gravestones from the churchyard were used in its foundations, but this cannot be verified. In *White's Directory* of 1844 the rectory was valued at £13.7s.1d. and had 50 acres of glebe and a yearly rent-charge of £630 awarded in lieu of tithes. The stable block was demolished in 1976 when storm damage made it unsafe.

Fred Holder: *Rev. Haslewood had a boat and would sometimes take us children for a ride round the moat. There was a boathouse then.*

The Church sold the house in 1979.

Poplar Hall

Poplar Hall, which stands at the western end of the village, was not within the parish boundary until the mid-1800s. A Grade II listed, sixteenth-century timber-framed house with eighteenth-century alterations, externally the ground storey is faced in brick with the timbers exposed on the upper storey. The chimneystack has four octagonal shafts with moulded stacks on a square base. Records show the house owned by Ebenezer Hitchcock and occupied by John Rootsey in 1787; owned by Simon Minns in 1824 with occupier William Freebourne, followed by John Freebourne in 1838. It was bought by the Westren family in 1915 and the land farmed by Claude Westren until it passed to Jack Gray in 1967. It has remained in the family.

Red House Farm

The house is set high and well back from the road, and looks out across meadows to Park Wood. It was originally a medieval hall house, altered and extended in the sixteenth century, and has eighteenth-century fenestration. It is timber framed and has

The Old Rectory in 1934.

Aerial view of Red House Farm, 1970s.

Aerial photograph of Rookery Farm, showing the barn which was exported to America.

Rookery Farm

The lane passing this farm on the eastern fringe of the village used to be known as Rookery Road, but is now Manor Road. Parts of the substantial red-brick house date back to 1485, but the earliest records of ownership state that in 1786 William and Mary Bull rented the farm from Jemina Nevin for £90.12s.4d. The annual tithe duty was £40. After a series of tragic suicides, two of which occurred in the adjacent barn, the Bull family left in 1861 and Robert Harvey took it over, together with nearby Manor Farm. Both farms were bought by Thomas Hubbard in 1900. Willie and Lillian Laflin were tenants from 1902 to 1918, but they decided to buy their own farm following a steep rise in the rent. In 1948 Rookery Farm was sold to **Edmund Green**, who farmed there for 30 years. He described the barn:

It was a beautiful lovely big barn, I used to keep my hay in it, and my old Ford 8... those timbers were as good as any in the country, they were massive.

In 1982 the owner decided to demolish the by then dilapidated barn, but instead it was sold to Sussex-based Heritage Oak Buildings, and was dismantled and stored until 1987, when it was bought by John Heinz III, an American anglophile, and erected in Idaho. His widow later married John Kerry, and during the 2004 presidential elections in the USA the history of the barn was revealed in a *Times* headline 'Kerry's Idaho hideaway is haunted by a British

some tall Tudor chimneys. The oldest part of the house is the kitchen, believed to date from the 1400s, and the deeds, some on parchment and written in Latin, date back to Elizabethan times. At some time it was owned by the Lott family, and later by the Veseys. A descendant of this family living in Canada contacted the present owner, Mary Hitchcock, and has visited the house. In 1921 it was owned by Herbert and Jessie Gibbons, who sold it to Alan Hitchcock in 1947. The large, cool pantry is typical of a farmhouse. Inside, the house is very distorted, with sloping floors and windowsills, and doorways are low. Renovations revealed another very large inglenook fireplace. There is a large timber-framed barn to the west of the house.

George and Kate Barber outside their cottage, now named the Thatched Cottage, in the 1920s.

Thirza Clarke's Sunnyside Cottage, c.1920 (now Tara's Cottage).

The Old Post Office, c.1925.

Potash Farm in the 1940s. Mollie Pryke on the right.

Mrs Beaumont outside her cottage on the corner of Ipswich Road. 1920s. (Now Nutters Nest).

The original Mill Farmhouse in Hadleigh Road viewed from the stack yard, 1935.

ghost'. It is said to be haunted by the ghosts of the Bull family and the present owners, Andrew and Julie Hunn, have occasionally 'felt a presence'.

The Thatched Cottage

The cottage is believed to date from about 1600 and was originally three dwellings known as Yeomens Cottages. Since that time the property has undergone many changes, most notable of which has been the gradual reduction in the number of homes within the property. At one time locals nicknamed it Tallow Row, on account of its long frontage (300 feet) with many windows, each of which displayed a candle. By 1920 it was only two homes, and the Barber family lived in the larger one.

Reg Barber: *It was a very large cottage, three rooms down and three up. The centre room had one door at the front and one at the back, and had a chimney block where mother baked the bread, enough for a week. Here also was a copper for washing. This had to be filled overnight. The water was fetched from the pond in the field. Also in this room up one corner was the coal put. In this room we had a wash down in a large bath. The floor was made of bricks.*

In the 1960s it was converted into one cottage and renamed 'The Thatched Cottage'.

Wall Farm

The oldest parts of the house date from the mid-seventeenth century. Its Grade II listing notes a double sash window in which the operating sashes and cords for the centre part go over the side windows to the 'mice', which are held outside the frame. A mullioned window has also been uncovered. The house was built in two parts and is L-shaped. In the mid 1900s it was a police house. Part of the garden is walled, but a six-foot high brick wall, constructed in the early-twentieth century, serves no purpose and could have been a sort of ad hoc job-creation scheme.

Wheelwrights

Wheelwrights was originally two seventeenth-century thatched cottages, one of which, as the name implies, was the home of Ben Harvey, a wheelwright in the early 1900s, whose workshop was adjacent. The Green family occupied the other cottage. In 1924 it was owned by Tollemache & Cobbold Brewery and was known as Rose Cottages. It is next door to the Rose and Crown, which also belonged to the brewery. More recently it has been converted into a single dwelling.

Yew Tree Cottage

Dating from the late-fourteenth century, Yew Tree Cottage was originally a hall house which later became two cottages. The roof is tiled, with a ridge chimneystack, the interior has cambered beams with arched braces and crown posts, and there is an inglenook fireplace. It was converted into a single dwelling in 1980.

During the depression between the two world wars farmhouses and cottages everywhere fell into disrepair and Elmsett was no exception. Some cottages were abandoned, others were condemned and many were demolished. Many had belonged to agricultural labourers and, as farming became mechanised, the young men had to look further afield for work, and the population declined. The first council houses in Elmsett were built in 1937. At about the same time ten bungalows were erected in Manor Road.

Rupert Cooper: *Father was speculating. Agriculture wasn't doing well, and he didn't think things would improve. We built the bungalows in Manor Road — people called them prefabs. I can remember going to London with father to look at them; they were originally put up to accommodate soldiers after the First World War. They were in Rye Lane, Peckham, and a very slippery character was selling them — he had long black pointed shoes! He sold father a dozen. They took them down and loaded them onto lorries in sections. Father paid very little for them, but he put them onto brick foundations, fitted brand new roofs and laid on water and a sewerage system. Each had an acre of land and he sold them for £300 each but they were slow to sell.*

The expansion of the village began in the early 1960s, when farmland started being sold for building and the ribbon development of bungalows in the Hadleigh and Whatfield Roads changed the character of the village to what it has become today.

✦ CHAPTER 9 ✦

Education

Elmsett C of E VCP School

The first school in Elmsett was held at Elm Farm, where young children aged five and six could attend for 6d. (2½p) a week. There are no known records of this school. Elmsett School was built in 1870, when the Government passed the first Education Act, which provided compulsory primary education in Britain. At the same time the teacher's residence was built. The funds for these buildings came from grants from the National School Society, the Diocesan School Society, donations from many local landholders and the rector, Revd Thomas Barber. The cost was approximately £400.

In 1873 attendance increased so much that an additional classroom was needed, and a small room was built onto the main building at a cost of £150. Miss Youngs became head teacher in 1896 and stayed for nearly 30 years. Some of the children walked up to two miles to attend the school. During outbreaks

Elmsett School, 1890s.

of whooping cough, influenza, chicken pox, measles or diphtheria the school would have to be closed for several days, on some occasions for several weeks. Once a year pupils would be rewarded for good attendance, good conduct and hard work when a special representative from the Education Committee would visit to present the prizes and medals. It was

Elmsett School in 1897/98. Back left: *Miss Kells;* back right: *Miss Young. The boy standing on the left is Alfred Barber, who married Jessica Hiskey* (front row, second from left).

Elmsett School, 1926. Left to right, back row: *Fred Holder, Leslie Pryke, Herbert (Tubby) Chinery, Victor Barber, Bobby Jarrold, George Holder, Alfie Holder, Miss Stowe;* middle row: *?, Olive Pryke, Bertha Holder, Edith Pryke, Billie Mark, Edith Richardson, Hilda Hiskey, Rona Kennington, Verdun Green, Hugh Gibbons;* front row: *?, Billy Scase, ?, Kenneth Gibbons, ?, Hilda Richardson, Nellie Richardson, Teddy Clarke, Basil Pryke, Madge Flowerdew, Alec Holder.*

Elmsett School, c.1928. Left to right, back row: *Miss Stowe, Teddy Clarke, Verdun Green, Alec Holder, Kenneth Barber, Hilda Hiskey, Nina Wilding;* middle row: *Walter Wilding, Cissie Barber, Marjorie Flowerdew, Evelyn Mowles, Reggie Mowles, Alfie Holder, Stanley Richardson;* front row: *Joe Skippings, Ronnie Robinson, Eileen Holder, Evelyn Holder, Robert Green, Daisy Taylor, Valerie Holder, Muriel Kennington, Russell Barber.*

Elmsett School in 1928. Left to right, back row: *Hugh Gibbons, Verdun Green;* fourth row: *Miss Perkins, Ken Barber, ?, ?, Teddy Clarke, Ben Barber, Reggie Mowles, Harry Beaumont, Miss Stowe;* third row: *Tom Richardson, Ruby Grant, Marjorie Flowerdew, Evelyn Eade, Hilda Grant, Vera Barber, Nellie Robinson, Cissie Barber, Evelyn Mowles, Dorothy Beaumont, Robert Green;* second row: *Freddie Richardson, Joe Skippings, Hilda Richardson, Eileen Holder, Daisy Taylor, Valerie Holder, Muriel Kennington, Evelyn Holder, ?, Sidney Last;* front row: *?, Aubrey Barber, Russell Barber, Ronnie Robinson, ?, ?.*

noted that in May 1907 22 prizes and six medals were awarded.

In 1912 there were 88 pupils on the school roll, but by 1918 pupil numbers had declined to 56, mainly due to the continued epidemics of influenza, measles and whooping cough. The Education Act was amended during this year, fixing the school-leaving age at 14. During the 1920s a report regarding the school building stated that the decoration, both exterior and interior, was in poor condition; classroom heating was poor and the floors dangerous, with nails standing proud of the wood; the seating for the infants was poor, the condition of the toilets offensive and there were inadequate hand-washing facilities (a bucket of cold water in the playground). In the 1930s each child received a third of a pint of milk a day. At the age of 11 the children had to cycle to Hadleigh School, the girls for cookery and the boys for woodwork, for which they received a bicycle allowance from the Education Department. Also during the 1930s the children would listen to wireless broadcasts.

The War Years

During the Second World War the school hours changed to 8.30a.m.–11.30a.m. Villagers opened their homes to evacuees from London – the 17 children joined in the lessons but some had to be taught in the Reading Room because of lack of space. Fortunately, when a bomb fell on the village in May 1941, the school was only slightly damaged. In May 1943 a canteen was arranged for, but it was February 1944 before it was up and running. Mrs Rose was appointed dinner lady and early in February 1944 a kitchen table, a Valor stove and an oven arrived at the school, and on 14 February children began having hot school dinners for 2s. a week. The meals were cooked at the junior school in Hadleigh and brought to Elmsett by van. Ten more London evacuees, admitted in July 1944, stayed until June 1945.

Postwar Years

When the Second World War ended the school was closed for two days for the victory celebrations. As the evacuees returned to their homes in June, the school roll dropped to 31. The school closed again for the day on 2 June 1953 for the coronation of Queen Elizabeth and the schoolchildren joined in with the village celebrations. On 21 June 1961 18 pupils from the school were taken to Sproughton Green to see the Queen when she visited the area. In 1962 further improvements were made when two wash basins were installed in the front porch with a five-gallon water heater, so at last the children had hot and cold running water instead of a bucket in the playground, but it was not until 1968 that a toilet block was built

Elmsett School, 1953. Left to right, back row: Lawrence King, Richard Groom, Michael Clarke, Graham Griffiths, Alan Perry, Chris Barber; middle row: Susan Barber, Daphne Leeks, Valerie Willis, Blanche Hiskey, Peter Hitchcock; front row: Leonard Pryke, Mary Clarke, Kenneth Cox, Trevor Gibbons.

Elmsett School pupils in 1956. Left to right, back row: Richard Groom, Richard Pryke, Alan Perry, Michael Clark, Graham Griffiths, Laurence King, Michael Edwards, Leonard Pryke, Christopher Barber, Trevor Gibbons; middle row: Mary Clarke, Blanche Hiskey, Daphne Leeks, Maureen Pease, Peter Green, Carolyn Barret, Ann Peter, Susan Barber, Valerie Willis; front row: Elizabeth Grant, Lionel Bradbrook, Muriel Fayers, John Perry, Desmond Barber, ?, Catherine Lambert, Rita Taylor, Helen Green.

Resting on school sports day in 1976. Left to right, back: *Denise Laflin, Irene Goodchild;* middle: *Helen Watkins, Jenny Hitchcock, Julia Woods;* front: *Paul Cage.*

and the building housing the Elsans was removed. Increasing numbers in 1966 meant that a temporary classroom had to be added, and a second temporary classroom was placed on the meadow in 1971, when numbers rose again. During the 1970s swimming lessons were introduced, children being taken to the new pool at Hadleigh. The opening of the new Village Hall in 1979 provided additional space which is still relied on for school lunches as well as for educational purposes. After the gales of 1987 the school was closed. Although structural damage was minimal, with slight roof damage and a broken window, the electricity was off and the wind had blown debris from the storage garage on the meadow into the playground. By the 1990s each classroom had acquired a computer and printer and in 1993 the temporary classroom on the meadow was moved and joined to the main school building. One teacher in particular, Mrs Sue Mackie, was very keen on organising a recycling centre at the school and formed a group of pupils into an ECO committee, which has raised considerable funds for the school. The 125th anniversary of the school was celebrated in 1995 with the publication of its history, researched

and written by Year 6 pupils Laura Davis, Naomi Holland, Ben Rumsey, Emma Sage, Charlotte Thorpe and Rebecca Ulph, assisted by villagers Melanie Lucas, Lynn Ulph and Celia Wright. A service of thanksgiving to commemorate the anniversary was held at St Peter's Church, officiated by the Bishop of Dunwich.

School Extension

The temporary classrooms were coming to the end of their useful lives and, with extra space badly needed and rules regarding disabled access to be applied, it was decided to remove one temporary classroom and extend the main building. After informal discussions, the Village Hall Management Committee negotiated a long-term lease of 50 years at an index-linked rent of £750, an income which helps to cover the costs of maintaining the meadow. Past and present pupils and many residents each bought a brick, thus contributing towards the extension, which was completed in 2004. At last Elmsett has a truly superb school and one in which the children can take great pride.

Matthew D'Sousa (aged 10): *In July 2004 there was the first sign of building. There were bangs and crashes, the sound of saws, hammers and cement mixers. Consequently my eardrums felt like they had burst. Soon it settled and the bricks were being laid and it was all coming together. One brick after another for days. Soon it was as high as I was. Soon it was higher than some trees. Soon it was high enough. Then the roof was going on, filling the gaping hole over the bricks. Next, summer was over. The building was getting nearer to completion, just a few more months. October came and the decoration in Class 2 was almost done. October was over and Class 2 was settling in, Class 1 still had a way to go, and Class 1 was getting excited. After Christmas Class 1 moved in. It was warmer and felt bigger. The building was finished. We are now enjoying our new classrooms as well as our main entrance and cooking area. It was worth the wait.*

Elmsett School, 1996.

Elmsett School, 2005.

School Log-Books

There are several log-books and a punishment book dating back to 1907 (earlier ones were lost during the Second World War). The teachers at the time were Miss Youngs and Miss Stowe. Miss Youngs, who arrived at the school in 1896, must have been an excellent teacher. The first Inspector's report in 1907 gives 'very good' for every subject:

There are no children who make no effort. Both teachers evidently taking pains to make the teaching thorough and interesting… the infants are being well grounded in and should be a credit to the other division in a short time. I report the school to be very good, and advise that the report be entered each year in the log book.

A year later a different Inspector gives similar praise, but states:

… not much attention has been paid to the Prayer Book subject this year and maps should be more frequently used. It seems to me that the particular group of children at present make instruction in anything beyond elementary questions rather difficult. There can be no doubt but that the teachers have done their best with the materials in their hands. I class the school as very good.

In 1909 the diocesan inspector also commented that: '… much careful and thorough work has been done; this school is in a satisfactory condition.'

The excellent reports on the teaching continue, with the children frequently described as '… below average in point of general intelligence and responsiveness' and in 1910 the inspector recommends: 'In the infants room an object lesson lasting 30 minutes is too long. Physical exercise should be taken for a short time daily.' A recurring comment is that:

… the boys' offices are in very bad condition, they are not properly partitioned nor screened from the play-

ground and the ventilation is so inadequate that they are offensive.

In 1916 the diocesan inspector, whilst praising the school's other subjects, found:

The Prayer Book work is not so well known as the Bible work. Perhaps with more time one may hope to find a little fuller knowledge of the meaning of the Catechism, etc.

Throughout this period the Revd Scratchley was making frequent visits to the school, often two or three times a week. Other regular visitors included the attendance officer, the nurse and the dentist.

Memories of School Days

Reg Barber was a pupil from 1905 to 1914, when there were three teachers at the school:

The first class was of five year olds. This was the start of learning our ABC and 1+1=2, and spellings and so on. The teacher's name was Miss Tipple. At seven years old children went into the next room, where the teacher's name was Miss Stowe. At nine years old children went up to the top class, taught by Miss Youngs, and if you were good enough to pass The Exam at a special school you left at 12 years old. Every morning was opened with a hymn and a prayer. The lessons included drill, arithmetic, writing, drawing, painting, reading, geography, history, singing, spelling and of course a little play time both morning and afternoon. Should anyone need the toilet in between lessons, you had to hold up your hand, and when asked you would say 'Please can I leave the room?'.

Pauline Watkins was a few years younger, and lived just outside the parish boundary at Camperdown on Flowton Road:

Elmsett School in the early 1900s.

Elmsett School in 1908. Second row, second from the right is Jim Steward. His friend, Bob Malster, is also in the group.

Elmsett School in the 1920s with the teacher's house on the right of the building.

I was five and a half when I started school in Elmsett. We had to walk all the way (two miles). Miss Youngs was a governess, a dear little white-haired lady and Miss Stowe was a tall motherly lady. Some of the time they lived in the School House, and some time in Threeways Cottage. They were lovely people. There were quite a lot of pupils, all different ages from big boys right down to little tots in the little room. We all had to do the same thing and were all taught together. How they did it I just don't know. We used to have Miss Annie Hiskey who was a pupil teacher. She took the infants in the little room. Children stayed at Elmsett

Elmsett School, early 1900s.

School until they left at 14. We had to do everything there, our sewing, and if it was wet and we couldn't go out, we did our exercises in the big room. There were some big trees opposite the school door and when it was nice weather we sat on the roots to eat our lunch. When it was very hot – I think 1921 was the hottest we'd ever known – we had our lessons outside. In wet weather Miss Youngs used to have a big guard in front of the fire covered with coats and hats drying ready for the children to walk home. Dad used to Vaseline our boots and put old socks over them so that we could walk in the ice and snow.

Cissie Holder: *I started school at the age of three the same time as my brother Ben, who was four. There were between 40 and 50 pupils and we had two classrooms and two teachers, Miss Youngs and Miss Stowe. I stayed until I was 14.*

Aubrey Barber: *Miss Stowe was my first teacher. She stayed in the village during the week and cycled home to Stoke-by-Nayland at weekends.*

From the punishment book it would appear that Miss Youngs was quite lenient, as there are only two entries for 1908 and no further ones until 1928, after she had left. A series of head teachers covered the next 15 years, including one whose duties were terminated. This coincides with the greatest number of punishments listed. Most of the miscreants were 'disobedient' boys aged 11–13, and their punishment varied from two strokes with the cane to one stroke with the ruler. In 1930 ten boys were whipped for disobedience. There were a few further entries for 1948 and 1949, all involving children from the same family – the boys were punished for playing truant, throwing stones, insolence, swearing, spitting and fighting.

Mrs Roberts is remembered with affection. She arrived in 1937 and stayed until 1955.

Brian Hiskey and **Brenda Woods**: *We remember Mrs Roberts. Everything at school revolved around her. She was never off work and she did everything – very strict. There was Miss Hollis and Mr Grant too, he was very fussy – he would check all the ledges for dust.*

Elmsett School, 1950, with Miss Hollis. Left to right, back row: *?, Gerald Riddlestone, Karolyn Barrett, Peter Green, Rita Fulton, Michael Foster, Gordon Watkins, Graham Hayes, Robin Barnes, Jean Harris;* front row: *Paul Robinson, Colin Taylor, Michael Clarke, Gwen Malster, Joy Riches, ?.*

Elmsett School, 1963. Left to right, back row: *? Richardson, Janet Mussett, Valerie Dunnett, Hilary Barber, Angela Skippings, Laura Barraclough, Valerie Patterson, Brian Skippings;* third row: *?, Linda Richardson, Susan Gant, Paul Patterson, Andrew Barnes, Janice Bradbrook, Robin Jeans, Ian Richardson;* second row: *?, Jenny Barraclough, Cynthia Green, Margaret Gibbons, Alan Grimwade, Christopher Patterson, Alison Barber, Jane Sillitoe;* front row: *Colin(?) Richardson, ?, Anthony Glenn, Jonathon Glenn, Richard Gidney, David Turner, ?.*

Going on the Hadleigh High School was a bit of a rude awakening.

Brian didn't like the noise there and would much rather have been out in the fields.

Michael King: *There were two classrooms, the big room and the little room each heated by a tortoise stove. We had wooden desks, with lids to hide behind. The big room had an attendance board on the wall. The teachers had no helpers or assistants. They did everything themselves from the start of day to the finish, even lunchtimes. We all went home, but Mrs Roberts or Mrs Grimwade supervised those who stayed. Mrs Rose dished up.*

Jean Simpson (née Harris): *Mrs Roberts was very bad on her feet. She walked with sticks and had calipers round her legs. She also had a wheelchair, which may have been worked by moving two handles. Discipline was very strict. If we made a noise in the little room, she would tap on the window and there was silence.*

Hazel King and **Gwen Horne (sisters, née Malster):** *Boys and girls were taught to knit. Our brother started to knit a baby's bonnet for Hazel but didn't get on very well at all. By the time it was finished Hazel had outgrown it so Gwen had it for her doll.*

Margaret Watkins: *In 1947 we didn't go to school for about six weeks. It was too dangerous to walk in the snow and there was no petrol. The school dentist used to come with his caravan – it hurt like mad!*

Mr Grant, who had been an assistant teacher in 1946/47, returned as head in 1955 and stayed for 20 years.

Hilary Wilson and **Alison Gillies (sisters, née Barber):** *We went to Elmsett School, but as the village grew some new families sent their children to Whatfield school. This caused some problems, as there had always been an element of competition between the two schools. Mr and Mrs Grant ran the school; they were disciplinarians.*

[Alison remembers being told off on her first day for not closing her eyes for prayers.] *We used to do mental arithmetic and 'problems'. There were about 40 pupils, and it was so crowded three older ones of us had to work in what is now the head's office.*

Judith Corble (née Bowell): *I started school when I was five. We did not have play schools or pre-school – we just went to school. When I started at Elmsett School there was just the original building, and my classroom, the juniors' was at the back. The two teachers were Mr and Mrs Grant and they lived in Hadleigh. He had the top class in the big room, and I can clearly picture the big desks, with inkpots, that were*

all round the room. They had to be moved around a lot, as we did everything in that room, we had all our lessons, we ate, and we even did country dancing! I can't recall where the meals came from, but I remember eating my lunch in there. There was a big old boiler in there with a large guard around it, and in winter when we had our milk and it used to be frozen we all sat around the stove. The toilets were outside.

In 1967 Miss Lawrence joined the staff as infant teacher and Mrs Grant became part-time.

Sheila Herd (née Hitchcock): *I remember Miss Lawrence, who used to cycle from Somersham every day, come rain or shine. I remember her as a little old lady, but I'm sure she wasn't – I think I just saw her with my child's eyes! She had two mice chalked on the blackboard and every day near going home time she would roll the mice to the front and tell a story about them, or she would tell us a 'My naughty little sister' story. Some children would fall asleep and their mums had to carry them out. Everyone was scared of Mr Grant – he had a really good aim with chalk or board rubber. I remember having to do country dancing every week and the embarrassment of having to pair up with a boy for this. When Mr Leeds came as Head [1975–84] we used to do lots of nature study and bird watching.*

Former pupils and villagers at the Service of Thanksgiving for 125 years of Elmsett School, 1995.

School sports day, 1995.

Another infant teacher at the school was Mrs Mackie, who took up her post in 1977 and stayed until 2002. The children benefited greatly from her promotion of the recycling centre, which helped to fund many projects at the school.

Mr Marshall became head in 1987 and has instigated many improvements.

The children who started school in the early 1990s wrote of changes which had taken place in their time at the school in their 125th anniversary commemorative book:

There used to be a red door to enter the main building. The infants' classroom and the toilets stood separately near to the main school, but one classroom was along the path at the edge of the meadow, and it was very hot in summer and cold in winter. It had no water, and this had to be carried there for art and science lessons. Pupils had to walk, in all weathers, to the infant block. There was a drinking fountain near the main door, and there was a pond across the playground surrounded by a fence and locked gate.

By 1995 all the classrooms were linked and the floors carpeted. At the time of writing the playground has been extended and the pond area has been developed into a managed nature area, which is used for teaching purposes. The school has achieved excellent results from Ofsted reports and in 2005 was featured on Anglia television.

Alice Kempson (aged 5): *I was a bit surprised when the teacher said we were going to be on TV. The whole school was really excited. But I was a bit sad because I wasn't on a lot. We got on TV because we got a really good Ofsted report.*

In 2004 the school won a BT Education Award to run a project in which the children decided to form a link with a school in Angola.

David Bray (age 10): *The whole school was involved with the book and all had their names printed in it. We heard the Angolan folk tale from Tommy, a relation of one of the pupils, and he lived in Angola. He came to visit us and he inspired us. We wrote the book to raise money for more books for Tommy's school in Angola. It has been great to have a connection with children so far away.*

In 2005 the school achieved a National BT Education Award of £10,000 to continue the project, which included having the book translated into Portuguese

The Fox and the Wolf
AN ANGOLAN FOLK STORY

Written by Class 1 Pupils (years 5 and 6) of Elmsett Primary School, with Nicci Gerrard and Sean French (Nicci French)
Illustrated by the pupils of Elmsett Primary School and Hilli Thompson
PROJECT FUNDED BY BT EDUCATION AWARD 2003/04

The book written by pupils of Elmsett School to raise funds for a school in Angola.

for use in Angolan schools.

The children run a School Council and an Eco Council.

Katrina Seeley (aged 10): *In the School Council we discuss how we can make money for people in Angola and Uganda. We also discuss matters in and around school. Every year we elect people to be on the School Council so everybody has a chance to be on. We've only been on TV once before. The teachers said we had to be sensible. It was a great day and the whole school had a fantastic time. They filmed us for a whole day, and I was a bit nervous. I like Elmsett School because it's so friendly. You know everybody and you never feel alone. You often see older children looking after the younger children that have just started school. The best thing about Elmsett School is that when you're upset there's always someone to play with.*

The school has won another BT Education Award for 2006 in recognition of the children's demonstration of good speaking and listening skills. The children will decide on the project they will undertake.

The School Council, 2005-06. Left to right, back row: Katrina Seeley, James Robinson, Matthew D'Sousa, Paul Midgley; middle row: Sarah Stock, Zoe Griggs, Amy Coleyshaw, Lewis Kempson; front row: Georgia Bearman, Alice Kempson, Catherine Funnell, James Grant.

The Eco Council. 2005–06. Left to right, back row: Linzi Hill, Matthew D'Sousa, Paul Midgley, James Robinson, David Bray, Olivia Sherred; middle row: Alistair Grant, Sarah Stock, Melissa Canham, Isaak Hitchcock; in front: Ranulf Gull.

Sam French (11) joined the school in 2005: *I remember coming to Elmsett School and meeting new people. It was very different working here with other people. I made a lot of new friends and had lots of fun, but I was still not used to the blue uniform and it was strange working with different teachers. The playground was different too, but still fun. I feel different here with new people, and happy that I am here.*

Community Recycling Centre at Elmsett School

In the early 1990s some older members of the Girls Brigade, who were studying environmental matters, asked the Parish Council to organise a bottle bank for the village. One was subsequently sited near to the Village Hall. Their initial idea has become a community recycling centre at Elmsett School which has raised over £110,000 for school projects since 1992.

Sue Mackie was a reception class teacher at the school, and describes how the scheme started:

I used to pass the bottle bank each day on my way to teach at the school. As it filled and overflowed quite quickly I started to contact the waste recycling company to ask for a collection. They suggested collecting aluminum cans too. Good idea, I thought – and placed an old dustbin next to the bottle bank. A letter arrived about recycling ink cartridges, photocopiers and fax machines, so we started collecting these, not knowing quite what to do with them! Then in 1992 the Government gave money to local councils to encourage recycling in the community, so with support from school governors we registered Elmsett School as an official recycling centre with Babergh District Council

and were able to claim credits for the weight of materials collected. 'Entrust' helped to fund fencing off the end of the playground, relocating the bottle bank and improving the access to our expanding recycling centre. It was officially opened in 1994. Over the years the school has received over £13,000 in the form of weight credits for the glass, paper, textiles, aluminum and steel cans, foil and shoes. The recycling of ink cartridges has raised over a phenomenal £120,000, and is supported by both local and national businesses. Old spectacles are sent to Vision Aid. Used stamps are donated to the local Hospice, where they help with fund-raising.

The work on recycling has helped pupils at the school to learn and care about the environment and the importance of sustainable lifestyles. Over the years the fund has paid for extra facilities, resources and projects which have benefited the children in many ways. Until the Early Years Unit became part of the reception class the funds paid for its teacher. It is currently helping with the purchase of computers. In 2002 Elmsett School applied for, and was granted, the top award from the international environmental Eco Schools Scheme and is entitled to fly the Green Flag, subject to regular reviews. The Eco Committee, which has adult and pupil representatives, meets regularly to discuss the new targets and how these might be achieved.

In 2005 Sue Mackie was awarded the MBE for her environmental enterprise and endeavours.

Elmsett Playgroup

Lorna Quick started the Playgroup in 1964: *Our first daughter was born in 1960, two weeks after we moved from a flat in London to Elmsett. By 1964 we had three children under four, and as there was no nursery school in the area and I was a trained nursery nurse, we converted our dining-room into a playroom, and invited eight pre-school children for two mornings a week to what was to become the first pre-school Playgroup in East Anglia, and one of the first in the country. We had a farm wagon in our orchard which the children loved, and on which we had many adventures and imaginary journeys. The children quickly learned to climb the wheels for storytime in the summer. When word got around more village children arrived, joined by others from Hadleigh and neighbouring villages. We moved to the Methodist Church and Elizabeth Cage became a permanent helper with other mothers taking turns to help out. Each year we had a Nativity play, and took part in the village fête with a marching band. When Mary Tait took over it continued at the Rectory. We left Elmsett in 1970, but still have happy memories of our time there.*

Sheila Herd: *I have faint recollections of playgroup. I went to the Rectory and I remember sitting round a table having a drink and Mrs Tait telling us a story.*

Playgroup children climbing into the wagon for story-time, 1966.

One time Doreen Ladbrook brought David in (as a tiny baby!) to show us bathing a baby.

The Playgroup continued to grow and when the Rectory was no longer suitable, in 1974 it moved to the Reading Room.

Lee Boniface: *My association with Elmsett Playgroup in the Reading Room began in 1974 as a mum on the Help Rota, then as Sheila Lawrence's assistant, and later as supervisor with Ann Furness as assistant. The Reading Room was by then looking a bit sorry for itself but made an excellent home for the Playgroup. The Committee were very easygoing about wet paintings left to dry along the walls; floors were not 'precious' and were easy to clean. Children were, in fact, welcome. Sunshine through the windows could make the old wooden walls look warm and cosy, but only in the summer. Winter sun still shone through the same windows, but the lack of insulation completely dispelled any illusion of 'warm and cosy'. Winter mornings before electric wall heaters meant hoping all the portable gas heaters would light, which could not be guaranteed; thank goodness for our extensive repertoire of action games. Health and Safety would have a field day now! Not a scrap of stainless steel anywhere in the kitchen and we even washed paint pots and drinking cups in the same old sink. How we all survived to tell the tale I do not know! There was a small outdoor area where the children could play and we were able to take nature walks in the meadow behind the building. One day I was approached and asked if we could use some extra help. There was a recently widowed lady, very fond of children, who would love to come along sometimes. Extra hands were always welcome, and soon Lily Holder was a regular and valued helper and, indeed, she stayed on long after Ann and I moved on in 1978. Margaret Berry followed me as supervisor and took the Playgroup into the new Village Hall and a new era.*

The Playgroup has run continuously since its inception. Margaret Leek was the leader for 17 years and for several of these was joined by Judith Corble. There have been many changes over the years and it now caters for three age groups. There is a weekly session for children up to three years old called 'Stepping Stones'. The three- and four-year-olds attend morning sessions of Playgroup, and an Early Years group runs in conjunction with the school, preparing the rising fives for full-time schooling. Maria O'Donnell is the leader in 2006, assisted by Victoria Gregory – Judith Corble's daughter – and Sarah Watkins, whose husband Joe's grandmother, Pauline Watkins, attended Elmsett School nearly a century ago!

Music time for Playgroup children, 1965. The picture includes: Jake Reynolds (standing), Katrina Moyes, Anne Sillitoe, Frazer Moyes, Keith Barber, Andrew Barber. front row: ?, ?, Diane Quick, Peter Quick, Marcus Booth.

CHAPTER 10

Accidents and Tragedies

The Cruel Winter of 1903/04

Around the year 1890, after John and Mary Ann Westren had settled in at Elmsett Hall, they had tennis courts erected for the enjoyment of their young family and to entertain their friends. Ernest, their eldest son, excelled at the sport when an occasional tournament was held. Besides enjoying his sport, Ernest had also taken over control of their flock of sheep. The Christmas of 1903 saw heavy falls of snow begin to build up into drifts. The fold was opened and the sheep released to roam and seek their own shelter under the thick hedges surrounding the nearby fields. In the early days of 1904 snow kept falling, with deep drifts developing and covering the land.

During the weeks which followed, with bags of meal and hay loaded onto a wooden hurdle which served as a makeshift sleigh, Ernest went out day after day to search for and feed as many of the buried flock as he could locate. From time to time he would go home, cold and wet, for a hurried snack before returning to continue his search until nightfall. Eventually, with the arrival of warmer spring weather, when the snow melted, it was revealed that a large proportion of the flock had not survived the long, harsh period of wintry weather. Unfortunately, the cold wet weather also took its toll on Ernest. Having been in soaking wet clothing for long periods he developed pneumonia from which he did not recover.

He died on 1 June1904, aged 31. As his coffin was carried from the church, members of the Tennis Club lined the path to his grave in St Peter's churchyard. He was buried beside his younger sister, Florence, who had died on 4 April 1897, aged 17 years. His mother was so distraught on losing her son that no more tennis was allowed. The courts were closed and eventually dismantled.

Rookery Farm

The Bull family were tenants on the 155-acre Rookery Farm in the 1800s. William Bull found it a struggle to feed his 11 children and to pay his annual tithe of £40. In August 1816 he hanged himself in the barn next to the house. The coroner recorded a verdict of 'lunacy'. Just 13 years later Robert, his 34-year-old son, also hanged himself, and on this occasion the verdict was 'temporary derangement'. His brother, John, had nine children to feed, and in 1839 his wife, at the age of 30, died in childbirth; by 1844 two young sons had also died. In addition to the suicides of his father and brother, another brother and a sister had died. Known to be mentally unstable, John was constantly watched, but on 2 January 1855 he went out during a thunderstorm to fasten the barn door, which was blowing in the wind. When he did not return a search was carried out. He was found hanging from a tree – at some time he had hidden a rope, waiting for the opportunity to end his life.

Marriage Tragedy

In 1932 Roly Kennington, who worked on the roads, married Ethel Mary Clarke. She was one of the foster children of Mrs Brown and lived with the family in one of the council houses on the Hadleigh Road. It must have been one of the shortest marriages on record.

After exchanging their vows they walked to the vestry to sign the register, then walked up the steps into the porch, where the bride collapsed. Although only in her thirties it is thought that she had a stroke. She died later that day.

Bonfire Accident

In 1894 some men had been hedging and, as was the practice at the time, any wood that could be used for fuel was saved and the rest burned on a bonfire. On this particular occasion the children from the Wilding family, who lived in a cottage at the bottom of Spinney Hill, used the embers of the fire to bake some potatoes. The little daughter, Martha, aged five, went too near the fire and her dress caught fire. The other children did not know how to smother the flames and she burned to death. She was buried on 27 November.

Drowning Accident

Occasionally adults tell children tales with the best of intentions but they don't realise that a child's curiosity is insatiable. In this instance some children who lived at the Old Post Office were told that if they looked over the top of a water butt into the water, they would be able to see their reflection. One young boy's curiosity got the better of him and he climbed up to look into the water. The level must have been quite low, because he leaned too far and toppled in. No one heard him and he was found drowned.

Killed by a Windmill Sail

In the early 1900s a man at the mill backed his tumbril (cart) to the door and got too close to the sail, which was turning quite fast. He was killed instantly when the sail hit him.

Disease among Children

When looking through old burial registers of the village one is always struck by the number of children listed. Many were the hazards they had to face in their early years. In Elmsett during the year 1864, a disease wrought havoc with one large family. This was diphtheria, which appeared every few years, at some times much more virulently than others. Few families could have suffered more grievously than the Ratcliffs, living at the time at Ostend Cottage. At about Christmas time Sarah, aged eight, developed the disease and by New Year's day she had died. By the first week in February seven of the children were dead. The fear of infection was so great that the little coffins were not taken into the church, but only as far as the porch.

Diphtheria continued to appear at intervals. There was a bad outbreak in the 1890s, with fatal consequences in the Hiskey and Pearl families. Its last appearance was in May 1940, when some of the London evacuee children and one adult were taken to the isolation ward at the hospital in Ipswich. Immunisation of infants began shortly afterwards and the disease has now almost been eradicated.

Fire at the Mill

Ladbrooks' Mill suffered a serious setback in 1963, when a fire destroyed the entire flour mill.

Trevor Gibbons gives an eyewitness account:
During the early hours of the morning on Saturday, 7 December 1963, a fire broke out in the flour mill. I was 15 years old at the time, living with my parents and five-year-old sister at Elmcroft in Whatfield Road. I vividly remember being awoken at about 4a.m. by loud cracking noises resembling gunfire, which instantly had me out of bed and hurrying to the window. A bright orange glow lit the sky over Mill Lane and flames were leaping into the air over the new flour mill. Asbestos sheets on the roof of the adjacent building were exploding, causing a noise which could be heard across the entire village. My father and I quickly dressed and made our way up Whatfield Road to the mill. The fire had taken such a hold; we assumed it had been burning for some time and the fire brigade must be there. As we passed Elm Farm I remember George Holder leaning out of a bedroom window shouting 'Fire! Fire!'. Turning into Mill Lane we saw that the fire service was not there and we were among the first on the scene. The fire must have been burning for some considerable time;

both the new flour mill and the older adjoining buildings were well ablaze and it was impossible to tell where it had started. The mill manager, Rex Barrett, was opening the office to fetch the keys for two lorries parked close to the burning building – two men who worked at the mill bravely drove them to safety. It was now 4.30a.m. and the fire was spreading quickly through buildings – the flour was exploding as it burned. Fire appliances began to arrive, firstly from Hadleigh, soon followed by several other crews. The large number of appliances available enabled the fire fighters to pump huge amounts of water into the building, thus preventing further spread. However, water supply soon became a major problem. I clearly remember Mr Rowlands, the Hadleigh fire chief, who I knew lived nearby, asking me where the storm water collected. The nearest large pond was some distance away – the horse pond at Maltings Farm. The fire appliances attending did not have the equipment to pump over such a distance and so the Auxiliary Fire Service was called in to assist. They laid a large hose from the mill to the pond at Maltings Farm and soon began pumping water. The contents of the pond were quickly drained, but it did enable the firemen to bring the fire under control. Daybreak brought a very sorry sight. The first and second storeys of the new building, which was only three years old, appeared to be completely destroyed, as was the warehouse which had contained hundreds of sacks of flour. The fire service was there for much of the next day damping down the smouldering timbers and contents of the buildings. One memory that will always remain with me is cycling past the drained horse pond on the morning after the fire. Many bewildered ducks sat around, staring at the black mud, with nowhere to swim!

The Great Field Fire of Elmsett

In the late summer of 1984, during a particularly hot spell, a field fire started in Elmsett which eventually led to about two square miles of standing corn being destroyed.

It started from a good deed. One of the villagers had been clearing the ditches around the Rectory Meadow playing-field. He then decided to burn the brush and rubbish, which turned out to be not such a good idea, as there was a gusty 20-knot wind blowing. A spark must have carried into the adjoining field, which immediately caught fire. As the fire spread, more appliances were called in to tackle the blaze. Local farmers and their workers joined the 80 men from 16 fire engines on the scene. There was also a huge airport fire tender from Wattisham airbase. This had a water canon driven by a gas turbine engine, and carried a warning notice advising people not to stand behind it, as the blast from the engine extended for about 20 yards. The strain on the water supply was too great, and the main water system collapsed – water had to be taken from the Old Rectory moat. The roads acted as fire breaks and the fast-moving fire was brought under control after about an hour, much to the relief of householders, many of whom had oil tanks and gas cylinders outside their homes. The villagers, who can be relied on in an emergency, opened up the Village Hall and took cold drinks to the firemen, so the WRVS, who always attend major incidents, found they were not needed on this occasion!

Sisters **Hilary Wilson** and **Alison Gillies** remember this fire in particular, as their uncle was the man who had been working on the meadow:

It was very eerie. One could hear the sirens coming from every angle. From the gardens in Whatfield Road (where Hilary was living) we could see masses of smoke. The fire was amazing and quite scary. Luckily, the wind took it along the backs of the gardens in Whatfield Road and across the fields towards Whatfield. Uncle Gerald never lived it down – it was even mentioned at his funeral! Field fires often occurred in hot, dry weather – one year we lost ten acres of crops to a fire. Another serious fire was when Dad's barn suffered an electrical fault and went up in flames.

The Story of Helen

Brenda Edwards tells Helen's tragic story: *It was a fine July morning in 1986, when Helen Edwards, then age five, boarded a train with her father, Roger, in Needham Market. It was a treat for Helen – her first train journey. They were going to Cambridge, where Helen was to have a minor operation to remove a strawberry mark from her head. The operation went tragically wrong and very soon villagers were discussing ways to help. The Revd Harrison opened the door of the church every evening whilst Helen was in intensive care. People who would not normally have attended sat in the church to pray for Helen. Cards, presents and flowers arrived at her home. From the very beginning the Ladbrook family, especially Doreen, who had taught Helen in Sunday school, offered help. Regular updates about Helen's condition were published in the village newsletter in the nine months that she remained in hospital. By then it was known that she had suffered irreparable brain damage and she was not expected to live for long.*

We would not accept this and decided to go to the British Institute for Brain Injured Children in Bridgwater, Somerset. Doreen helped us to take Helen by train for her initial assessment. The programme of exercises the Institute designed for her was for six hours a day, seven days a week and involved lots of volunteers. The Ladbrook family took Helen for two days each week and continued the programme in their home. To our amazement the villagers and friends provided over 160 volunteers. The youngest was 11, the oldest 79. Of these volunteers 32 continued to help for the whole five years Helen was on the programme. All came at their allotted time, did as they were instructed and went away. They asked nothing of us and gave lots. The result is that Helen is still with us as part of our family. Although still very damaged, she is now a lively and happy young lady. Her accident brought the whole close-knit community of Elmsett together and from our sadness came hope and friendships which are still alive today. Thank you everyone.

In the Reading Room, c.1970. Left to right, in the foreground: Eric Fison, ?, Barbara Briscoe, Sheila Barber, Rosemary Hitchcock, Richard Hitchcock, Rachel Hitchcock; in the background: ?, Mervyn Hiskey, Alan Barber, Ken Kemp, Lorna Quick, Margaret Sharp, Ann Barber, ?, Robert Hitchcock.

The Reading Room in a derelict state, 1995.

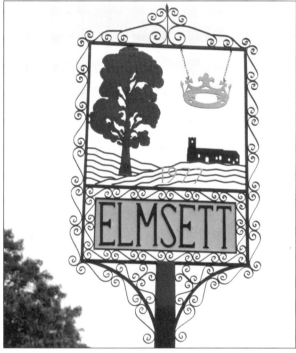

The ancient oak on Rectory Meadow in about 1950. It measured 21 feet 8 inches in girth 6 feet from the ground just before it fell in 1963.

The village sign, erected in 1977 to commemorate the Queen's silver jubilee. It was designed by Ron Kerridge from a doodle he had made during a Community Council meeting. Ron, a skilled draughtsman, worked in engineering and was well known for his doodles which, he claims, help concentrate the mind. The sign was unveiled by Mrs Jenny Barnes, Chair of the Parish Council during the jubilee celebrations.

CHAPTER 11

Village Amenities

The Reading Room

The Reading Room was built in 1934 on a small piece of land given by Ernest Ladbrook in a corner of the meadow adjoining his garden at Laurel Cottage. Prior to this all social events took place in the school, including plays and concerts.

The Reading Room was a rectangular, timber-framed, asbestos-clad building with a slate roof, heated by a tortoise stove. Newspapers were placed there for villagers to read and the room was soon put to good use as a hall for village activities. The Scout group, the Girl Guides and the Parish Council used to meet there. At the outbreak of the Second World War in 1939 it became the centre for many activities. It was used for the assembly of the 50 evacuees from Bethnal Green, for the supply and fitting of gas masks and as a classroom to accommodate the children for their lessons, as the school was too small. The Home Guard and ARP firewatchers used it as a base during the winter. After the war and throughout the 1950s and 1960s it became a focal point in the village. It was used by doctors for weekly surgeries and the district nurse used it for baby clinics. For a while in the 1950s films were shown there each week, with the projector situated in the room at the back. Fund raising resulted in an extension being built in 1958, making it an L shape and providing much-needed extra rooms. Events were popular; many people remember an entertainment put on to raise money for the purchase of the Rectory Meadow, where Eric Fison, suitably attired, sang 'Lily the Pink' to rapturous applause. Bessie Taylor, who is fondly remembered, was the caretaker for many years, and visiting speakers would comment on the cleanliness of the room.

Jenny Barnes: *Bessie used to struggle to light the stove, and if the wind was in the wrong direction it burned badly and filled the room with smoke.*

In the 1960s the sanitation remained rather primitive, but improvements were made in the early 1970s, when electric heaters were installed and the main sewer connected. For a short while the Playgroup and other village organisations continued to use it. However, as the village outgrew the building it became necessary to plan for a new Village Hall and to provide a playing-field. A Community Council was formed in 1966 to raise money and obtain grants, initially to buy and drain the Rectory Meadow. The Reading Room continued in use as a Village Hall until 1979, when the new hall was opened. The Village Hall Management Committee took over the management of the Reading Room in 1979. For a few years it was rented for use as a piano workshop. It was sold in 1996 to John Simmons and Lesley Woor and converted into a holiday home.

Elmsett and Aldham Community Council

The Community Council was set up in 1966 in order to raise money to buy the Rectory Meadow from the Church. Eric Fison was elected to chair the committee and two years later the seven and a half acre Meadow was purchased for £2,000. In 1969, with the assistance of many villagers, Eric Fison and Derek Rose supervised the planting of trees around the periphery of the meadow. Later, in 1978, more interesting varieties were planted. Frank Knight (former director of RHS Garden Wisley) advised on the selection, which was purchased and planted under his supervision by volunteers. In 1970 the Council became 'The Elmsett and Aldham Community Council'. There was great enthusiasm for raising money for village amenities, largely led by Eric Fison, who had a way of persuading people to volunteer their help, and the Community Council was selected to produce a display for HM the Queen when she was in Ipswich for her silver jubilee visit in 1977. Ron Kerridge and Cecil Bowell were proud to man the display.

There were many imaginative fund-raising activities. A weekly lottery started in 1967 and ran for over 12 years and there was a craft weekend, a picture auction and an open evening at the mill, in addition to social events. Principal amongst these was the annual fête, which continued until 1976.

Throughout the 1970s a considerable amount of work was undertaken to improve facilities. The meadow was drained, ploughed and seeded, a tractor shed built, a tractor bought and children's play equipment scrounged or donated and constructed from old scaffolding poles. The total cost of all this work amounted to nearly £3,000. Subsequently, the Co-op Funeral Parlour, which was a portable building, was purchased and converted into a sports' pavilion. This cost another £350.

The Village Hall

Planning started in 1971 for a new hall to be built on the meadow and, after lengthy investigation of several options, the proposal to go for a sectional building at an estimated cost of £30,000, with the wide use of voluntary labour, made this a realistic project. The Community Council had raised over £8,500 and Alan McCusker, as project manager, having secured the grants from various sources, took on the organisation, costing and building arrangements.

Knights & Hill were awarded the contract and in June 1977 the 'shell' of a Banbury building was erected on a prepared base. Of the many volunteers who worked on the project, one, Ron Kerridge, co-ordinated the work as director of works, and Richard Hitchcock was treasurer. Dennis Hill made an invaluable contribution in helping to alleviate many of the problems, and also supplying time and materials at no extra cost.

After a year progress was such that the Community Council formed a management committee for the day-to-day running of the Hall. As completion neared, more help was forthcoming – especially from young mums – but in order to keep the project on schedule a lot of the decoration, both internal and external, was carried out by young offenders on probation. Robert Dougall, a national TV presenter, officially opened the Hall on 29 May 1979. In 2003, with Russell Leek as project manager, the toilet block was rebuilt to accommodate facilities for the disabled.

Guy Fawkes Night

The guy, made by village children, would travel in style in the comfort of an old armchair perched on the trailer behind Richard Hitchcock's tractor. For some years he was attended by a boys' band and a procession of people and children carrying lit torches. Cecil Bowell usually made these torches by nailing baked bean tins to strong pieces of wood and filling them with rags soaked in a mixture of paraffin and diesel. The torches were lit at Aldham Corner by Cecil and carried in procession to the meadow along Hadleigh Road, with other people joining in along the way. In the meadow a huge bonfire would have been prepared and, once the Guy was ceremoniously carried to the top, the torches were thrown onto the pyre. This was the signal for the festivities to begin. Hotdogs, burgers and a firework display followed and usually raised up to £70 a year.

Jenny Barnes*: Bonfire night was a great occasion. I remember well the night the WI had a tarpaulin shelter outside the village shop. We had hurricane lamps, and oil stoves to cook the sausages on. It was a blustery night and we had problems – but all the sausages were cooked and sold.*

Sadly, the event ceased in 2000, a victim of economics and increasingly stringent regulations.

The Elmsett and Aldham Newsletter

Since October 1975 a monthly newsletter, which Revd Harry Tait originally started in 1970 for the two churches, has been distributed to every household in both parishes. After he left the area, Muriel Cook became the editor and it expanded to become the newsletter for the two villages, with a small committee collecting news from the parish churches, the Methodist Church, the school, clubs and village organisations. Family news was also covered –

Muriel Cooke at a surprise party in 1990, given on her retirement from compiling the village newsletter. She was presented with a cheque for £100 from grateful villagers. 1990.

Village pump, c.1940, drawn by Edna Maynard and used for a newsletter cover.

births, deaths, engagements, weddings, examination successes and local achievements. Muriel wrote the earlier material by hand, which was then stencil typed by Janet Crick and run off on a duplicator. It was then collated and delivered to each house monthly by a team of distributors. In 1990, when Muriel reached 80, she handed over the editorship to Rachel Hitchcock, with Margaret Leek and Jackie Parkinson as sub-editors. Janet Crick continued to type until Rachel, helped by her son William, conquered her computer. In 1992, to get a more professional look, it was printed and stapled by a local printer. Today it is a compact booklet with an attractive cover drawing of a village scene. Advertisements are included to assist with production costs. Each February a list of the local facilities is included in a fact sheet.

Elmsett Parish Council

Since its establishment following the 1894 Local Government Act, Elmsett Parish Council has been actively supportive of all village developments, ventures and enterprises. For 92 years the chair was held by members of the Ladbrook family, first by William, who was succeeded by his son, Ernest, and later by his grandson, Jack. Jenny Barnes, who had been the first woman on the council, then took the chair, followed by Cecil Bowell. William Ladbrook's great-grandson, John, presided until 1996. Roger Horne was elected to the chair until 1999, and the current chairman (2006), Nick Bird, has held office since. The Parish Council has kept firm and benevolent control of such matters as planning applications, working closely with both county and district councillors. It has seen many changes in membership over the years – too many to name. Some have been long-standing representatives and well-established Elmsett residents, others relative newcomers. This book could not have been produced without its support and encouragement.

Amenities

Elmsett did not have modern facilities until the middle of the twentieth century, with mains electricity arriving in 1952, although outlying houses and farms relied on diesel generators and were not connected until the mid-1960s. Mains water was available to most properties by 1955. The main sewerage system did not arrive until 1969.

Sewage

Before the sewerage system arrived most houses had their own or a shared septic tank. Anglia Water initially wanted to site the treatment plant in a good arable field belonging to John Hitchcock, but he resisted this, and offered a less productive field further from the village – he did this free of charge to

compensate for the additional cost of the installation. Some houses still rely on septic tanks.

Brian Hiskey: *Everyone buried waste in their gardens. Luckily everyone had big ones with plenty of room and it was good for the rhubarb! The outside toilet at Elm Cottage was a cricket pitch length away from the house. There were two privies side by side for the two cottages. After you had 'been', a layer of earth was spread over. The pit underneath was emptied about three times a year. I remember emptying it once. A big hole was dug near the damson tree; the pit was opened up at the back and emptied into the hole using a long handled tool called a swangler – a Suffolk word. Then the hole was covered over. Later on we got modern and the toilet was made, with a bucket that was emptied once a week. In winter it could be quite frightening going there in the dark, and we used to wait for someone else to go too. The best month to use the outside toilet was June, when the honeysuckle climbing over the privy was in flower.*

Water
Originally, water was taken from the village pump and ponds.

Aubrey Barber remembers the pump being a focal point in the village: *It was in the centre of the village – a real gathering place. The pump itself was unusual in that it had two spouts. One was high enough to make it useful for filling water carts and the other low enough to fill pails of water to take home. There was no general system for mains water; just a few people had their own arrangements, for example Chequers Farm had an outside tap supplied by Elmsett Mill. All water for the household had to be carried into the house. Think of family night when the bath was filled or wash day, when the copper had to be filled and the fire lit under it. Rainwater was always collected and used. We had a herd of cows so needed a lot of water when using the milking utensils, the churns and the ladles, and for dealing with the butter and cream.*

The village pump, c.1950. Aubrey Barber's sister, Vera Bowell, is on the bench.

Cecil Barber pumping water at Laurel Cottage in the late 1920s.

Above: *Preparing the site for the pump, 1995.* Left to right: *Arthur Jeans, Robin Jeans, Aubrey Barber, Bill Simpson, Roger Horne.*

Below: *Aubrey Barber making a symbolic gesture at the unveiling of the pump.*

My brother Victor, sister Vera and I must have carried hundreds of gallons of water on our bicycles. In times of drought the water cart was used to take supplies of water to Aldham village. Alf Pearl, who kept the Rose and Crown, used to do it and charged a halfpenny a bucket. The cart was filled by fixing a length of troughing from the top spout of the pump to channel the water in. The lower pump was blocked off with a piece of wood. It was quite a little operation, but then there was always someone around to lend a hand. There were railings around the pump and bench seats, so you could lean your cycle against the rails and have a sit down, a chat and enjoy this popular meeting-place. There came a time when it was felt the village pump should be removed, as it was reckoned a danger. Several of the residents, particularly the older people, were saddened by this, so to commemorate the fiftieth anniversary of VE Day in 1995, a new one was found and readily installed as a memento of former years. Sadly, a double spouted one could not be found, and in spite of many enquiries through the local council and other likely contacts the original could not be traced.

Brian Hiskey: *We had a set of wheels with a water butt on top for carrying water from Pump Corner.*

It took eight buckets full to fill the copper. Later there was a standpipe outside our house taken off the supply to the mill.

Some outlying houses and farms still have their own boreholes. Others were connected to the mains much later than the village.

✦ CHAPTER 12 ✦

'Yarnin' round the Pump'

Sport

Reg Barber: *It may be of interest to mention village sport. I just mention the obstacle race; I cannot say the distance. The start was a run and jump over various heights, crawl under a net, which was pegged flat and tight to the ground. This net was one used by the farmer over the vehicle to keep pigs in on transport. Next they had to crawl through the rungs of a ladder, and run to the finish. Men had a game of quoits – a bed of clay with a peg of iron in the centre, throwing steel quoits a distance to see who could get it nearest to the pin. If one circled the pin it was called a ringer. I cannot say if competitions were held in this sport.*

Brian Hiskey: *I believe the quoits bed was near the Chequers. Men would walk miles along the footpaths after work to play a game.*

Pigs Might Fly!

Rupert Cooper: *My brother John and I were sent to bring a pig back from Bildeston. We had a two-seater car in those days and a trailer. When we were coming back we got to Naughton Straight Road and I said to John, 'Bet you can't get up to 60m.p.h. before we get to the T-junction.' 'Bet I can,' he said. Then disaster struck. While we were building up speed the pin jumped out of the towbar. The trailer followed the car for a while and then suddenly veered off to the left and the towbar dug into a gully and catapulted the pig into Mr Juby's wheat field. A few minutes later a policeman came biking by. 'What are you boys doing in that field?' he asked. 'Looking for our pig,' we replied. 'Humph,' he said. 'I expect it flew there.' 'Well actually, yes it did!' we replied.*

Driving Difficulties

John Cooper (1916–2000) used to tell a tale of his youth: *I remember the water coming over the bridge at the bottom of Church Hill. I was driving my car to a dance when it got stuck in the water, so I had to get out and go back to the farm for a horse and rope to pull it out. I tied the car to the rope and fixed up the horse, and then realised I had got to steer the car and lead the horse at the same time. I rolled down the top of the car and climbed in, and steered it with one hand and the horse with the other.*

Alfie Holder: *The lads used to congregate in the evenings outside Ben Harvey's workshop and have a confab and then we would go for a walk. One night it was pitch black and we could hear this noise coming towards us but couldn't see a thing. All of a sudden we saw a glimmer of light and it turned out to be an old Model T Ford lorry and the only light on it was a hurricane lamp hanging on the radiator cap.*

Flo Barber: *We had an old Ford 8 car, which cost £65, and I drove this without having to take a test. One day I went up Cornhatches Lane… and had to turn the car round. I asked Vic [her husband] to turn it for me but he said 'You brought it here, you get it back' and I did! We had the car for years and then sold it for £95 – quite a profit.*

Funerals

Reg Barber: *If there was a bereavement in the village Mother would go and do all that was needed. Father would take her if it was too far out. The older children would look after the younger ones. Father was a bearer at all funerals. In those days coffins were carried shoulder high and the undertakers always had men of the same height. Should the corpse be too far away for the men to carry, the undertaker would ask Father, with his pony and cart, to assist. This was not difficult as the back of the cart could easily be taken off so the coffin could be put in… every house would have its curtains drawn when the funeral procession passed along. This was a mark of respect.*

Michael King remembers the bier used later on for carrying coffins. It was kept at the rectory.

Music

Ben Harvey had a fine voice. When there were events in the village he would sing old English ballads.

Pauline Watkins: *The school used to put on concerts – people would get up on stage and sing and do all sorts of things. My father used to get a party of people to come over. He used to go to other country concerts and sing for them – he couldn't play an instrument, but he would stand up and sing without a pianist.*

Reg Barber: *Father was a very great musician. For years he played the clarinet in the Methodist chapel. Also at home on a Sunday he would play the accordion and us family would sing along at the tops of our voices.*

Clothes

Reg Barber: *As children grew in those days the clothes were handed down one to another. I must say that in those days the material was good. The best was called cord. Boys never had long trousers until they left school. The trousers we wore were called knickerbockers, which buttoned tight below the knee. Clothes were ironed by what is known as a flat iron. It was heated in front of the fire. The next to follow these was the box iron. This was heated by little pieces called the heathers, which were put in the fire to get hot. The iron had a section which was pulled up and the heathers put in, not by hand but by a special instrument called the tongs. All fires had a guard in front, roughly three feet high. It had many useful purposes, and of course it kept the children off the fire.*

Chimney-Sweeping

Trevor Clarke: *Fred Holder told me of a supply of gunpowder in the village which was put to good use for blasting soot out of chimneys. He told me how to put it into the stove, where to hold the pole to keep the door closed – and which wall to stand behind!*

The Toy Fair

Ruby Pryke, one of seven daughters who lived at Lucy Wood Cottages, told Janet Cooper about the toy fair. Given sixpence to spend, she bought sweets for her sisters for one penny, some beads for two pence, a present for her mother for two pence, and a stick of rock for herself for a penny. Besides toys and sweets, haberdashery and kitchen items were also sold. The fair came every year during Whit week and was an event which was eagerly awaited and enjoyed. It was held to the north of the village at the top of the hill by the Hall. The last one was held in 1914.

Coronation Celebrations

For George V's coronation in 1911 a bicycle race was held from the cricket pitch down Ipswich Road to Gate Farm, on to Aldham Corner and back to Elmsett along the Hadleigh Road. It caused a great deal of fun as the roads were just tracks and wheels kept getting stuck in the ruts, so people were falling off and going over the handlebars.

In 1937, for the coronation of George VI, a dance was held in the rectory garden. Harold Cooper fitted an iron bracket on the branch of a tree to hold lights powered from a battery. He wonders if it is still there today.

A Visit to the Doctor

Taffy Skippings, who always has a mischievous twinkle in his eye, visited his GP in 2006, and was asked his age and when his birthday is. 'Boxing Day,' says Taffy. 'Which year?' asks the doctor. 'Every year!' says Taffy.

Weather

Edmund Green: *In July 1948 there was a terrific thunder and hailstorm at around 3.30p.m. It was dark as night with huge hailstones which cut crops down to three or four inches. There was no harvest that year. The storm also killed a lot of young chickens. It lasted about ten minutes, but stripped all the apples and leaves from the trees – they were as bare as in winter. The storm missed most of the village, but it covered a front two miles wide, and Rookery Farm was in its path. The NFU had a collection for farmers who lost their crops, so there was some compensation.*

Flo Barber: *In 1921 there was a very bad drought. Everyone relied on pond and well water. If this ran dry there was a problem. In that year the only water was at*

Snowed in – Manor Road, 1947. Left to right: *Jim Donovan, Walter Wilding, Alf Holder, Billy Osbourne, John Rouse, ?, Percy Cooper.*

Flowton brook, so my father had to strap barrels to his horse and collect water from there. It was the only water available.

June Skippings: *I remember one really bad winter when all the roads were blocked. One of Ladbrooks' drivers, Roger Leeks, got as far as Clay Hill in Aldham but had to leave his lorry there. The next morning several of us went and dug him out, and two or three of us went home with him and helped him to unload his lorry. All the men from the mill went out clearing the roads.*

Allotments

One feature which has disappeared from village life is the allotments that were in existence when cottages were not very generously provided with gardens. Some were opposite the Hazelwood, some more in the rectory kitchen garden. There were also some in a field called Monks, glebe land, which the Revd Spear made available in 1831. Conditions to be observed were listed thus:

1. *The rent for each lot consisting of one rood or there-abouts to be seven shillings and sixpence a year, tithe free, to be paid punctually on the first day of November, the occupier paying rates. NB The rent is due at Michaelmas.*
2. *No occupier to be allowed to plough his land, but to cultivate it by spade husbandry only.*
3. *The ditches and drains to be kept clear and the fences and paths in good order by each occupier.*
4. *No work to be done on the Sabbath day.*
5. *No lot to be underlet.*
6. *Any occupier breaking these conditions to quit on three months' notice, and*

7. *Any occupier convicted of stealing or dishonesty or of any other offence against the laws of the country immediately to forfeit his lot with the crops thereon.*

Brian Hiskey remembered that his grandfather paid rent for a vegetable plot on the site of the Quaker burial ground.

Elmsett Settlers in the New World

When the *Elizabeth* sailed from Ipswich in April 1634, among her passengers was a family from Elmsett. Sam Smith and his wife Elizabeth, both aged 32, and four small children, survived the long voyage and helped to settle Watertown, Massachusetts. A few years later they moved on and helped to settle Hadley, Mass. (mindful of Hadleigh?). Sam Smith was a fellmonger – a dealer in hides and skins.

Snippets from the Press

Suffolk Assize 5 August 1829
Geo. Smith for entering the property of Samuel Cole at Elmsett and stealing divers articles. James Schofield and Haggai Hines for stealing six hogs from John Vincent at Elmsett. 7 years deportation. (Voluntarily sent to hulk at Portsmouth before deportation.)

Bury Post 1838
8 August 1838. James Waddell, 37, a land agent in the employ of the Eastern Counties Railway, was charged with ravishing Henrietta Shipp aged 13 at Elmsett. Her father kept the Chequers at Elmsett and the prisoner dined there on the 29th; he then joined the others in the taproom, she shew him upstairs where he committed the offence. Guilty of gross conduct. 2 years to be kept at hard labour.

The Carpet Bowls team, 1989. Left to right, back row: Roy Cutts, Brian Lee, Marion Brown, Derek Brown, George Dunnett, Joyce Skippings, Taffy Skippings, Tony Skippings, Phil Crick, Jim Humphries, Barbara Lee, Gladys Bovington, Frank Bovington; front: Jeremy Brown, Andrew Crick, Gerald Barber.

The cricket team, 1950s. Left to right, back row: Ken Kemp, Paul Clarke, John Barber, Chris Barber, Gerald Barber, Harold Waspe; front row: Derek Rose, Ray Perry, David Leeks, John Perry, Eric Bowell.

CHAPTER 13

Sport and Leisure

Rose and Crown darts team, 1931. Left to right, back row: *Victor Barber, Alf Mower, Jim Taylor, Leslie Taylor, Edmund Green, George Malster;* front row: *Tom Green, Jack Hiskey, Billy Osborne, Gerald Barber, Roger Leeks.*

Aubrey Barber giving his grandchildren, Anna and Alex Gillies, a lesson in carpet bowling, 2000.

Like most villages, Elmsett has always had sports facilities for its residents. It had a tennis club in the early part of the twentieth century, football has been an important part of village life, with the Elmsett Lads team preceding the Rose and Crown team, and the cricket club founded in 1912 is still in existence. The Rose and Crown Darts Team, which enjoyed a period of success in the 1930s, ran until the 1980s, and for a while the pub was home to a cribbage team.

Carpet Bowls

Ken Kemp, Frank Bovington and Aubrey and Gerald Barber introduced carpet bowls into the village in the 1980s. The first captain was Ron Skelton, who died very suddenly, but the members were pleased to receive a cup in his memory, which was donated by his widow. There is an annual competition for this trophy. After Ron died, Taffy Skippings, previously vice-captain, took over as captain and, in his words, 'The club keeps muddling along'. The members travel far and wide to take part in competitions, sometimes as far as the Isle of Wight and Cornwall. They have won a considerable number of trophies over the years and in 1988/89 were Suffolk Carpet Bowls Association Division 3 champions. One of the founder members, Aubrey Barber, is the club's

chairman. Every month Taffy reports on the club's progress (or lack of it!) in an amusing article in the village newsletter.

Cricket

First organised by Percy Cooper and Jim Scratchley in 1912, the original players had no pads or gloves, but plenty of black eyes! Percy Cooper suffered a broken arm at the age of 60, but continued playing until he was 65. He was a good batsman and notoriously difficult to get out, sometimes refusing to accept an LBW verdict. The Leeks family were very athletic – Harry, George and Roger were all cricketers.

Rupert Cooper: *Father used to take the team in a twin cylinder, chain driven Trojan car with about ten horsepower. He could get ten people in it, but on the hills some had to get out and push, and jump on once it got going. When it broke down we used Ladbrooks' little yellow lorry, which we called 'Ladbrooks' Banana'. Arthur Skippings used to drive it. There was a chap called Sidney Lloyd… he was a good cricketer, and if he and father could get settled down, they'd want a bit of getting out. They made a good pair. Father once put a ball straight over the road into the thatched roof opposite. All the old folks, Bill and Dick Beaumont, Arthur and Bob Skippings, would lean over the hedge to watch.*

Elmsett Football team, 1940s. Left to right, back row: *Jack Bradbrook, Leonard Taylor, Peter Mitchell, John Hynard, Harry Leeks, Taffy Skippings;* front row: *Jim Marchent, Gerald Barber, John Rouse, Ken Grimsy, Neville Tampion.*

Elmsett Lads football team with the Lavenham Cup in 1959. Left to right, back row: *Derek Rose, Gerald Dean, Alan Barber, Ray Leeks, Eric Bowell, Jack Bradbrook;* front row: *Ken Kemp, Brian Hiskey, David Leeks, Peter Clarke, Michael Page. Taken on Brian Hiskey's 21st birthday.*

The Revd Haslewood moved the cricket from the Rectory Meadow to the field behind the Reading Room, which was not suitable as a cricket pitch, and after he died matches resumed on the meadow, where Elmsett Cricket Club still plays. In the 1960s and '70s the pitch was prepared on the day of the match, and players and spectators sat around the big old oak tree to watch the game. In those days all Elmsett players lived in the village, and matches were held against teams from other villages and from Ipswich. Elmsett was famous for the quality of its cricket teas – not just sandwiches, but cakes and scones. Players' wives provided teas for the teams, which they had in the garden of Mr and Mrs Bob Skippings. The left-overs were enjoyed by the spectators.

Football
By K.P. Wood

Five Score Years 1896–1996

The Elmsett football team, established in 1896, was known for many years as the 'Elmsett Lads'. They played on the Rectory Meadow until the Revd Haslewood arrived in 1926. He disliked the noise of children and the footballers, and to solve his problem he offered a field at the other end of the village for use as a playing-field. The Elmsett Lads accepted his offer with alacrity, but after his death in 1942 they returned to the Rectory Meadow. In 1976 it was decided to improve the changing facilities by replacing the old shed. A new pavilion was erected –

Elmsett Athletic, 1999. Left to right, back row: *Justin Mayes, Peter Beardsell, Julian Bingham, Joseph Cardy, Dale Avis, Lloyd Dodsworth, Ashley Hills, Samuel Paterson, Ashley Davis, Nicholas Woods;* front row: *Nicholas Bell, Leigh Gibson, Thomas Tawell, Ian Kirk, Benjamin Upson.*

this new building had previously belonged to the Co-operative Society undertaking business – and it is still in use as the sports pavilion. Visiting teams claim the dressing-room to be as silent as the grave!

Brian Hiskey: *The boys had a very good football team, which played other villages and was in the Ipswich and District League. We started playing on the Rectory Meadow, but when the village bought it the ditch, which ran through the middle, was filled in and it was ploughed and reseeded, so we played on the Haslewood field again for a few years. At one time, before I was a player, the boys played on the meadow at the corner of Manor Road and Flowton Road.*

Brenda Woods: *Sometimes cows had been in the field, so the players had to look out for cowpats.*

Taffy Skippings: *There used to be a girl we called 'Blondie'. If she came onto the meadow we used to be able to gather enough young men to have a complete team.*

Our Sporting Heroes
Mick Grimwade and Denzil Sillitoe were both keen footballers. They first played for Hadleigh and progressed through various clubs and teams. While doing his National Service Mick had had the opportunity of teaming up with professional players, which proved an invaluable training ground. In 1952/53 they both played for Tottenham Hotspur in the Metropolitan League; Denzil had to retire through an injury which still plagues him today. After retiring from playing for Ipswich, also through injury, Mick then played for Elmsett for several years.

Elmsett Athletic Youth Football Team
During the summer of 1999 Steve Tawell and Mark Cardy left Hadleigh United to set up a youth team. This was to be for children from Elmsett, Hadleigh and surrounding villages. Elmsett and Aldham Village Hall Management Committee, Elmsett Cricket Club and a whole host of people from the village assisted in getting the club up and running and ready for the first season, and sponsorship was obtained. An Under-11 team was quickly established and joined the Colchester and District Youth League.

The following season (2001/02) an Under-13 team had the excitement of a tour to Belgium before the season started, and Mark Cardy set up an Under-8s team. In the 2002/03 season the club expanded to three teams: an Under-14 and two Under-10 teams. The club entered its fifth year with a move to the Ipswich and District Youth League. An Under-15 team went into Division 1, and two Under 10 teams into Division 2. During this season work commitments forced Steve Tawell to stand down as manager, and Steve Robinson took over. He and Mark Cardy have kept the club running. The 2004/05 season was less successful, and at the end of this season the Under-16 team folded as the players moved to different schools and colleges. The club now runs an Under-12 team, but only two Elmsett boys still play for the club. Over the years it has also run children's discos, played exhibition matches and run mini tournaments, as well as providing noise and excitement on Sunday afternoons in the winter months.

Netball

From 1997 to 2001 an Elmsett Ladies' Netball Club ran. It rapidly attracted enough interest in the area

Scout camp, 1935.

Muriel Ladbrook with scouts at a camp in the 1930s.

Setting off for scout camp in a Ladbrooks' lorry in the 1930s.

Cinderella *in 1981.* Left to right, back row: *Kathryn Challis, Jenny Hitchcock, Susan Challis, Julia Woods, Sally-Ann McCusker;* front row: *Caroline Furness, Angela Day, Melanie Tricker, Michaela Hines, Katrina Hines, Suzanne Hamlet.*

Table Tennis

Soon after the new Village Hall opened, John Sherwood and Alan Newman established and ran the club for youngsters. Having acquired two tables and equipment, they held weekly sessions for about eight years. To stimulate interest, all village organisations were invited to take part in a knock-out competition. Selwyn Parry and Derek Rose gave coaching, and the club became part of the District League and had a number of successes, winning several trophies.

Clubs

Boy Scouts

Jack Ladbrook started the group in 1933. When the annual camp was held at Walton, near Felixstowe, his wife Muriel accompanied him to give assistance. There was a band of five buglers and three drummers, which used to march from the Reading Room to the church in summer. In winter Jack Ladbrook found wood and supervised its chopping and sawing, distributing it in bags from his lorry to old age pensioners a few days before Christmas. The Scouts carried on until the outbreak of war.

Girl Guides

Mrs May Ladbrook and Mrs Margaret Turner started a company in the 1930s, which was taken over by Flo Barber in 1936. As captain she took the girls camping to Bawdsey Manor and Stutton Hall, where they slept in bell tents and cooked over open fires. They also had to dig latrines.

to form two teams. They practised weekly at Elmsett School and were coached by the late Pam Orton, an international netball coach and referee, and resident of Elmsett. The team competed in many matches in the Suffolk Netball League, never quite managing to win, but enjoyed themselves trying.

Tom Hitchcock, a pantomime producer, making up for the 2001 pantomime Mother Goose.

Pauline Watkins: *I didn't like being under canvas… but we had a good time. We worked for our badges – my granny, who was very old, had a list of the Morse Code. She used to say the word and I did the dot dash to her. Poor granny – she didn't know a mite what I was doing! We used to do knots, sewing and cooking for badges, which were all down our sleeves.*

When Flo had to give up running the Guides she couldn't find anyone to take over, so the company folded. 'Things don't change,' she said.

Elmsett and Aldham Players

The Elmsett and Aldham Players have produced an annual pantomime in the Village Hall since 1981, so 2005 was the 25th anniversary year. The programme for this special occasion included historical notes from two of the original cast, Robert (Mac) Mackie and Ron Kerridge.

Mac, writing in the spirit of the pantomime, begins:

I wanna tell you a story…
Once upon a time, long ago in the village of Elmsett two relatively young men talked together in the grounds of the chapel. They spoke of many things, not cabbages and kings but of the New Village Hall and the talent of their neighbours, who were able to entertain with songs and sketches to raise money to pay for this new edifice

The cast of Aladdin, *1982.* Left to right, back row: *Marion Brown, Cecil Bowell, Sheila Hitchcock, Fred Richardson, Sally Ann McCusker, Adrian Bowell, Jill Robinson, Gavin Barber, Carl Mann, Frank Cadell, Robert (Mac) Mackie, Mandy Norman, Clare Skipping;* middle row: *Catriona Cadell, Susanne Hamlet, Melanie Tricker, Louise Hamlet, Caroline King, Jonathan Gatiss, Naomi Ladbrook, Joanne Crick;* front row: *Suzy Perry, Elizabeth Hitchcock, Angela Day, Morag Mackie, Franne Sherwood, Joanne Woods.*

Alice in Wonderland, 1994. Left to right: *Laura Beardsall, Richard Newman, Rebecca Hadrill, Robert Leek, Michael Challis, Geoff Wilson, Katie Simmons, Chris Woods, Peter Moore, Alisa Newman, David Leek, Paul Nugent, Ian Tarling, Anna Mackie, Sarah Hadrill, Paul Moore, Jane Jones, Helen Shackleton, Melanie Lucas, Steve Davis, Jan Woods.*

that had been created on the meadow. The bearded man, (Mac himself), said to the clever wordsmith and musician (Jonathan Tricker) 'Have you ever written a pantomime?' to which the clever one replied, 'No, but I would like to!' A third man (Ron Kerridge), who was a great leader of the Boys' Brigade and impressive in his uniform, joined them and said he was available to direct and help with such a performance. And so it all began!

During the early years music was composed by Jonathan Tricker and played by his wife Rosemary

and their children, Tim and Melanie. Gloria Sherwood made many costumes, taking time off work to do this. Her mother and parents of children in the cast assisted her.

Owen Corble: *It is still very much a 'home grown' effort with scripts, having been written by locals, encapsulating local ideas and ideals. The casts have been an enormous mix of talent, attracting old and young alike to perform. Dick Whittington in 1983 had an age range of six (Anna Mackie) to 80 (Fred Richardson).*

Alice in Wonderland, 1994 – *the children*. Left to right: *Janet Bird, Laura Davis, Katie Tiernan-Coulson, David Wilson, Julia Cox, Eleanor Moore, Rebecca Wilson, Tommy Tiernan-Coulson, Helen Wilson, Lucy Barnett, Daniel Nugent, Vicky Wright, James Barnett.*

Pantomime children – Aladdin, 1987. Left to right, back row: Purdy Chambers, Simon Skippen, Lesley Boden, Laurie Tarling, Anna Mackie, Katy Simmons, Rebecca Hadrill, Clare Kistner; front row: Simon Hitchcock, Rebecca Hobson, Jane Elliott, Paul Skippen, Laura Smith, Alisa Newman, Allie Chambers, Sophie Hill.

Finances were difficult in the first year, but the Community Council came up trumps with a small loan, and many people paid hard-earned coins of the realm to watch. Today the children of some of the first players are mainstays of the cast. No one is ever sent away. During its existence the Elmsett panto has raised a great deal of money for charity. Panto has had its peaks and troughs like everything, but this is for sure – panto is here to stay in Elmsett!

Ron Kerridge, who calls himself an OAP (Old Aged Producer) wrote:

In the beginning a courageous few people performed solo sets in the Reading Room at social gatherings. Cecil Bowell, Fred Richardson, Marion Brown, myself and others whose names escape me (senility?) used to appear on stage to a packed house. Then, a year or two later, these solo acts formed the Elmsett and Aldham

The cast of Aladdin, 1987. Left to right, back row: Kevin Bloomfield, Jenny Skippen, Michael Challis, Paul Moore, Helena Robinson, Peter Moore, Chris Woods, Sarah Griggs, Ian Kempson, Simon Skippen, Ian Tarling, Trevor Clarke; front row: Richard Newman, Laurie Tarling, Anna Mackie, Purdy Chambers, Katy Simmons, Katy Llewellyn Jones, Lesley Boden, Rebecca Hadrill, Clare Kistner.

Players and the annual pantomime was launched. We needed scenery; Mac volunteered and also proved himself a versatile actor! And who will ever forget Marion Brown as a Fairy Godmother? Music was composed and played by Jonathan Tricker, who also wrote the script, and lighting was provided by Freddie Barber, who operated a single spotlight from the lighting box which he had designed and built at the rear of the hall. As the years passed by, more and more children and adults added their talents to the 'Players'. Home-made costumes have been replaced by professional costumiers, lighting and sound are now state of the art, and a group of talented writers, directors and musicians add to our pleasure.

Anna Reily (née Mackie): *I was first in the village pantomime in 1983. I was six years old, and the pantomime was Dick Whittington. I'd watched rehearsals the previous years, as Dad, Mum and my sister were all involved. Watching was all that I did, as I was too young, until Mrs Bennett asked if I wanted to join in with the dancing. The young people then were only in the chorus. Feeling a bit unsure I did join in, and I liked it a lot. It was fun being with the older girls and learning all the songs and steps for the dances. I was to be a rat, the smallest one, and so always the last*

to go on stage! We went on with the Queen Rat and even had to dance with her. She had to hold me up high at the end. The whole dance was under ultraviolet light and we had costumes that glowed in the dark. I remember being the tester rat for the costume. While I was wearing it my Dad painted it with ultra-violet paint. I remember it being very cold, but it worked. Since that first performance I have been in many more pantomimes, progressing from chorus to actual parts! It always involved a lot of laughs on and off stage, and I am glad that I took the first steps all those years ago.

Zoe Griggs (age 8): *I did my first panto in 2004. My character was mouse. I liked doing the rehearsals, and my favourite real show was Saturday night – we had a party after it.*

Memories of a former performer, by Paul Moore
The first Elmsett Panto I took part in was the 1990 version of Cinderella, *written by Trevor Clarke and directed by Richard Ledger. My brother Pete, when the call for auditions appeared in the* Elmsett and Aldham Newsletter, *persuaded me to join him in applying. We were unable to make the auditions and were therefore very surprised when Carol the Costume Lady came round to say they would like us to play Rupert and*

Legless Theatre Company – original cast, 1991. Left to right, back row: *Michael Challis, Ian Tarling, Helen Shackleton, Paul Moore, Chris Woods, Paul Nugent;* front row: *Ian Kempson, Peter Moore.*

The Legless Theatre Company meet Princess Anne in Ipswich, 1994. Left to right: *Ian Tarling, Ian Kempson, Michael Challis, Peter Moore, HRH The Princess Royal, Carol Russell.* (EADT PHOTO)

Rodney, a couple of toffs who appeared in the 'front of curtain' scenes. We were delighted (I was also daunted) as it turned out that these were quite big parts. Pete's experience of 'am dram' was that all the best parts went to the same people year after year, and that newcomers had to wait for someone to die before getting a decent part. One of the great strengths of the Elmsett panto is that this was never the case; very big parts were given to relative newcomers. Having got the scripts, the roller-coaster ride of rehearsals and 'homework' leading up to the performances began. I remember clearly the first time I went onto the stage to read the part. Legs shaking, throat dry, very conscious of (seemingly) a hundred faces watching to see what the 'new boys' were like. Richard Ledger was very gentle with me; he could see what I was trying to do with that soppy, fey voice but, 'Could I please project it to the back of the hall?' Weeks passed; Pete and I were quickly assimilated into the panto family. Finally, the first night arrived. I stood behind the curtain and listened to the expectant hum of the audience. A sudden, huge rush of adrenaline swept over me. My hair stood on end, all the tiredness and anxiety evaporated, and I knew I was about to have the time of my life. Pete and I did our bit, people laughed out loud and clapped when we'd finished. Rupert and Rodney were a success. The natural 'high' from the panto lasted until the Sunday evening after we had taken down the scenery, etc., and returned the Village Hall to normal. I was hit by my first bout of 'Post Panto Blues'.

The Legless Theatre Company

Many of the cast of the Elmsett and Aldham Players experienced withdrawal symptoms when the annual pantomime finished in the spring. It was in the early spring of 1991 that the Legless Theatre Company was first conceived when, noticing signs of 'Post Panto Blues', Lynne Moore suggested to her brother-in-law, Peter Moore, that he might do something for the May Day Fête. Her suggestion was a Punch and Judy show that used actors instead of puppets.

Peter Moore: *I did a little research into the origins of Punch and Judy and was not surprised to see that pantomime came from essentially the same source, a form of comedy from sixteenth-century Italy. The spirit of pantomime could be carried into this new venture. The old scripts were all too violent, but I had read enough to get a flavour of the originals and of the character of Punch: a lovable rogue.*

With lots of ideas milling around in my head, I went one sunny Sunday morning to nearby Groton Woods and sat in a quiet clearing surrounded by birdsong. My mind cleared suddenly and I wrote the outline of the plot in a few minutes. Now I needed the actors; all the panto friends I approached were willing to take part. I decided to give them a short description of their characters and an outline of the plot and asked them to develop their own script.

Although demanding, it gave the show a freshness and spontaneity and ensured they were never 'thrown' by unexpected incidents. Roy Bartlett from the village loaned a large marquee and the costumes had been borrowed or hired. We felt we were ready for an audience. On the day of the May Fête everything was ready for our first show. As we put on the makeup in the small area behind our makeshift 'playboard', we could hear the excited buzz of a large audience filling the marquee. We found the show funny – but would they? We began somewhat nervously, little realising that we would be doing this show for the next seven and a half years! It was a great hit, not least with a reporter from the East Anglian Daily Times. A picture of the show appeared on its front page, together with an article headed 'That's the way to do it', and the publicity meant the Legless Theatre Company was inundated with requests from villages and charitable organisations eager to book a novel attraction. We decided to keep going for the rest of the summer. We chose Save the Children Fund (SCF) as a charity we were all happy to support. Helen Shackleton came up with our name – because we could only be seen from the waist up. Carol Russell, County Organiser for SCF, gave us invaluable and unstinting support from the outset. Soon we had a 'fit up' (marquee) and 'playboard' (stage), sponsored by Elmsett resident Dennis Hill, all our own costumes and a diary full of bookings. The rest is history. We performed all over Suffolk and beyond and twice at Punch and Judy Fellowship annual conventions in Covent Garden, London. When Japanese tourists ignored other high-class street theatre to watch our show we really felt we had arrived. Another highlight of our career was being presented to, and performing for, HRH the Princess Royal (Princess Anne) in Ipswich in 1994.

In November 1998 the members decided to call it a day. After the final show Peter Moore was proud to accept, on behalf of all the 'Legless' members, a Certificate of Appreciation from the Regional Director of the Save the Children Fund.

Elmsett Fellowship Brass Band

In early 1980, Rupert Starling was inspired to start a brass band. Having acquired some musical instruments, he started to teach a small group from the Girls' Brigade. Because of Rupert's initiative and teaching skills, numbers soon increased to include some Boys' Brigade members and other interested children and adults from Elmsett and the surrounding district. The band's first proper engagement was in October 1981. After this, more people showed interest and Rupert enlisted the help of Tim Clarke, who has given faithful service as deputy bandmaster and teacher ever since. From thence the band has been known as the 'Elmsett Fellowship Brass Band'. It is an interdenominational organisation and plays music mostly for church services, village fêtes and other charitable events. For more than 20 years, the band has supported the National Children's Homes charity with an annual village

Above: *Elmsett Fellowship Band, 1983. Left to right, back row: Tim Clarke, Derek Moyes, Miles Hitchcock, Sheila Hitchcock, Melanie Tricker, Justine Barber, Marion Brown, Mick Grimwade, Derek Baker; middle row: Adrian Bowell, Timothy Tricker, Rosemary Tricker, Janet Crick, Jill Clarke, Jim Kelly, Deborah Laflin, Ann Laflin, Duncan Boniface; front row: Denise Laflin, Gavin Barber, Joanne Crick, Rupert Starling (Bandmaster), Geoff Wilson, Alison Barber, Hilary Wilson.*

Left: *Pram race in aid of Elmsett Fellowship Band, 1980s. Left to right: Janet Crick, Revd Roy Harvey, Rosemary Tricker.*

Christmas concert. There have been four bandmasters: Rupert Starling, Malcolm Cox, Brian Stansmore and, at the time of writing, Jon Tricker, and all have contributed much to the band. It plays regularly at the village fête, the Remembrance Day Service, carols around the tree on Christmas Eve, in addition to a busy programme of concerts, church services, festivals and fêtes around the area.

Above: *Elmsett Fellowship Band, 2005. Left to right, back row: Tim Clarke, David Allen, Joy Sillitoe, Don Tyler, Barry Carter, Kath Stock, Jonathan Tricker (Conductor);* middle row: *John Glazin, Jill Clarke, Rita Allen, Ken Wilding, Janet Crick, Rosemary Tricker;* seated: *Russell Allen, Marion Brown.*

Left: *Junior band players in 2005. Left to right: Alex Gillies, Michael Holt, Arthur Glazin, Sam Kingston.*

The band performing at Naughton fête in 2005. Left to right, back row: Sam Kingston, Alex Gillies; front row: Tim Clarke, David Scarfe, John Glazin, Don Taylor.

131

The Boys' Brigade, 1982. Left to right, back row: *Marion Brown, Ian Caddell, Toby Simmons, Barry Chambers, ? Carter, Simon Hiskey, Michael Challis, Michael Perry, Jeremy Brown, Adrian King, Brenda Woods;* middle row: *David Woods, Andrew Crick, Paul Buckle, Mark Skippen, Ron Kerridge, David Berry, Rev Reg Edmunds, Richard Carter, Gavin Barber, Andrew Laflin, Rodney Buckle;* front row: *Barnaby Simmons, Simon Skippen, John Boden, James Horne, Richard Sherwood, Robert Watsham, Robert Simpson, James Fanshaw, Robert Leek, Nigel King, David Llewelyn Jones.*

The Boys' Brigade, by Ron Kerridge

The 1st Elmsett Company was formed in 1975 with guidance from the 10th Ipswich Company. Captains have included Ron Gunn, Ron Kerridge, Marion Brown and Marilyn Watsham. It proved very popular, and attracted a large membership both from the village and surrounding area. Some of the highlights were in 1982 when the centenary of the founding of the movement was celebrated. A raft race was held on the river Gipping, and a summer camp took place at Mundesley, in Norfolk. The company also participated in the Eastern Division Fanfare at the Suffolk County Showground. The Post Office produced a first-day cover, which contained an insert stating the objectives of the Boys' Brigade: The advancement of Christ's Kingdom among boys and the promotion of habits of obedience, reverence, discipline, self-respect and all that tends towards a true Christian manliness.

Ranger Boys

The Ranger Boys is for five to 11-year-olds and is currently led by Russell Leek, who runs a lively club which is becoming increasingly popular.

Oliver Mires (aged 9): *'My favourite thing is Ranger Boys because of all the fun things we do, like making things and playing great games. I go every Thursday and try not to miss a single one.'*

Edward Seeley (aged 8): *'It was fun making paper chains. Ranger Boys uses all of your energy up in the games. In summer we play rounders. We have a tuck shop in winter.'*

Adam Coleyshaw (aged 10): *It's my favourite thing in Elmsett. In winter we play the chocolate game, when you have to roll a dice and if you throw a six you have to dress up as a bugler and eat a Mars bar with a knife and fork. We also play volleyball with a balloon. We have such fun and one day I might end up being the leader.*

The Girls' Brigade

Ellen Barber: *After the new church was built we heard that two girls from Elmsett planned to go to Whatfield to see if they could join the Girl Guides. We felt, as we*

The Boys' Brigade, 1976. Left to right, back row: *Stephen Ladbrook, Gavin Barber, ?, Adrian Bowell, ?, Stewart Day, Chris Regan, Jason Mann, ?;* third row: *Matthew King, Mark Kerridge, David Bloomfield; Christopher Rose, Paul Buckle, Andrew Walsh, Timmy Lowne, James Hitchcock, Michael Bovington, Simon Hiskey;* second row: *Ron Kerridge, Colin Boniface, Ron Gunn (Captain), Marion Brown, Terry Clark;* front row: *Rodney Buckle, Kevin Bloomfield, David Norman, Timothy Tricker, Duncan Boniface, Philip Ladbrook, Martin Hiskey, David Woods.*

Boys' Brigade camp, 1983. Left to right, back: *Adrian Bowell, Gavin Barber;* front: *Toby Simmons, Adrian King, Andrew Laflin, Andrew Crick, Jeremy Brown, Mark Skippen.*

Left: *Boys' Brigade raft race, 1983.* Left to right: *Paul Buckle, Rodney Buckle, Adrian Bowell, Chris Regan.*

The original members of the Girls' Brigade in 1964. Left to right: *Cynthia Green, Alison Barber, Valerie Patterson, Hilary Barber, Angela Skippings, Linda Robinson, Janice Bradbrook, Linda Patterson, Judith Bowell, Lesley Barber, Muriel Fayers, and officers Joy Grimwade, Ellen Barber and Susan Barber.*

Girls' Brigade cast at the Royal Albert Hall in 1978. First Aid in Nursery Rhyme Land.

had adequate premises, that we ought to provide some organisation for our village children. I knew someone running a Girls' Life Brigade at Polstead Methodist Church, so got in touch. Within days she visited the village to meet anyone interested in helping with a similar scheme in Elmsett and with total enthusiasm she arranged a starting date and suggested a minimum of ten girls should attend. Just ten arrived, and Mrs Morton (the advisor) ran a typical evening to show us what was done, and later arranged for the leader's training. The Girls' Life Brigade ran from strength to strength. It has been running continuously from 1964, and has seen many changes, including a change of name to 'Girls' Brigade' and a new, less formal, uniform. Over the years the Brigade has taken part in National Rallies at the Albert Hall in London, and also a cookery

Girls' Brigade members taking part in Songs of Praise *in St Mary's Hadleigh, September 1979.* Left to right: *Susan Challis, Alison Barber, Irene Goodchild, Helen Walsh, Mrs Ellen Barber, Julia Woods, Jane Nathan, Elizabeth Hitchcock.*

competition at national level. For the tenth anniversary the girls produced a long-playing record of songs and hymns. Girls have been very successful at swimming and sports events in both the local and district divisions. The Duke of Edinburgh Award has been a feature for several girls who have had the pleasure of receiving their awards at Buckingham or St James's Palace. Two members, Gillian Barber and Helen Walsh, reached the Queen's Award in 1984 – the highest accolade in the Girls' Brigade work. Three of the present leaders, Wendy Tawell (née Grimwade), Valerie Dunnett and Becky Hobson, were members of the company when

Original members of the Girls' Brigade at the 30th reunion in 2004. Left to right: Cynthia Green, Alison Barber, Valerie Patterson, Hilary Barber, Linda Patterson, Judith Bowell, Lesley Barber, and Lt Joy Grimwade and Capt. Ellen Barber.

Ellen Barber and Margaret Leek planting rose bushes at the Girls' Brigade 40th Anniversary reunion in 2004.

young, and have now returned to help with the ongoing work.

Both Ellen's daughters, Alison and Hilary, became officers, the latter running the Duke of Edinburgh Award scheme which enabled several girls to gain their Gold Award.

Margaret Leek (present captain): *Girls' Brigade is still going strong in 2005, with girls coming from Elmsett, Hadleigh and surrounding villages. There are now four auxiliaries and myself. Last year we celebrated our 40th anniversary with a reunion of present and 50–60 past members and helpers. There was a display of the changes in uniforms, scrapbooks and*

favourite memories. The Company is still very active in District competitions and events, and Elmsett does well in the sports and swimming. We are lucky to have parental support for these events, both vocal and with transport! As well as working for badges, the Company also has some form of fund-raising venture at least once a year. Camps, which used to be a full week and were often the only holiday some of the girls would have, are now held for a weekend, but the girls still enjoy them. I can see the Brigade carrying on for many more years.

Sheila Herd: *Girls' Brigade was a big part of my memories of growing up in Elmsett, lots of happy memories including* First Aid in Nursery Rhyme Land, *where I got to be Little Miss Muffet and we all performed in the Royal Albert Hall in London. Everybody pulled together to make the costumes and I have a memory of Mum and Dad making things like crowns for this. We entered a cookery competition and practised making cheese scones for weeks on end. I think other groups of girls practised as well. Then we went up to London, I think, where we had to cook what we'd practised and present it to be judged – presentation was very important. I loved the games and activities we did with the Girls' Brigade.*

Georgia Bearman (aged 5): *We sing songs and play games, like when one person says 'tomato sauce' and we have to guess who said it. We say prayers. We make Christmas cards and decorate them with glitter.*

Alice Highland (aged 10): *We learn about Christ. We go on trips and go to swimming galas and play games like ladders, chubby bunnies and fishes in the sea. We have squads and then go into age groups do a service, spiritual, physical and educational activities. Going to Girls' Brigade lets you make new friends and at the same time have lots of fun.*

Elmsett and Aldham WI
by Jenny Barnes
In 1952 we decided to start a Women's Institute in our village. We contacted the office at Bury St Edmunds for West Suffolk, and the office at Ipswich for East Suffolk. Speakers from both East and West came out to explain the rules and regulations – they were both anxious for us to join their respective Federation. After much discussion the vote was taken; the majority was for West Suffolk.

We were very fortunate to have Mrs Margaret Hitchcock to start us off, explaining all the rules and regulations, including no first names to be used, no meetings in members' houses, and keeping meetings at the same time and place, and day of the month. Our first President was Mrs Jack Ladbrook, and I was Vice Chairman. Mrs Ladbrook was on holiday for our first meeting, so I had to chair it. Later on we had our first group meeting, which again I had to chair. The Reading Room was packed with delegates of eight other WIs from neighbouring villages.

In the early days the County Federation ran a produce guild, with monthly meetings. We had a wide choice of speakers, instructors and demonstrators on a variety of topics to choose for our meetings – from jam making and bottling fruit to glove making, basket making and many other crafts, in our early days. They were all available, and we were very keen to take part.

We had a party in the early part of every December, with committee members bringing refreshments, and every year we produced a 30 minute costume play – what fun we had rehearsing. The Reading Room in those days had a tortoise stove for heating. It was very temperamental and when the wind was blowing in a certain direction the room was full of smoke. For our committee meetings and rehearsals we used oil stoves, very smelly and temperamental, but gave a little warmth on cold evenings. But with the laughter and fun of rehearsals the cold conditions were forgotten.

One year we felt ambitious and entered the County Drama Group Competition with a costume play, The Lawn. We won the cup – it was such an achievement we couldn't believe it. That year the Theatre Royal in Bury St Edmunds, which had been used as a barrel store by Greene King brewery for several years, had a face lift and had been fitted out as a theatre again. The West Suffolk Federation was asked to use it for the opening and we were asked to perform our play there. This was a great honour, and we enjoyed it. We were also asked to portray the five Canadian ladies who started the Women's Institute. We had to dress ourselves, as far as we could, like the five ladies, and a large picture frame

was made for us to sit in. The hat that I used was borrowed from Mrs Mower, who died before I could return it, and I kept it for years – it was blue straw with pink roses round the brim. A catch-phrase developed whenever a hat was needed '… you can use Mrs Mower's hat!'

WI enactment of the five Canadian founders, c.1950. Left to right, back: *Mrs Griffiths, Jenny Barnes, Miss Milton;* front: *Flo Barber, Mrs Cook.*

Five sets of sisters at the WI party in 2004 – Elmsett is still a close-knit community. Left to right, back row: *Joy Sillitoe, Ellen Barber, Sylvia Hiskey, Gwen Horne, Ann Kerridge;* front row, each seated in front of her sister: *Marion Brown, Joy Grimwade, Sheila Barber, Hazel King, Brenda Foulger.*

In the early years, when married women didn't work, we were able to attend most of the area meetings. We entered into and helped with everything that happened in the village.

We also went litter picking with a Womble and invited the children to join us. We led them round the village, and they loved it. It was a great success. In fact we entered into the spirit of everything, county and village, and enjoyed our WI's enthusiasm. Many new crafts and hobbies were embarked upon after the talks and demonstrations. The WI is a great asset to the village.

Jenny is now 91 and still attends meetings regularly.

The Girls' Friendly Society

During Archdeacon Browne's time as rector (1946/56) meetings were held at the rectory and led by Mrs Browne. It was a Christian-based society with many activities for girls to take part in. Joy Sillitoe remembers croquet on the lawn, cookery in the kitchen, and being allowed to explore the rectory and its grounds. Brenda Woods remembers trying on Mrs Browne's hats. After the Brownes left, meetings were held in Laurel Cottage kitchen with the Misses Ladbrook. A drawer and cupboard were put aside for the girls to use.

Blanche Seager: *We were about ten years old and were allowed to cook and eat outside long before barbecues were popular. We made dampers – a flour and water pastry mix wound round a stick and cooked over a fire, then filled with jam and eaten. They didn't taste very nice! We had competitions – I won first prize (a china dog) for a hat made out of newspaper. We knitted wrap-over vests for babies in Africa and listened to stories of foreign places. Sometimes we had guests – the vet came to talk to us, and Lady Faulkner from Aldham – I remember having to curtsy and present her with an orchid.*

Mary Watt (née Clarke): *We made models out of soap; I made a cat. One Christmas we were invited into the drawing-room to meet Mrs Ladbrook.*

The Over 60's Club

Flo Barber and Jenny Barnes have memories of how and when the club started.

Mrs Ranson, who lived in Hadleigh Road, used to invite a few people to an afternoon tea party in the Reading Room on alternate Friday afternoons. She did this on her own, making sandwiches, cakes and scones. Jenny then started helping her, and Bessie Taylor helped to get out the tables and chairs. Flo then began to help with the baking of cakes and scones. The numbers increased, and Flo used to organise a game of whist, and Jenny other games, including table tennis. After tea the people who came always wanted to play bingo – Jenny said they would have played all afternoon, but it was rationed to after tea! In about 1956 it officially became the

Over 60's Club, and qualified for a transport grant from the County Council. This enabled people from the neighbouring village of Aldham to join. There was always an outing in the summer, fund-raising whist drives in the evenings and a Christmas party. For several years members won many prizes in the craft exhibition, which was held either in Bury St Edmunds or Ipswich. Flo continued on the committee until she was 88. Now aged 93, she is still an active member. Marion and Peter Rowe took over the running of the club when they moved to Elmsett in 1983, and continued until Peter's death in 2005. Marion is still running the club.

The Senior Citizens' Christmas dinner and social evening was held in the Reading Room for several years in the 1970s. Cyril Wyatt had the idea one evening in the Rose and Crown. Gerald and Renee Barber's daughter, Lorraine Coleyshaw, remembers them taking on the organisation and fund-raising events with John Hodson. Companies were asked for donations, collections made in workplaces and the brewery approached for free beer and sherry. Many people volunteered their help with the cooking and serving of the meal and providing transport. After the meal, entertainment was provided by the Cass family and friends.

The Young Wives/After 8 Club,
by Rosemary Tricker and Janet Crick

In the early 1970s Mary Tait had the inspiration to form a Young Wives group to provide some relaxation and entertainment for the younger female 'stay-at-homes'! In those days very few of us were able to stay in full-time employment after starting a family, so we were delighted to have the opportunity, on at least one evening per month, to meet as a group. After eight years, we felt calling ourselves 'Young Wives' was a little optimistic, and we changed to the 'After 8 Club'. It soon developed into a thriving club and ran for many years. Until 1983 we helped to organise the programme of talks, demonstrations, visits, parties and money raising ventures for charity. We gave ourselves plenty of food for thought (in our case 'food' was paramount!).

Here is our irreverent A to Z of recollections of some of the many activities:

Accident prevention, AGM, Auction… some remained accident-prone, but the auction got rid of the junk.
Books… provided much needed escape from children, nappies and young husbands.
Cake decoration, Conservation, Crime, Couscous... some turned to conservation, some helped charity but no one turned to crime. The cakes and couscous went down well.
Dinner Dances, Discos and Drugs… the first two were extremely popular.
Embroidery… an escape for the arty ones.
Freezers (full of food!), Felixstowe Docks, First Aid, Flower arranging… Felixstowe docks represented an escape route to the big wide world.

The prize winnning WI collage made in 1989 by Ann Kerridge, Rachel Hitchcock, Joy Grimwade, Mel Plumley, Margaret Bowell to depict the British Food and Farming Year. The guest speaker at the meeting was Ashley Cooper.

Gardening, Ghosts, Guide Dogs, Gym & Trim (not us!)… *very few of us ventured out on dark nights, so didn't need guiding and did the ghost hunting at home.*
Hampton Court, Health Food, Heraldry, HMS Ganges… *two trips out and where all the nice girls, even healthy eating ones with a family tree, simply loved the sailors!*
India, Ipswich Hospital Maternity Wing… *where we went to have our babies much closer than India.*
Jigsaw factory… *a reminder to look for the missing pieces.*
Kew Gardens… *the flower arrangers were reminded not to 'pick 'n' mix' rare species.*
Lunch and dinners out… *it was good to let someone else do the cooking.*
Make-up, Musical instruments… *subtlety, sensitivity, gentle application and a good foundation – no problems here!*
Nick (Police Station)
Oops – nothing!

Pancakes, Pantomime, Patchwork, Pottery, Poetry… *of course the pancakes came out top!*
Quilts… *quaint work.*
Radio Orwell, RAF Wattisham… *lots of talent here, girls!*
Sewing machine, Scholl shoes… *shoes were needed for the catwalk – yes, we did give fashion shows.*
Tea planting, Theatre, Tooks bakery… *a cup of tea, a seat at the Wolsey Theatre and a crusty loaf – just the job.*
Uxor, uxoris… *it's Latin for wife, you know – and we were the 'young ones'.*
Very hard to fill!
Walton-on-the-Naze, Weaving, Wine tasting… *spinning on the coach to Walton, where we loved the sun, sand and sea breeze, and a bottle of fine French Claret.*
Xmas social… *Xmas fayre – cake, mince pies, wine, chocolate – food as usual.*
Yoga… *mystical, but very stretching.*
Zest, Zabaglione… *we had plenty of both, which is just as well because no one gave us a talk about Zucchini. Or did they?'*

CHAPTER 14

Some People of the Parish

Many of the quotations in this book have been taken from previously recorded living memories of the older residents of the village.

Elizabeth Bennett, who moved to Elmsett with her family in 1982, explains how it all began:

When I moved to Elmsett some of the windows in St Peter's were boarded up and, mistakenly, I thought it was because of vandalism. I could not have been more wrong. In fact the windows were being repaired at considerable expense. When the boarding came down, the clear Suffolk light poured back into this beautiful medieval church and it glowed. The project to replace the hassocks was coming to completion and the warm, rich colours of the materials could be seen properly. Repairs and restoration have continued to need money and in 1988, when a fund-raising village festival was being planned, I was very pleased to help. My part was to borrow old photographs and, as people lent them to me, they often told me the story behind the pictures. As several residents of the village could remember details of life here spanning most of the twentieth century it seemed an ideal opportunity to ask them to tell their stories. When I revisited them later with my tape recorder I had only to turn it on to capture the richness of their memories. It was enjoyable, entertaining and educational to listen to these stories from lovely people who are no longer with us. It gave me insight into families whose lives were intertwined in a small community. The tapes were played during a Flower Festival at the church, and I only wish I had done the job properly by recording some of the amazing conversations between elderly people who returned to see the village and were reunited with friends they had last seen decades before.

Since then many more recordings have been made during the compilation of this book, and villagers who were born and grew up in Elmsett have added their memories to the archive. Below we have given a brief summary of those who have since died.

Cecil John Barber (1904–94)

Cecil was one of ten children, seven boys and three girls, born to George and Kate Barber, and resided in Elmsett all his life. He lived in Thatched Cottage in Flowton Road until 1936, when he married Sallie Garrod of Bildeston. They began their married life in a new council house just down the road from his parents' house and it remained their home for the rest of their lives. Two boys, Charles and Gordon,

Cecil Barber in 1926 – the fencing was probably made by his father.

were born to them; Gordon died in infancy. When Cecil was a boy life was hard and he had to help his father with his work. He left school at the age of 12 and went to work at Elmsett Hall Farm for Charles Westren; he moved later to work until the 1950s on the two Ladbrook farms. During that time he became Head Stockman and set up their prize-winning herd of pedigree Wessex Saddleback pigs, which he showed at various agricultural shows in the east of England. To supplement his low farm worker's wage he kept chickens, pigs and bees. In the 1930s he rented an old cottage in Flowton Road and kept chickens upstairs and pigs downstairs. After Sallie died in 1986, Cecil remained active and he could still be seen riding his bicycle around the village when in his 80s.

Frederick (Freddie) Barber (1933–2000)

Freddie was born in Elmsett and attended the village school; after leaving he served an apprenticeship with the Eastern Electricity Board. Having

John, Monica and Fred Barber, 1940.

completed his National Service he returned to work for the EEB until retirement. He married Sheila Pitt in 1959 and they had three children. He was involved with many local activities, and used his electrical skills to great effect during the building of the Village Hall, where he spent untold hours working. He organised PA systems for the village fêtes and stage lighting for the panto. He also enjoyed restoring classic cars.

Gerald Barber (1920–1999)

Most people in the village knew Gerald as 'Racey' from his habit of challenging his boyhood friends meeting at Pump Corner to 'race you round the block'. He was born and lived in Elmsett all his life except for time served in the RAF during the war. A sports enthusiast in his younger days, he played cricket and football for Elmsett and Hadleigh. He was an active fund-raiser on the Community Council and for the village sports clubs.

Brian Hiskey (1938–2004)

Brian was of the sixth generation of Hiskeys in Elmsett, and took a particular interest in village matters, past and present. When he left school he worked on Ladbrook's farm until his enforced retirement due to arthritis in 1994.

He married Sylvia Pitt in 1962 and they had three children. After retirement he took great joy in passing on his knowledge and love of the countryside to his grandchildren and taught them to 'talk Suffolk'! He spent many hours tending family graves at St Peter's and helped with the churchyard wildlife management. He is remembered there, not only with a fine headstone, but also with a wooden seat which bears his name and that of his lifelong friend, Tony Skippings.

Alfie Holder (1917–2001)

Born in Lucy Wood Cottages, Alfie moved to Aldham when he was 13. He left Elmsett School at 14 and started work for Mr Turner at Gate Farm, where he was a stockman. He later worked at Flowton Brook Farm before taking a job as tractor driver at Elmsett Hall. He also worked as a lorry driver for the Coopers and subsequently for Ladbrooks' Mill.

Frederick (Fred) Holder (1917–2001)

When Fred left Elmsett School at the age of 14 he worked at the Rose and Crown doing odd jobs. For a while he worked on a farm in Burstall but spent most of his working life at Ladbrooks' Mill. He had a

Brian Hiskey, 1938–2004.

Fred Holder scything the grass verge outside his cottage in Ipswich Road in 1994.

The last Holder family to live in the village, 1930s. Left to right, standing: Fred, Bertha and George; seated: William and Alice.

strong interest in the past but was very much in touch with the present and had many friends of all ages. He never lost the relaxed and unhurried manner of a true countryman and his quiet thoughtfulness was a reminder of a bygone era. After retiring he took great pleasure in helping others – he walked dogs, cleared paths and ditches, watered wilting plants – all without any fuss. He had a great passion for both steam engines and old fairground machinery and travelled to rallies near and far on his old motorbike. A Rassin street organ was played at his funeral.

George Holder (1915–98)

At the age of 14 George left school and went to work as a backhouse boy at Laurel Cottage. He was paid 10s. a week for 50 hours' work. At 16 he joined the men on the farm doing the same arduous work as them. He and Cissie were married in St Peter's, where he later became churchwarden. He also

Alice Lilian (Lily) Holder, 1998.

served on the Parish Council for several years. After working on the farm he became a driver at Ladbrooks' Mill, first on the lorries and later driving fork-lift trucks. During the war he served in the Royal Artillery and many people still recall his poignant reciting of Binyon's 'For the Fallen' at the annual Service of Remembrance.

Lily Holder (1914–2002)

At the age of 14 Lily arrived in the village, where she worked as a nursemaid to John Westren at Elmsett Hall. In 1955, after a long courtship, she married Robert Holder, who also worked at the Hall. They moved into Rose Villa in Ipswich Road, where they kept 40 hens to bring in extra income. When Robert became seriously ill, Lily nursed him for several years until he died in 1977. She loved children and was always ready to baby-sit and give help with childcare. She entered into village life with great enthusiasm and served on many committees, as well as being caretaker of the Village Hall for some years. She was a regular churchgoer, delivered newsletters, played darts and bowls and attended all fund-raising functions, where she invariably organised a raffle.

Bryony Clarke (aged 12): *When I think of Lily I remember all the great times we shared together… I always accepted the treat of being taken to Hadleigh… we would often get fish and chips. I used to teach her how to dance to the latest songs (and I'm pretty sure she enjoyed it). She used to win raffles and now her luck is still with me. Some days I went to church with her and*

The 'Elmsett Mafia' of the 1950s. Left to right, back row: Tony Skippings, John Barber, Ken Kemp; second row: Sid Malster, Tom Green, Malcolm Laflin; front: Brian Hiskey.

we would often wander around the gravestones, where she would tell me who the people were and what they were like. Now she is gone… she was loved very much in this village, by my family and many others.

Tony Skippings (1933–2002)

Tony was one of the survivors of the wartime bomb incident, in which his childhood home in The Street suffered serious damage. After leaving school he worked for his father at Potash Farm. He married Joyce Green in 1955 and they had three children. Having completed his National Service, he worked at Ladbrook's farm before moving to the mill, where he was a lorry driver until he was made redundant when it closed. His hobbies were many and various, from fishing to carpet bowls; he loved his garden. He was often seen cycling round the village with his grandchildren and enjoyed visiting his daughter, Mary, and her family in New Zealand. In retirement he was always willing to drive people to hospital for appointments or to help with visiting. He also helped to maintain the churchyard.

Some Elmsett Families

Inevitably, research into village history reveals that some families are well documented and details of others have become obscured with time. Family history, however, was not the objective, but some facts have emerged which have helped to give an insight into land ownership and the employment structure of a rural community over the past two centuries.

George Barber outside the Thatched Cottage in 1951.

The Barbers

George Barber (born 1846) was a thatcher who moved to Elmsett when he married Mary Ann Gant (born 1847). Between 1847 and 1891 they had 12 children and the eldest son, also George, followed his father's trade. He married Kate Smith in 1891 and they lived in Flowton Road, where they had 10 children. A younger brother, Arthur, married Jessica Hiskey and they lived at Baybrooks, where they had four children. They moved to Mill Farm where Arthur farmed. He and his wife retired to the newly built Moat Farmhouse in 1938 and his eldest son, Victor, took over Mill Farm.

In the 1950s Hadleigh Road was known locally as 'Barber Alley' because so many Barbers lived there. There are many descendants of George and Mary Ann still living in the village.

Kate Barber with a grandchild in 1937.

Frank Barber with Sarah Hitchcock in 1983.

Percy Cooper (1889–1961).

Robert Fison and his father, Fred Fison, with their cows on church meadows, 1969.

Sheila Herd: *No book about Elmsett would be complete without a mention of Frank Barber (youngest son of George and Kate), who lived next door to us and was like an extra Grandad, especially for my sister Sarah, who he doted on. He was the youngest child and legend had it that when he was born his mother was told he wouldn't survive, but he lived until well into his seventies. He always suffered ill health but he was self-sufficient and grew all his own vegetables. He also made sloe gin; one year he made it in a jar which had previously been used for pickled onions and every time my Mum called on him she was offered some. Frank always drank shandy so he never knew how Mum suffered with that gin – it was foul!*

The Coopers

John Cooper moved to Manor Farm with wife Hannah (known as Polly) and son Percy in 1906. Percy married Mabel Jackson in 1914 and farmed in Semer until he took over the management of Manor Farm in 1917. Percy was a far-sighted and innovative man who diversified during the depression of the 1930s. He was very active in the village; he served on the Parish Council, was a churchwarden and was also an enthusiastic sportsman. During the Second World War he was the Parish Organiser and Billeting Officer. He and Mabel had four children, whose memories have been invaluable during the compilation of this book. His daughter, Janet, has been the Parish Local History Recorder for over 30 years. Percy's grandson, Oliver, now manages the farm.

The Fisons

Fred Fison bought Elmsett Hall and Church Farm from Charles Westren in 1945 and moved into the Hall with his wife Sarah and their family, Eric, Daphne and two-year-old Robert. Fred ran the 365-acre farm with a workforce of four, growing cereals and sugar beet and fattening the progeny of his 60-sow herd of pigs. Like many other farmers, Fred benefited from the availability of prisoners of war to work on the land, and he provided accommodation for some in the attic bedrooms. Some of these men, appreciative of family life and the food cooked by Mrs Fison, enjoyed the company, especially of young Robert. One, Gunter Peter, married Molly Clarke and continued to work in the village, on farms and later at the mill, remaining in Elmsett for the rest of his life. Robert married Pauline Garrod in 1965 and moved into Church Farm; they had two children, Josephine and William. After Fred died in 1972, Eric and Robert ran the farm until Eric left farming in 1974. Eric and his mother moved to Church Farm; Robert and his family moved into the Hall. Eric left the area after Mrs Fison's death in 1977. Robert sold the farm to Nick Bird in 1989.

The Hiskeys

The Hiskey family has lived in the village for seven generations. John Hiskey of Chattisham, born 1775, married Mary Bragg in 1805 and they moved to Elmsett soon afterwards. From the children of this generation other family names start to appear in the marriage register, many of them still present in the village today, notably Holder, Clarke and Green. The Hiskeys's occupations were always listed as 'agricultural labourer'. The second generation of Elmsett Hiskeys married into the Keeble, Cousins, Gant and Warren families. A particularly well documented branch of the family stems from a son of the second generation. Thomas Hiskey was born in 1849 and in 1871 he married Eleanor Warren (born in 1853). Between 1872 and 1898 they had 13 children. The Hiskey family became related to another local family when Thomas and Eleanor's oldest son, John Thomas Hiskey (1872–1957) married an Ellen Barber. This couple had nine children. One of these, named Alfred (1910–43), married Kate and they had two children, Brenda and Brian. Blanche Seager is the daughter of Alfred's brother John (born 1905) and Diane Diss is the granddaughter of their youngest

The Holder family outside the Brick Cottages in the early 1900s.

sister, Gertie (born 1912). Diane's children are the next generation of Hiskeys descended from Thomas and Ellen living in the village.

The Holders

The Holder family first appeared in Elmsett in around 1750. A marriage between Thomas Holder and Elizabeth Archer took place in 1770, but of their ten children only five survived childhood. One of these was Robert Holder, who married Sarah Warren in 1798 in Hadleigh. This couple had nine children, several of whom moved to neighbouring villages in adulthood. Robert and Sarah's first child (also Robert) was born in 1799 and married Martha Hubbard in 1824. They had 13 children who, in their turn, married into the local families of Hiskey, Mower, Meadows, Sparks and Green. The tenth son of Robert and Martha, Jonathan (1841–1920), married Lydia Meadows in 1873 after his first wife died. From this union there were nine children, one being William Robert (1882–1952), who married Alice Miriam Meadows in 1911. They had three children, George, Frederick and Bertha. George married Cissie Barber, still living in the village. Bertha and Fred never married. Fred lived at No. 2 Brick Cottages all his life; it has been renamed Fred's Cottage.

The Ladbrooks

The founder of the Ladbrook milling family was John (1808–65), who purchased a windmill from the Stearn family in 1848. He had learned the art of stone milling in Bures, where he met and married Ann

Ernest Ladbrook (1873–1946).

Dupont (1814–65), the daughter of a carpenter. They moved to Elmsett with their two sons, bought the village grocer's shop and settled into the adjoining house (the Old Post Office). John helped to establish a Primitive Methodist chapel in the village, although he and his wife worshipped at the Baptist chapel in neighbouring Somersham, where they are both buried. John outlived his wife by only a few months. Their youngest son, Alfred (1840–71), was an enterprising and caring man who started a night school in his home for the youth of the village who, having started work at an early age, had been unable to receive an education. He joined his father in the milling trade, but died young, leaving his wife to run the grocery business to support their daughter. His brother, William (1835–1925), married Elizabeth Sarah Green in 1867 and they made their home at The Maltings, bought for them by William's father. Two sons were born to them, George William in 1870 and (Alfred) Ernest (1873–1946). George William, on coming of age, left home and travelled widely to Australia and South Africa, and on to the Klondyke, where he engaged in gold prospecting. He returned after ten years and moved to Red House Farm in Hintlesham. Ernest married Mary (called May) Bailey Grimwade in 1902, and settled into Laurel Cottage. They built a small room onto the side of the house and started a successful non-denominational Sunday school. They had three children, John, called Jack (1904–79), Sybil and Christine. Ernest was diagnosed with disseminated sclerosis (MS) in 1936 and for the next ten years, although unable to work as previously, retained his interest in the mill. He watched with satisfaction as the business expanded under the management of his son Jack – the fourth generation of Ladbrooks to manage the milling firm. Jack married Muriel Willey in 1931 and they made their home at the Maltings, where two children were born, Rachel and John. Jack took his share in village life, becoming a Methodist lay preacher in the Ipswich circuit and serving as chairman on the Parish Council, as his father and grandfather had before him. For some years he represented Elmsett on the old Cosford Rural District Council. The fifth generation of Ladbrooks at the mill began when John joined in the 1960s. He married Doreen Jeffrey in 1966 and, after a few months, they were able to move into their new bungalow, built close to the mill on Cassocks field. By remarkable coincidence Rachel married Richard Hitchcock, a member of an Elmsett farming family who are directly descended from Cornelius Hitchcock, who bought Bures mill in 1875, where the first John Ladbrook had learned his trade. Rachel and Richard have four children, John and Doreen have five, one of whom is adopted.

The Stearns

The Stearn family farmed in Elmsett for around 200 years. The first reference is to Edward Stearn, who was living at Elmsett Hall in 1690, but the family may have been there before that date. The trustees of the Bishop Andrewes' Charity owned the farms they rented. In about 1780 the Old Hall farmhouse, which stood near the brook, fell into disrepair and the new house was built a short distance away at the top of the hill. At about the same time, Benjamin Stearn married Sarah, daughter of Robert Mirrington, who owned Chequers Farm and Ale House. They had a large family of eight sons and four daughters. In 1790 Benjamin acquired Chequers, but they continued to live at the New Hall and in 1825 Chequers was sold. The Stearns appear to have been an enterprising family who played an active part in village life, and members of the family were involved with the church in such roles as churchwarden, treasurer and overseer for a number of years. However, after a dispute with the rector, Revd James Spear, they transferred their allegiance to Flowton. The sons attended Needham Market Grammar School, riding daily the six miles there on donkeys, which were bred on the farm. The boys were musical and, as they grew up, joined the church band, all of them sitting in the gallery to play for services. Ben (1783–1860) was the only one to move any distance away from Elmsett, and even he returned as a widower in old age. Thomas (1791–1843) purchased a mill in Hadleigh, replacing Cousins Mill, which had been at Mill Farm. Three other members of the family died young, Edward (aged 25), Daniel (aged 27), and Charlotte (aged 17). After their father's death in 1816, John, William and Patrick managed the land for their mother until she died in 1835. The Stearn brothers became noted breeders of Suffolk Punch and hunting horses. They had a nephew – also Ben – who lived with them along with his cousin, Mary, who was their housekeeper. When the last uncle, Patrick, died in 1841, Ben married Mary. They built a small cottage on the corner of Flowton Road to retire to – a plaque above the porch says 'BMS 1879'. Ben died in 1882 and Mary in 1890 – the last of the Stearns to live in Elmsett.

The Turners

Robert Edwin Turner moved to Elmsett at around the time of his first marriage, in 1881. He is listed in *Kelly's Directories* as:

Landowner, farmer and thrashing machine proprietor, clerk to the Parish Council, assistant overseer, agent Sun Fire & Life, Horse Insurance & Railway Accident & Employers' Liability Offices.

He owned eight farms by 1911. After his wife's death he married Ada Emma Gooderham in 1885; they had five children. The oldest son, another Robert Edwin (born 1887), and his younger sister, Ada Grace (born 1891), married a sister and brother of the Woodward family. The youngest of the Turner

Mr and Mrs John Westren with their 15 children in 1896. Left to right, back row: *Ethel, Ernest John, Laura Emily, Edwin Claude;* middle row: *Lily, Mr Westren, Reginald, Maud, Mrs Westren, Ellen;* front row: *Cecil, Florence, Arthur, Mabel, Lionel, Leonard, Charles.*

family, Gwendoline (born 1910), married a nephew of this family, Thomas Godderham. Alfred, the third son, married Norah Gage from Aldham. All had families and have descendants still living locally. The second son, Makens, did not marry until relatively late in life and until his father's death in 1941 he lived and farmed with him at Gate Farm. He continued to farm in partnership with his brother Robert. Their mother died suddenly in 1947 and four months later Makens married Marjorie Walker. Gate Farm was sold in the 1954.

The Westrens
John Westren was born in 1842 in North Devon, where he grew up on a farm. In 1869 he married Mary Anne Bailey and they had 13 children. In 1882 John, leaving the family to manage the farm in Devon, travelled to Elmsett, where he had obtained a

two-year lease on the Hall and Church Farm, with an option after this period of a further long-term lease or a return to Devon if he was not satisfied. Apparently he liked the 'feel' of Suffolk soil and prospects were encouraging. He sent a message to his family to join him in Elmsett. After the necessary transactions and sales were negotiated the younger children and their mother travelled by rail, while the older ones loaded their possessions and furniture onto wagons; drawn by horses, they made their way to Elmsett, where they took up residence in 1884. Two further children were born after the move and the family remained at Elmsett Hall, where Charles was farming at the time of the tithe dispute. His brother, Claude, farmed at Poplar Hall, helped for a while by his nephew, Edwin, who still lives in the village. The Westrens have scattered far and wide, to Canada, New Zealand and Australia.

CHAPTER 15

Down Memory Lane

Gone Forever
by Janet Cooper

It is difficult for anyone now to understand what life was like for a child in rural Suffolk in the years between the First and Second World Wars, so great have been the changes since 1945. In those days a farmhouse was almost self-sufficient: milk came by the pail, flour in a sack, eggs galore, rabbits, poultry and game if the butcher couldn't get round. Mother made the bread and the yard was full of faggots (bundles of sticks) for the bread oven. We also had an abundance of fruit – apples, pears, plums, etc. We enjoyed the simple pleasures of being a country child. Mechanisation had not really begun to take over rural life; even the postman sometimes came round in a pony and trap. Horses were still used. What a time children had at harvest time, riding in the empty wagons, riding the trace horse or taking meals into the fields and sitting among the workers while it was eaten. Some of the things we did were seasonal, such as going to the wood on Good Friday to collect primroses and violets for the church at Easter. We also got bunches of palm (willow) but this was left outside, it being considered unlucky to bring it indoors. Spinning tops, hoops and skipping ropes came out in the spring when the roads had dried up. Our road had not been tarred and grass grew in the middle in places. A lot of our toys were home made – catapults, stilts and popguns, and whistles made from ash. Acorn cups became dolls' tea cups and a plank over a barrel made a good see-saw, while a length of wagon rope made our swing from the walnut tree, and in the orchard we had a hammock. Sunday was a day completely different from the rest of the week. Games and toys had to be put away on Saturday evening, Sunday clothes laid out and shoes cleaned ready for church. No work was done, other than the essential – like milking and feeding stock. No cooking, except for the vegetables, no knitting, needlework or mending. We usually walked to church with our parents, two miles there and back. We had Sunday books and Dad had a Sunday paper, but my grandfather, who spent the last three years of his life with us, would not read this until Monday. When we were very small we were allowed to play with a Noah's Ark and the animals – this was kept for Sundays only. In summer we went for long walks, or went to see relations or they came to see us. Sunday winter evenings were usually spent looking at a variety of books; we had three attics at Manor Farm, one of them was choc-a-bloc with books, bound copies of the London Illustrated News and other magazines of all sorts. The day finished with Mother at the piano for our favourite hymns. Such was Sunday in one Suffolk farmhouse in the 'Thirties'.

Harold Cooper

Harold was born in 1918, and as a small child remembers watching the sails of the windmill going round from his bedroom window. The windmill blew down in about 1926. Elmsett was a quiet rural village, and one of the differences he notices now is the absence of garden gates. Every cottage had a

Janet Cooper with her pony, Gipsy, 1930.

Whatfield Road, c.1920, looking towards Pump Corner, with the Old Post Office on the right. The fence was necessary to keep passing livestock out of the garden.

Hadleigh Road, 1935, showing the elm trees from which the village takes its name. Many of the trees have since succumbed to Dutch Elm disease.

garden fence and gate, as sheep were often driven through the village. Several villagers owned goats, and these were pegged along the roadside to graze. Gypsies used to come once or twice a year and park on the verge where it was wide enough to camp. They were Romany gypsies and the women wore a lot of jewellery – gold bangles and necklaces. There would usually be a tinker (tin maker) and peg maker among them. No one was afraid of them. Two meeting-places in the village were the smithy, where the farmers' boys congregated, and the village pump. Some cottages had a well; others took water from ponds and field drains. Mr Pryke at Lucy Wood used to place a bucket under a field drain in the morning on his way to work, and collect it at lunch time, when it would be full of lovely clear water. The allotments in the village were very well tended. They covered three to four acres and were used by 12–15 farm workers at weekends. In the autumn they used little handcarts in which to take their produce home. The cobbler in the village was Joe Skippings. He was crippled as a child and trained to repair shoes and harnesses. Many houses and cottages have disappeared, but evidence of their existence can frequently be seen. Sometimes there will be a pond, sometimes a fruit tree in the hedgerow; bulbs appear in spring where the garden used to be. At the bottom of Spinney Hill some daffodils flower every year where Harold remembers a cottage once stood. He remembers that it was abandoned and fell into disrepair, and eventually all that was left was a pile of bricks from the chimneystack. When the roads were tarred in about 1928 no extra strengthening was done; they were simply tarred over. The signposting was always very good.

Moving to Elmsett, 1947
by Jenny Barnes

We moved to Elmsett, temporarily for six months, in 1947, but found it so lovely we decided to stay. We moved from a large farmhouse with running water, hot and cold, but no electricity. No. 2 Flowton Road had no mains water or electricity. We had a pump in the corner of our front garden which was used by the other three houses and the cottages down the road. The water was full of iron and stained the galvanised buckets. We had 'Aladdin' lamps and smaller paraffin lamps. Candles were too risky with young children. The outside loo luckily was attached to the house, so no trailing down to the end of the garden. The contents were disposed of in the garden. We had a large black range in the sitting room for heating and cooking (lots of black lead and elbow grease). We also had a three-burner Florenco oil stove (named Flo) in the kitchen, which I used for baking. For washing and heating bath water we had a large copper in the corner of the kitchen. We had radios, 'the wireless', but no television. The radios were worked by accumulators, which were collected every week by the man who delivered the papers. They were taken to a shop in Hadleigh to be recharged, and were delivered back a week later. Christine, our daughter, was five when we moved to Elmsett. She attended the village school, where Mrs Roberts was the Headmistress. They had large open fireplaces which had to be cleared out and re-lit every day in time to warm the classrooms by 9.00a.m. for the start of school. The school was also used for meetings of the Parish Council and for lectures once a month. Sunday school was held at Laurel Cottage, in the small room on the corner of the house. This room was also used as the village library. Boxes of books were exchanged regularly so there was always something new to read. When we arrived our garden was one large chicken run – no vegetable patch or flowerbeds or grass. It entailed lots of hard work, both digging and planting. I think we started with the smaller front garden. The hedges everywhere were tall, but kept trimmed regularly and the grass verges were full of wild flowers. A lovely hawthorn hedge, about ten feet tall, stretched from Red House Farm gate across the field to the bridge on Offton Road. In May, when it was covered in blossom, it was absolutely magnificent – a sight never to be forgotten. Church Road had beautiful spreading hornbeams, and the walk to church was really lovely. The brook at the bottom of Spinny Hill ran over the road – there was no bridge. Bob [her husband] would say to the children, 'We'll go and wash the car,' and there would be a rush for wellies and buckets and brushes. He would disappear with the children, Chris and Rob, to the ford and an hour later they all came home soaking wet and happy, having seen no other traffic to interrupt them.

From Red House Farm to Elmcroft
by Margaret Aggiss

My grandparents, Herbert and Jessie Gibbons, moved to Red House Farm in 1921 with their sons, Hugh and

Ken Gibbons with his mother, Jessie, outside Red House Farm in 1942.

Kenneth (our father). Later on Hugh remained on the farm with grandfather, but when war broke out Dad joined the RAF and was on active duty when the two bombings occurred in Elmsett. He told me once of a disturbing incident whilst he was on leave. Some aircraft had been involved in a 'dogfight' in the skies above the farm. Father did not think any more of this until the next day when walking his dog. He found a dead German pilot hanging in his parachute from a tree by the brook. He also recalled a Spitfire crashing in the area of Spinney Hill around the same time. When Dad left the RAF at the end of the war he was employed at the mill as a representative. In later years he became Sales Director. He met our Mum, Myrtle, at a dance in Naughton. They married in November 1945 and moved into the old School House where my brother Trevor was born in 1948. Mum told us that when Trevor arrived the teacher told the children in class to be very quiet, and not to wake the baby. A devout Christian, Dad was elected churchwarden at St Peter's alongside his good friend, George Holder, and later Arthur Foulger. Dad had a wonderful sense of humour – I'm told when he was a teenager he set fire to his bicycle wheels and cycled through the village wheels ablaze for a dare! He also played the trumpet in the Boy Scouts. In the early 1950s Dad built Elmcroft on Whatfield Road. Sadly, Dad died suddenly in 1971 – he was in his early 50s. Following his death our mother took on the Post Office. We left Elmsett in 1975. It had been a wonderful village to grow up in, and both Trevor and I have very fond memories of the village.

Memories of an Elmsett Childhood, 1952–54
by Peter Hitchcock

Like most of us, I still remember my first day at school. Every time I heard the latch on the front door of the school, I thought it was my parents coming to pick me up! At that time, the Headmistress of Elmsett School was Miss Roberts, a rather stern and formidable lady in the eyes of a child. She arrived each day in a black, open three-wheeled invalid car with tiller steering. Everyone walked to school in those days, unless lucky enough to be offered a lift once in a while. Walking up the hill from Red House Farm I invariably met Robin and Christine Barnes and we walked together. On the way we would sometimes see Mr (Cecil) Barber who lived in one of the cottages, now a single house known as 'Thatched

Potash Farm and Acorn Cottage, c.1935.

Cottage'; Christine usually had to tie my shoelaces again there. Once a week, Revd Brown would come to take morning prayers. On Coronation Day in June 1953, he presented each child with a copy of the New Testament. Attached to the school was the School House, occupied by Ken and Myrtle Gibbons and their son Trevor, who was not yet of school age. I have fond memories of the nature walks we went on, particularly up past the church, where the hedgerows were tall and untrimmed, with many wild plants including blackberries and old man's beard in the autumn. There was also Sunday school held at Laurel Cottage – this was a voluntary activity and I gather I was not a good attender. Often we would meet the 'road men' – three council employees whose job it was to repair the roads and keep the verges cut neatly, all done by hand.

Most of the outlying farms did not have mains water or electricity in the early fifties. Red House Farm was no exception but this did not mean that we lived without all 'mod cons'! We had an oil-fired generator which produced about two kilowatts – enough to light the house or barns, but rarely both together. An electric fire was an occasional luxury but if both bars were on the lights would dim. We also had television, which was used only when special programmes were on. This was the era of Muffin the Mule, with other programmes such as 'Renfrew of the Mounties', 'Champion the Wonder Horse' and 'The Lone Ranger' following in later years. I remember that we watched the Coronation – in black and white, of course.

Water was pumped from the well and stored in elevated tanks which provided the necessary pressure to supply taps around the house and piggeries – and the all-important sanitation facilities. The quality of water was never questioned until many years later health officials suggested that it wasn't fit to drink. To coin a phrase 'it never did us any harm'! Farming in the fifties had almost completely moved away from horsepower, although I do remember that we had one old carthorse for a time. His name was Short because he only had one eye (think about it!). Mechanisation was developing fast but it still meant that three or four men were required on a typical farm, whereas today one or two men can handle three times the area. A lot of work was done by hand then, especially the sugar beet and potatoes, and harvest time needed even more manpower – there were jobs then for children helping out and pocket money to be earned. Those were very different happy times for children – just half a century ago!

An Elmsett Childhood
by Andrew Barnes

Born in Elmsett in 1953, I lived in the village for 17 years and still return regularly. Living in Flowton Road, my earliest memories are of my family drawing water from the pump which served the four houses. Domestic facilities were quite different at that time – baths were taken in a 'tin-bath' using water brought from the pump and heated in a wood or coal-fired 'copper'. With no mains water there was no WC and facilities were accessed from outside the house. The advent of mains water in the late 1950s changed our lives considerably. In those days my grandparents lived in Burstall and we regularly walked over to visit and it was quite possible to do so without seeing any car on the way.

The winter of 1963 was the worst for many years. It must have been a time of difficulty for many, including my parents, but for a ten-year-old it was heaven sent – no school and a white wonderland to explore. Dick Mayes lived at Hill Crest in Flowton Road and I remember him admonishing me on the first day of the snow when I set out to explore. 'Don't go down there boy, you'll get lost.' Didn't he know that I was ten and that I knew my way to Flowton? The easterly wind had whipped the snow into huge drifts, completely blocking the road on the hill down towards Red House Farm. Taller than a man, the wind had sculptured them into amazing shapes and the images of that day are some of the most vivid I have. When the village school finally reopened we were still in the grip of winter. It was staffed by a husband and wife team, Fred and Barbara Grant. Where the snow was compacted in the playground, a 'slide' was formed and on occasions, when the ice wore so thin that the playground surface came through, we asked Fred whether he could pour water on the slide overnight so we could have a better sliding surface the following day. He would inspect the slide, and if the weather was still freezing, he would often oblige. He would tell us that he didn't want any complaints about wearing out shoe leather – it was for each one of us to decide whether to slide or not – but no mention of Health and Safety. This was before the litigious age that we live in now. At that time there were around 25 pupils and rumour abounded of the intention to close the school for economic reasons – thankfully it didn't happen but it was a close call.

Coughs and colds were usually treated at home, but when the need arose there was a regular surgery held at the Reading Room. Medicine was dispensed from a big container held there and was diluted with water in the medicine bottle. It seemed to me that the same medicine was always dispensed. Only the concentration of it varied with the severity of the symptoms and this could be distinguished by the depth of its brown colour – the memory of its taste is something that will always stay with me. Weekends and school holidays were spent outdoors on the nearby farm, whatever the weather. I would never venture onto the farm without my sheath knife strapped to my belt. Whilst not comparable with a 'Crocodile Dundee' knife, it would nevertheless be completely unlawful to carry it today. Used for anything from cutting bailer twine to slicing an apple, it was completely acceptable and the thought of using it as a weapon would never enter into anyone's head.

Most schoolboys at that time had a collection of birds' eggs – 'bird nesting' was considered quite an acceptable pastime in the spring. An egg was removed from the nest and 'blown' by making a small hole in each end and blowing out the contents. Care was always taken not to cause any undue disturbance other than removal of one egg and blown eggs were frequently swapped between us to enlarge our collections. Whilst this practice of taking eggs is quite rightly illegal today, it did give us an appreciation and knowledge of wildlife which for me started a lasting interest. Childhood soon turned to adolescence and as usual the need for pocket money was of prime importance. Fruit, potato and vegetable picking were the main piece-meal activities that brought in the pennies at weekends. At one time I tried sugar beet hoeing, which was a lonely activity; each person intent on his allocated block of rows, working through them alone, eyes glued to the ground and with an almost permanent stoop. Time was money and there was hardly any interaction between the hoers.

Living in a small village, everyone knows you and you know everyone. This has distinct disadvantages when you want to try something you shouldn't, such as smoking. You could never go to the village shop for cigarettes as a young teenager. Flowton didn't have a shop but there was a house which sold tobacco. Being tall for my age and not being well known to Bill Butcher and his wife, ten Woodbines were handed over without question to fulfil the adolescent need for exper-imentation. Summer holidays were spent working on any one of the local farms. Working at Elmsett Hall is where I came to know Eric Fison. He was the only person I knew who regularly wore old-fashioned hobnail boots, but what made it even more unusual was that he had to have them hand made as they were a very small size. Eric was always unmistakable with his

noisy boots and he always hummed to himself wherever he went. I am sure that to him his tunes were the very height of musical talent, but to all who listened to him his humming was tuneless and was often the cause of much mirth, all taken in good heart by Eric. It was working at the Hall that I also met Ivan, a big man, very strong; I remember him trying to teach me how to move coomb sacks of grain. A coomb is a measurement of volume and, depending on the contents, could weigh anything between perhaps 16 and 20 stone. Apart from the obvious strength needed, there was also a knack and, having neither, my efforts were always doomed to failure. Not so for Ivan, who moved the sacks around as though they were 1cwt. Today there are Health and Safety training courses on lifting just ten kilograms and I have often thought back to my struggles with sacks weighing ten times as much. As anyone else brought up in the country, I was taught how to kill and prepare birds for the table and to skin and gut a rabbit or hare. At the time it seemed the most natural thing to do, but it is only when, in later life, you meet those who were not brought up in the same circumstances, you realise it is far from universal knowledge. Although now working for a bank in the City, I will always be a 'country boy' at heart and proud of it and I couldn't think of a place I would have rather spent my childhood.

Miss Elmsett

In the late 1960s there was a competition in the county for the 'Miss Spirit of Suffolk' title.

Miss Elmsett, 1970. Janet Crick being driven by Gordon Watkins to open the village fête.

Miss Elmsett, 1962. Mary Clarke (centre) *with her attendants, Valerie Willis* (left) *and Joy Riches* (right).

Miss Elmsett, 1971. Janet Westren (centre) *with her attendants.*

Janet Crick: *I believe I was the first 'Miss Elmsett' to take part in the county competition. I was chosen at a social evening held in the Reading Room, and organised by the Community Council, whose chairman was Eric Fison. A number of girls were 'persuaded' to enter this competition on the night! The first round of 'Miss Spirit of Suffolk' was held at the Melton Grange Hotel and I was one of the 14 girls picked to go forward to the final in Bury St Edmunds. Alas, I did not manage to take the title! However, as 'Miss Elmsett', I opened the next summer fête and was transported in a pony and trap by Gordon Watkins of Flowton from our home in Whatfield Road to the meadow adjacent to the Reading Room. I have no recollections of any more duties, other than handing over the title to Janet Westren at the end of the year.*

Assorted Reflections
by Jonathan Tricker

We moved to Elmsett in October 1966 when Britain was well into the swinging sixties, at about the time the Beatles gave us 'Yellow Submarine' and 'Paperback Writer'. It was a particularly wet autumn as I remember and the Elmsett clay soil was very new to me and very slimy. We set about making our new home and from the start the locals appeared friendly. Over the years we have witnessed the changing face of village life but we are still here and, happily, very likely to remain. Like many other rural Suffolk communities, Elmsett embraced the progressive sixties rather tentatively but things were so very different then. There was no main drainage and on clay soil the cess-pools filled remorselessly in wet winters. The provision of gas, too, remained a pipe dream. It was an Elmsett without 'Sawyers' and 'Windings', without 'Hazelwood' and a village sign; the rector lived in The Old Rectory and the Post Office lurked at the end of Whatfield Road, down which pigs were frequently driven from their farm quarters to nearby meadow pasture. There was no village hall as we know it; social gatherings took place in the Reading Room which, when tightly packed like a warm wooden cigar box, permitted very little free movement inside it. In spite of this, quite ambitious shows such as Old Time Music Hall evenings and small-scale dramatic entertainments were enthusiastically staged. It was the age in which large creamy-coloured Ladbrooks lorries plied their way to and from the mill along roads not yet subject to 30mph, and fighter planes rather than helicopters screamed over from nearby Wattisham. In those times the rectory meadow was far from a level playing-field and suffered from several hollows and boggy areas. Tolly Cobbold beer was the brew served in the Rose and Crown, which had no proper bar. I remember on one of my first nervous visits opening the door on a small room of 'natives' sitting on wooden benches round the walls, singing folk songs quite lustily to the accompaniment of an ancient squeeze-box accordion. It was a far cry from 'Yellow Submarine', but I stayed long enough to assure myself that this really was Suffolk in the swinging sixties and not a scene from a nineteenth-century malthouse in a Thomas Hardy novel. It seems likely that Elmsett never rivalled the likes of Kersey, Monks Eleigh or Cavendish for the quaint and cottagey picturesqueness sought by the water-colourists but as time went on the new Village Hall and extensive new housing expanded the possibilities for the community. A strong sense of identity and independence seems responsible for much that followed – the annual pantomime, torchlight processions and fireworks on bonfire-night, table tennis, carpet bowls, the Fellowship Brass Band and, of course, bigger fêtes, fayres and festivities. The ravages of Dutch Elm disease removed much of the hedgerow wood which gave the village its place name, but the spirit and the character of its people remains solidly rooted in its country soil.

The Postman
by Trevor Ford

Trevor has worked for the Royal Mail for almost 24 years, and for most of that time has been delivering mail to Elmsett and Aldham residents. He was delighted to be asked to write a contribution for this book.

There are many aspects of my job that I really enjoy. Working out of doors, and in particular the changing seasons. As I write this we are well into autumn, the trees and the hedgerows are shedding their leaves of beautiful autumn colours. The wildlife is something I particularly enjoy, especially the occasional sighting of foxes, deer, and the hares on the fields near to Poplar Hall, and very occasionally a heron taking off from a pond. Add to these the various other species of birds – owls, woodpeckers, finches, etc. and the birdsong from the Cornhatches Wood on a spring morning. There have been a lot of changes over the years, including a considerable increase in the volume of mail, and a large amount of new properties built in the village on Windings, Sawyers and the Hazelwood estates. Also the sad sight of the recent demolition and redevelopment of the Ladbrooks' Mill site. Some great characters worked there over the years. Meeting the customers and having a chat as I go about my daily round is also a very enjoyable part of the job. One of the real village characters who readily springs to mind, sadly no longer with us, was the late Fred Holder, who lived in Ipswich Road. Fred was always the same, very cheerful and extremely polite. If I called round and knocked on his back door with a package for him, he would always thank me four or five times before I left. Fred did not have a lot of modern conveniences in his little cottage, but he was very happy and contented – a lot to be said for that! I think it was a very nice touch that Anne, the present owner of the property, decided to rename it 'Fred's Cottage'. I will always remember Fred Holder with great affection – a lovely man. So I consider

myself to have been very fortunate, and have thoroughly enjoyed my time over the past 20 or so years as the rural delivery postman to the villages of Elmsett and Aldham.

In October 2005 the following article, written by Peter Wenham, appeared in the village newsletter:

Trevor's Diploma
Trevor knows everyone by name, even newcomers such as myself. Which is all to the good because it was that knowledge that enabled Trevor to deliver two very important pieces of mail that had totally mangled addresses. On one the complete address of a large Ipswich based firm had been substituted for my name and address, although the correct postcode had been used; and on the other item my name but the same incorrect address. Trevor realised that both items could be for myself, which they were! Such service is so rare in today's society that I felt it needed a special 'thank you', so I contacted Lesley Dolphin at Radio Suffolk to do an 'on air' thank you. The result, including a slightly embarrassed Trevor, was an interview with Trevor and myself broadcast on Lesley's morning show on 24 August, and the presentation of Lesley's very first 'Dolphin Diploma' to Trevor for services above and beyond the normal.

Memories of My Childhood in Elmsett
by Jenny Hitchcock

I always cycled to school with my brother James and we left our bikes in Lily Holder's garden. If it was wet, Lily would cover our saddles with plastic bags so that we didn't get wet bottoms on the way home. I remember the heavy snowstorms, and the drifts that blocked Slough corner. This meant that my sister and I had to walk across the fields to Granny's at Red House Farm in order to feed our ponies. We used to take the opportunity to make 'angels' in the snow on the way. We made bread at my great aunt's home at Laurel Cottage. The smell was always wonderful but the bread was rather heavy and dense. I loved going to Girls' Brigade, especially Camp. One holiday that will always be dear to me was the week we spent at Alnwick in Northumberland, as this was where we met Brother Cecil, a Franciscan

The green and smithy, showing a horse-drawn roller, probably newly repaired and awaiting collection, c.1930.

monk who I wrote to for many years. My sister and I had ponies – Moses and Frosties, who was a devil to catch, but nice to ride. In the summer, if the flies were bothering us, we used to walk slowly and then suddenly shout 'Go' and charge across the fields in the hope of leaving them behind. Unfortunately they were always still with us when we stopped.

Elmsett as a Place to Live
by Jean Lawrence

I shall always remember the bright, sunny, early June day I arrived in Elmsett 20 years ago in 1985. Even before I had got the children out of the car a neighbour had wandered across the road to welcome us, and we were invited to join her family and other neighbours for lunch the following Sunday. I found this rather strange, as she had no idea who I was, but this was just the start of a completely different way of life. That afternoon I took the children for a walk to introduce them to the village, especially the school which my seven-year-old daughter would attend. As we walked along people of all ages greeted us with 'Good afternoon' or 'Isn't it a lovely day'. 'People keep talking to us,' whispered my daughter. I explained that people in villages do talk to people they have not met before. I was brought up in a village and I longed for the same sort of life for my children. Within days faces became familiar, we began to know where people lived, and most importantly, whom they were related to. The biggest problem with being new was that everyone knew who we were; numerous people would cheerily greet us, and the brain became tired with trying to remember who they were. We were sucked into the routine of the village, much of which is dictated by the seasons. A walk down to the school in the morning, with a visit to the Old Post Office Stores for a newspaper on the way back. After lunch there would be a walk with my toddler son, perhaps to feed the ducks on the village pond, visit the pigs in the fields, find tractors or combines working or up to the mill to watch the lorries coming and going. Tuesday afternoons I would enjoy a cup of coffee and chat with other mums at the toddler group, where Ian learned to play and socialise with other children, many of whom would go to Playgroup, the village school and Hadleigh High School with him. In the winter Revd Harrison would join us for a toddler service, rather than braving the weather and having to sit in a cold church. The old play equipment still provided a dilapidated swing, on which Ian would sit and wait for Abbi to come out of school. On the way home we would visit the other village shop to pick up necessary provisions, with a small treat for the children. Every few weeks there would be a visit to Lesley at the hairdresser's. Because there were only a few children in any age group they were very good at playing in mixed-age groups and it was lovely to see how the older ones helped and cared for the younger and less able. Some parts of life in the village have changed. The mill is no longer there, the Old Post Office Stores has gone, and we no longer have a village bonfire night, but we are blessed with many amenities other villages have lost, and a population that appreciates our churches, school, pub and shop and, above all, one another.

The Maltings and village pond, early 1900s.

✦ CHAPTER 16 ✦

Looking to the Future

The people born in the early-nineteenth century lived through a period of great change, not experienced by any previous generations and unlikely to be equalled in the future. At the beginning of the century the combustion engine was in its infancy and farming, which was the mainstay of villages like Elmsett, has moved quite literally from sickle to satellite. Oliver Cooper, who used this phrase for his harvesting demonstration in 1998, has interesting thoughts on the future of farming:

Elmsett's environment, like much of Suffolk's, is changing in that some of its residents now commute between here and London. Many of the farmhouses, rectories and cottages now have quite different owners from 40 years ago, and there are many former urban dwellers in the countryside. During the 1980s there were high levels of over-production and the terms 'wine lake', 'beef, butter and grain mountains' attracted atten-

tion to this aspect of the Common Agricultural Policy. The public began to question how this had come about and the extent of the funding into European agriculture came under the spotlight. Farming practices – the use of fertiliser, pesticides, animal welfare, the effect of over-production on the environment, the pollution of ground water – all of these areas and more became topics of public debate. Side issues such as access to the countryside, and, more recently the hunting debate, reflect the increase in interest into how the countryside is managed. The previously insular farming industry has had to listen to the concerns of the wider community and reflect this in its practices. The growth of organic farming has been a commercial response to a market-led demand for food free of pesticides, with 'sustainable production' as a driving ethos. Average farm size is on the increase and this trend will almost certainly continue. Many farming families supplement their income through other businesses and ventures and this

Traditional haymaking at St Peter's churchyard in 2002. Left to right: *Brian Hiskey, Taffy Skippings, Phil Crick.*

trend has become known as diversification. Farmers remain custodians of the land, and most would wish to pass their piece of England to a new farming generation in better shape than when it was taken on. That is part of our stewardship. Agriculture has responded to these changing times. Environmental policies go hand in hand with production strategies. The harsh government-led production policy incentives generated after the Second World War have become agricultural history – and thankfully so have food shortages.

Conservation

Within the parish there is an important colony of rare arable weeds at Bushy Ley Farm which has been farmed organically since 1948. In 1993 it was estimated to have 90 per cent of the corn buttercup population growing in the UK, and seed from these plants and other rarities are collected for the national seed bank at Kew.

The churchyard at St Peter's has been managed for wildlife by volunteers since 1997, and is home to many plants, animals and insects previously struggling to survive. In 2005 it was one of six sites to reach the finals in the *East Anglian Daily Times* wildflower competition.

Laurel Cottage meadow is 3¼ acres of unimproved herb-rich grass, and it is believed that it has only been ploughed once, probably during the Second World War. It retains a good range of flora indicative of a traditionally managed hay meadow, including some rarities among the 50 species found. It was granted the status of a County Wildlife Site in 2000.

A small area of recently planted woodland is situated on the Hazelwood land and is also managed by volunteers, and the latest initiative, a community wood, is well under way.

Buckle's Wood

In the winter of 2004 a small group of village people met and listened to a presentation by Elizabeth and Grenville Clarke from the Green Light Trust. They were invited to the village fête to promote their work and, following this, a steering group was formed at the beginning of 2005 and the Elmsett Greenlife Grove Scheme (EGGS) was formally constituted in March. A bank account was opened with a start-up grant of £300 from the Green Light Trust and letters were sent to local farmers and landowners seeking their support for the wood. With EGGS gathering momentum, the village school became central to the project. Volunteers built a tree nursery in the school garden and villagers and children brought an assortment of native seedlings from their gardens which, together with the young trees grown by schoolchildren, were planted in the nursery bed. The project was launched on 16 June, when the children buried a time capsule and planted a young hawthorn tree which was dressed with their wishes for the woodland. The highlight of the day was the meeting with Mr James Buckle of Semer, who offered us Wood Field which is located behind the school. It was decided to call it Buckle's Wood in recognition of his generous donation. This is a long-term project. It will take many years for the woodland to be established, and hence perhaps only our children will live to see the wood reach maturity. Because it will become their job to maintain this woodland, it is fitting that they be involved right from the start.

The first trees to be planted in Buckle's Wood, January 2006.

James Buckle with his daughter, Emma, ready to help with the tree planting.

Alastair Grant (aged 7): *At Golden Wood in Lawshall we saw a yew tree that had been planted by Kaku Yafei, a young chief from Wagu in Papua New Guinea. We learnt a tree blessing in Kaku's language. At school we planted our tree and said the blessing.*

Paul Midgley (aged 9): *On 14 January most of the village turned up to plant 500 trees. It was very exciting and it was good fun. After a lot of planning and preparation and when a lot of trees had been planted the wood started to take shape. We started to put mulch round the trees, but ran out, so when the farmer went to get some more everyone went to get some refreshments. And they were very refreshing refreshments! Afterwards everyone got back to work. The trees were planted very quickly – it was a fun day.*

Elmsett Parish Plan

In 2001 Elmsett Parish Council discussed the possibility of drawing up a Community Action Plan, later known as a Parish Plan, and decided to sponsor the idea for the village. Promoted by the Countryside Agency, Parish Plans cover environmental, social and financial issues and help to define needs for the future. It involved a major survey of every household and the forming of an action plan to implement them. An open meeting, held in March 2001, was well attended, and it was decided to go ahead. With Alan Newman taking the chair, a steering group was formed. Alex Bass, Thomas Tippett and David and Helen Wilson produced a separate plan for youngsters. A grant application was submitted to the Countryside Agency and Elmsett became the first Parish Council in the Eastern Region to be awarded the maximum grant of

Muddy boots outside the Village Hall after tree planting – soup was being served inside!

157

£5,000. With funding secured, the Parish Council purchased a laptop computer and software for the project and a questionnaire was drawn up on issues relating to the village and its inhabitants. An exhibition, held in the Village Hall in November 2001, coincided with the delivery of the survey to every house. Analysis of the replies gave a clear indication of residents' requirements. As Elmsett was a pioneer parish, the committee members were asked to advise other parishes and appeared on local radio and TV. Replies were received from 659 people – the actual population of the village was estimated to be 725. There was overwhelming support for Elmsett School and Playgroup, and also for the Village Hall, churches, pub and shop. There was concern about speeding traffic and road safety and appreciation of the environment but improved maintenance was sought. There was great concern about the need for affordable local housing and other planning issues, and a wish to know more about issues discussed at Parish Council meetings. In response to the survey a Good Neighbour Scheme was launched, a new pavement was made along The Street, a footpath map was produced and an Environment Group formed which initiated the Community Woodland scheme.

Elmsett also has a team of Rapid Responders – a group of people trained to provide a quick response to deal with a suspected heart attack or breathing difficulties as it can take up to 30 minutes for an ambulance to reach the village.

Afterword

Exploring the past reveals far more than can be encompassed within these pages. A huge amount of research has been undertaken to peel back the layers of history that surround us. Wherever we look we see evidence of the past in the landscape. Wherever we walk, someone was there before us. If we stop and listen we will hear the sounds of nature that were so familiar to our forebears. Many of our older residents have shared their memories with us and have added life and reality to their period in history. So also has a ten-year-old pupil at Elmsett School. Having heard Beethoven's *Für Elise* in assembly one morning he remarked that he had heard it before 'when I was young'. History can be as brief as five years, as it was to this young man, or a lifetime, or an indeterminate period in history. It is inexhaustible. Life as we know it now will be part of history too – one day.

Bibliography

Akhtar, M. and Humphries, S. (1999), *Far Out. The Dawning of a New Age in Britain*, Channel 4

Cocksage, Edmund (1991), *Vagabond for Peace*, Fast Books, Australia

Glasswell, Samantha (2002), *Earliest English*, Tempus Publications Ltd

Higham, N.J. (1997), *The Death of Anglo-Saxon England*, Sutton Publications Ltd

Mountfield, Allan R. (2000), *St Peter's Church, Elmsett. A Brief History*

Rackham, Oliver (1994). *The Illustrated History of the Countryside*, Weidenfeld & Nicolson

Savage, Anne (2002), *The Anglo-Saxon Chronicles* – collected and translated, Salamander Books.

Shoberl, Frederic (1821), *Description of the County of Suffolk*

Seymour, John (1984), *The Forgotten Arts*, Dorling Kindersley

Twinch, Carol (2001), *Tithe War 1918–39. The Countryside in Revolt*, Media Associates

Whitlock, Dorothy, MA (1930), *Anglo-Saxon Wills*, Cambridge University Press

Subscribers

Mrs Margaret Aggiss (née Gibbons), Battisford
Mr and Mrs B. Ball, Hintlesham
Aubrey and Ellen Barber, Elmsett
Charles Barber, Needham Market, Suffolk
Mrs Deborah Barber (née Laflin), Felsham, Suffolk
Mr Desmond Barber, Whatfield
Lorraine Barber, Elmsett
Sheila R. Barber, Aldham, Suffolk
Linda Beaumont (née Patterson), Peterhead, Scotland
Maurice and Sheila Beckett, Monks Eleigh
Mark E. Bedford, Elmsett, Suffolk
The Beesley Family, Higham Ferrers, Northamptonshire
 Bennett, Whatfield Road, Elmsett
Timothy L. Berrett, Alfriston, East Sussex
Mike and Gill Billington, Cornhatches, Elmsett
John Bird, Elmsett Hall
David Bird, Elmsett Hall
Nick and Jane Bird, Elmsett Hall
Amanda and Simon Bishop, The Old Post Office, Elmsett, Suffolk
Rosalind P. Blakesley, Cambridge
Mervyn Bloomfield, Stowmarket
Jim and Angela Boden, France
Clare Boniface, Bramford, Suffolk
Duncan Boniface, Shirebrook, Derbyshire
John and Doris Botwright, Elmsett
Adrian Bowell
Sally Bowell/Frazer
Buff and Andy Branton, Hoo, Woodbridge
Ivy Claire Brown, Elmsett
Teresa and Denis Brown, Hexham, Northumberland
The Chambers Family, Elmsett, Suffolk
Elizabeth Christman
Karen Clarke, Ipswich
Beverly, Ashley, Jody and Emily Clifford, Elmsett, Suffolk
Ken and Anne Clinch, Elmsett, Suffolk
Tom and Margaret Cocks, Elmsett, Suffolk
A., J. and M. Connolly, Elmsett, Suffolk. 2006
Ashley Cooper, Gestingthorpe, Essex
Harold Cooper, Gestingthorpe, Essex
Janet Cooper
Stan and Ann Coram, Elmsett, Suffolk
John Cousins, Flowton, Suffolk
Andrew Crick, La Trimouille, France
Mrs Dorothy Crow (née Shortland), Elmsett
Elton and Sue D'Souza, Elmsett, Suffolk
Mark and Helen Davies, Elmsett, Suffolk
Jill and Terry Day, Hadleigh, Suffolk
Teresa De'Ath, Elmsett, Suffolk
Mr Frank and Mrs Linda Dearle, Elmsett
George, Joanne, Sophie and Alicia Demetriades, Elmsett, Suffolk

A.B. Dunnett, Flowton, Suffolk
Mervyn and Josephine Eade, Elmsett, Suffolk
Evan, Sue, Bethany, Joshua, Evangeline & Jacob Edwards, Elmsett, Suffolk
Roger, Brenda, Helen, Russell and Miriam Edwards
Roy and Rita Edwards, Washbrook, Ipswich
David M. Ellesley, Elmsett, Suffolk
The Pupils of Elmsett C. of E. V.C.P. School, Elmsett, Suffolk
Trevor Ford, Hadleigh, Suffolk
Arthur and Brenda Foulger, Elmsett
John and Hilary Furlong, Elmsett, Suffolk
Mr Ken Gant, Hadleigh, Suffolk
Mrs Mercie Gant, Boxford, Suffolk
Mr Philip Gant, Sudbury, Suffolk
Mr Russell Gant, Lower Layham, Suffolk
Cliff, Donna, Matthew, Thomas and Chloe Garnham, Elmsett, Suffolk
Debbie Lynne Gidney, Elmsett, Suffolk
John and Alison Gillies, Aldham
Russell and Ivy Goodchild
Danny and Betty Grace, Bacton, Suffolk
Mrs Alison Grant, Elmsett, Suffolk
Mavis and Peter Gray
Simon A.H. Gray, Amersham, Buckinghamshire
The Green Family, Coates Farm
Anne Griffiths, Elmsett
Michael J. Grimwade, Elmsett, Suffolk
Russell and Margaret Hamlet, Elmsett 1966–1991
Grace Hammond, Elmsett, Suffolk
Mike Harris, formerly Village Hall Chairman, Judy Harris, formerly After Eights Playgroup
James and Pippa Hart, Aldham, Suffolk
Joyce Hawes, Ipswich, Suffolk
Robin Hawes, Sudbury, Middlesex
Sheila Herd (née Hitchcock), Bramford, Suffolk
Clive and Gladys Hiskey, Somersham
Mervyn Hiskey (née Beckett), Attleborough
Sylvia Hiskey and Family, Elmsett
James and Liz Hitchcock, Elmsett, Ipswich
Jenny Hitchcock, Somersham, Ipswich
Mary Hitchcock, Elmsett, Suffolk
Mr Matthew W. Hitchcock, Flowton, Suffolk
Miles Hitchcock Brown, Elmsett, Suffolk
Peter Hitchcock, Formby, Lancashire
Rachel and Richard Hitchcock, Elmsett, Ipswich
R.J. Hitchcock, Elmsett, Suffolk
Sarah J. Hitchcock, Elmsett, Suffolk
William and Rachel Hitchcock, Nayland, Colchester
Witgar Hitchcock, Glemsford, Suffolk
Beryl Hoey, Adelaide, S.Australia
Jo, Paddy, James and Michael Holt, Elmsett, Suffolk
James Horne, Market Harborough

Roger and Gwen Horne, Elmsett
Philip How (Croxley Green, Hertfordshire), great-great-grandson of George A. Fenning of Elmsett (1842–1914)
Brian and Dorothy Jacobs, Ipswich, Suffolk
Robin and Anthea Jeans, Elmsett, Suffolk
The Jones Family, Sawyers, Elmsett
Emma Judd, Elmsett, Suffolk
Betty D. Kemp (née Skippings), Elmsett, Suffolk
The Kempson Family, Middlewich
R.L.W. Kerridge, Elmsett, Suffolk
Hazel and Michael King, Elmsett, Suffolk
Jason and Nicky King, New Zealand
Jackie and Geoff Kistner, Elmsett, Suffolk
Roger and Sue Kistruck
David P. Ladbrook, Stroud, Gloucestershire
John and Doreen Ladbrook, Worlingworth, Suffolk
Philip J. Ladbrook, Irun, Spain
Stephen Ladbrook, Bury St Edmunds, Suffolk
Jean Lawrence, Elmsett
John and Hazel Lee, Elmsett, Suffolk
David Leek, Ipswich, Suffolk
Robert Leek, Pozzo D'Adda (MI) Italy
Russell and Margaret Leek, Elmsett, Suffolk
Andrew, Melanie, James, Sadie Lucas, Newlands, Elmsett, Suffolk. 1985–2001
Claire Maddison, Felixstowe, Suffolk
Jason R. Mann, Elmsett, Suffolk
Carl Mann, Virginia, USA
Paul Marshall, Elmsett School, Elmsett, Suffolk
Mr and Mrs Matthews, Elmsett, Suffolk
Mr and Mrs S. McQuaker, Kersey, Suffolk
Roy, Sarah, Paul and Kate Midgley, Elmsett
Gill and Ken Millns, Nottingham
Peter W. Moore, Hintlesham, Suffolk
Peter Mowles, Whatfield, Suffolk
Robert W. Mowles, Ipswich, Suffolk
Stanley A. Mowles, Ipswich, Suffolk
Carolyn and Steve Murrell, Duston, Northampton
Margaret Nelson, Elmsett, Suffolk
Alan and Andrea Newman, Elmsett, Suffolk
Alisa Newman, Woodbridge, Suffolk
Richard Newman, Colchester, Essex
Valerie Norrington, Bredfield, Suffolk
Julia, Ross, Benjamin and Jessica Nowland, Keep River N.P., N.T. Australia
Richard and Jean Oakes, Elmsett, Suffolk
Chris and Michelle Parkinson, Preston, Lancashire
John and Jackie Parkinson, Elmsett
Malcolm Patterson, Elmsett, Suffolk
Paul Patterson, Elmsett, Suffolk
Stephen Patterson, Elmsett, Suffolk
Valerie Patterson, Elmsett, Suffolk
Mr John Frederick Perry, Hadleigh, Suffolk
Karl Peter, formerly of Flowton Road, Elmsett
Molly and Guenter Peter, Elmsett, Suffolk
Mrs J. Prentice, Saxmundham, Suffolk
Bessie Pryke, Elmswell, Suffolk

Mr and Mrs D.A. Pryke, Crowfield, Suffolk
Richard J. Pryke, Potash Farm, Elmsett
Lorna and Bob Quick, Glemsford, Suffolk
Carol and Ken Rackham, Caldham, Suffolk
Mr and Mrs M. Ratliff, Bildeston, Suffolk
The Rees Family, Hill Farm, Elmsett
Ann Rivers, Elmsett
Jim, Jean and Dan Roberts
Carol and Paul Robinson, Hemingstone
Stephen, Janette, Simon, Sarah and James Robinson, Elmsett, Suffolk
Ida Roper, Elmsett, Suffolk
Ruby and Derek Rose, Elmsett, Suffolk
Mr and Mrs K. Sanderson, St Annes-on-Sea, Lancashire
Evelyn M. Scurrell, Bradfield, Essex
Mrs Blanche (Hiskey) Seager, Elmsett, Suffolk
Katrina, Edward, Alexander, Iona Seeley, Elmsett
Naomi M. Seffar, Worlingworth, Suffolk
Les and Kathy Selby, Elmsett 1972–5
John and Gloria Sherwood, formerly Elmsett Stores
Mr and Mrs D. Sillitoe
Mr W. and Mrs V.L. Simpson, Elmsett, Suffolk
Brian Skippings, Hadleigh, Suffolk
Joyce Skippings, Elmsett, Suffolk
H.J. Smith, Elmsett, Suffolk
Mike Smith, Stowmarket, Suffolk
Simon and Yvonne Southey
Dave Steward, Stowmarket, Suffolk
Ray Steward, Felixstowe, Suffolk
Jacqueline Stoneman, The Barn, Aldham, Suffolk
Maria Taddesse, New Jersey, USA
Wendy Tawell, Elmsett, Suffolk
J. Taylor, Aldnam
Mrs Jane A. Taylor, Elmsett, Suffolk
The Thoroughgood Family, Bushy Ley, Elmsett
Dr Tim Tricker, Aberdeen, Scotland
Miss Mel Tricker, Ipswich, Suffolk
John F.W. Walling, Newton Abbot, Devon
David and Arabella Ward, Coates Farm, Elmsett, Suffolk
David and Helen Ward, Garden Cottage, Walliswood, Surrey
The Watkins Family, Flowton
Robert and Jonathon Watsham, Aldham, Suffolk
Peter and Loraine Wenham
Mr D. Westren, Carlisle, Cumbria
Edwin Westren, Elmsett, Suffolk
Mike and Helene Westren, Calgary, Canada
Joanne White (née Crick), Royston, Hertfordshire
John and Jean Whitelock, Elmsett
R.E. Wilding, Hadleigh, Suffolk
Chris Willey, Kensal Rise, London
Cyril and Brenda Woods, Elmsett
Graham, Penelope and Henry Woods, Thorpe Bay, Essex
Mrs Debbie L. Wray, Hadleigh, Suffolk
Celia Wright, Elmsett, Suffolk

There are now over 160 titles in the Community History Series. For a full listing of these and other Halsgrove publications, please visit www.halsgrove.com or telephone 01884 243 242